Charles P. Otis, Edmund F. Slafter

# Voyages of Samuel de Champlain

With historical illustrations, and a memoir

Charles P. Otis, Edmund F. Slafter

**Voyages of Samuel de Champlain**
*With historical illustrations, and a memoir*

ISBN/EAN: 9783742837639

Manufactured in Europe, USA, Canada, Australia, Japa

Cover: Foto ©ninafisch / pixelio.de

Manufactured and distributed by brebook publishing software
(www.brebook.com)

Charles P. Otis, Edmund F. Slafter

**Voyages of Samuel de Champlain**

CHAMPLAIN (SAMUEL DE)
d'après un portrait gravé par Moncornet

# VOYAGES

OF

# SAMUEL DE CHAMPLAIN.

TRANSLATED FROM THE FRENCH

BY CHARLES POMEROY OTIS, PH.D.

WITH HISTORICAL ILLUSTRATIONS,

AND A

# MEMOIR

BY THE REV. EDMUND F. SLAFTER, A.M.

———————

VOL. I.

1567–1635.

FIVE ILLUSTRATIONS.

Boston:

PUBLISHED BY THE PRINCE SOCIETY.

1880.

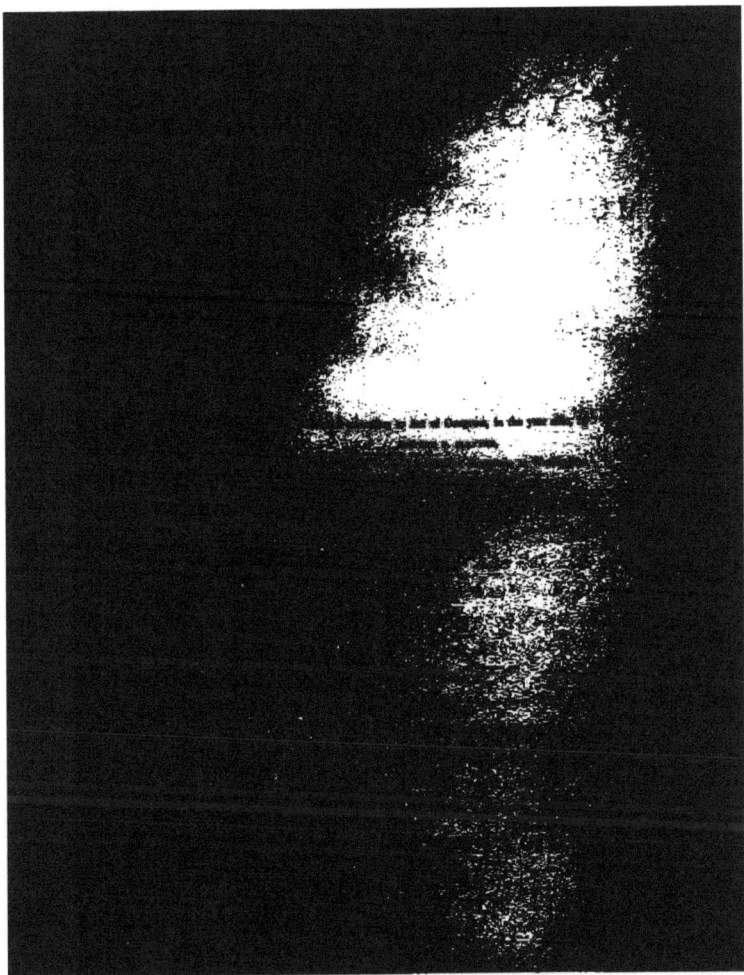

# PREFACE.

HE labors and achievements of the navigators and explorers, who vifited our coafts between the laft years of the fifteenth and the early years of the feventeenth centuries, were naturally enough not fully appreciated by their contemporaries, nor were their relations to the future growth of European interefts and races on this continent comprehended in the age in which they lived. Numberlefs events in which they were actors, and perfonal characteriftics which might have illuftrated and enriched their hiftory, were therefore never placed upon record. In intimate connection with the career of Cabot, Cartier, Roberval, Ribaut, Laudonnière, Gofnold, Pring, and Smith, there were vaft domains of perfonal incident and interefting fact over which the waves of oblivion have paffed forever. Nor has Champlain been more fortunate than the reft. In ftudying his life and character, we are conftantly finding ourfelves longing to know much where we are permitted to know but little. His

early

early years, the proceffes of his education, his home virtues, his filial affection and duty, his focial and domeftic habits and mode of life, we know imperfectly; gathering only a few rays of light here and there in numerous directions, as we follow him along his lengthened career. The reader will therefore fail to find very much that he might well defire to know, and that I fhould have been but too happy to embody in this work. In the pofitive abfence of knowledge, this want could only be fupplied from the field of pure imagination. To draw from this fource would have been alien both to my judgment and to my tafte.

But the effential and important events of Champlain's public career are happily embalmed in imperifhable records. To gather thefe up and weave them into an impartial and truthful narrative has been the fimple purpofe of my prefent attempt. If I have fucceeded in marfhalling the authentic deeds and purpofes of his life into a complete whole, giving to each undertaking and event its true value and importance, fo that the hiftorian may more eafily comprehend the fulnefs of that life which Champlain confecrated to the progrefs of geographical knowledge, to the aggrandizement of France, and to the diffemination of the Chriftian faith in the church of which he was a member, I fhall feel that my aim has been fully achieved.

The annotations which accompany Dr. Otis's faithful and fcholarly tranflation are intended to give to the reader fuch

information

information as he may need for a full underftanding of the text, and which he could not otherwife obtain without the inconvenience of troublefome, and, in many inftances, of dif-ficult and perplexing inveftigations. The fources of my information are fo fully given in connection with the notes that no further reference to them in this place is required.

In the progrefs of the work, I have found myfelf under great obligations to numerous friends for the loan of rare books, and for valuable fuggeftions and affiftance. The readinefs with which hiftorical fcholars and the cuftodians of our great depofitories of learning have refponded to my in-quiries, and the cordiality and courtefy with which they have uniformly proffered their affiftance, have awakened my deep-eft gratitude. I take this opportunity to tender my cordial thanks to thofe who have thus obliged and aided me. And, while I cannot fpread the names of all upon thefe pages, I haften to mention, firft of all, my friend, Dr. Otis, with whom I have been fo clofely affociated, and whofe courteous man-ner and kindly fuggeftions have rendered my tafk always an agreeable one. I defire, likewife, to mention Mr. George Lamb, of Bofton, who has gratuitoufly executed and con-tributed a map, illuftrating the explorations of Champlain; Mr. Juftin Winfor, of the Library of Harvard College; Mr. Charles A. Cutter, of the Bofton Athenæum; Mr. John Ward Dean, of the Library of the New England Hiftoric Genealogical Society; Mrs. John Carter Brown, of Provi-dence,

dence, R. I.; Mifs S. E. Dorr, of Bofton; Monfieur L. Delifle, Directeur Général de la Bibliothèque Nationale, of Paris; M. Mefchinet De Richemond, Archivifte de la Charente Inférieure, La Rochelle, France; the Hon. Charles H. Bell, of Exeter, N. H.; Francis Parkman, LL.D., of Bofton; the Abbé H. R. Cafgrain, of Rivière Ouelle, Canada; John G. Shea, LL.D., of New York; Mr. James M. LeMoine, of Quebec; and Mr. George Prince, of Bath, Maine.

I take this occafion to ftate for the information of the members of the Prince Society, that fome important facts contained in the Memoir had not been received when the text and notes of the fecond volume were ready for the prefs, and, to prevent any delay in the completion of the whole work, Vol. II. was iffued before Vol. I., as will appear by the dates on their refpective title-pages.

E. F. S.

BOSTON, 14 ARLINGTON STREET,
    November 10, 1880.

# TABLE OF CONTENTS.

## ILLUSTRATIONS.

ENGRAVED PORTRAIT OF CHAMPLAIN ON WOOD, AFTER THE EN-
     GRAVING OF MONCORNET BY E. RONJAT, *heliotype.*
MAP ILLUSTRATING THE EXPLORATIONS OF CHAMPLAIN, *heliotype.*
ENGRAVED PORTRAIT OF CHAMPLAIN, AFTER A PAINTING BY
     TH. HAMEL FROM AN ENGRAVING OF MONCORNET, *fteel.*
ILLUMINATED TITLE-PAGE OF THE VOYAGE OF 1615 ET 1618, *helio-
     type.*
CARTE DE LA NOVVELLE FRANCE, 1632, *heliotype.*

*CALCUL des lieux du Soleil & de la Lune à Paris au temps du passage observé de la Lune au Méridien, le 16 Novembre 1750, à $15^h\ 14'\ 24''$ temps vrai, & $14^h\ 59'\ 41''\frac{1}{2}$ temps moyen, suivant l'équation du temps, prise d'abord dans la Connoissance des Temps, où on la trouve pour cette heure de $14'\ 42''\frac{1}{2}$ soustractive.*

## CALCUL DU LIEU DU SOLEIL.

| | |
|---|---|
| Moyen mouvem. du Soleil pour 1750 | $9^s\ 10^d\ 00'\ 21''$ |
| Pour le 16 Novembre | 10. 15. 24. 25 |
| Pour $14^h\ 59'\ 41''\frac{1}{2}$ | 0. 0. 36. 57 |
| Longitude moyenne du Soleil | 7. 26. 1. 43 |
| Equation du centre du Soleil | − 1. 19. $57\frac{1}{4}$ |
| Lieu du Soleil ♏, ou | 7. 24. 41. $45\frac{3}{4}$ |

| | |
|---|---|
| Moyen mouvem. de l'apogée du Soleil pour 1750 | $3^s\ 08^d\ 35'\ 5[illegible]$ |
| Pour le 16 Novembre | 0. 0. 0. 5[illegible] |
| | 0. 0. 0. [illegible] |
| Longitude moyenne de l'apogée du Soleil | 3. 8. 36. 5[illegible] |
| A soustraire de la longitude moyenne du Soleil | 7. 26. 1. 43 |
| Anomalie moyenne du Soleil | 4. 17. 24. 53 |

| | |
|---|---|
| La première équat. du temps | − 5' 20" |
| La seconde | − 9. 27 |
| Equation du temps | − 14. 47 |
| Temps vrai | $15^h$ 14. 24 |
| Temps moyen corrigé | 14. 59. 37 |

Si 60' : 1' 30" :: 24' 53" ! Equation du centre pour $4^s\ 17^d$ ..... $1^d\ 20'\ 35''$
16021 ..... − 0. $37\frac{1}{2}$
3822
19843 R. 0' $37''\frac{1}{2}$ Eq. du cent. pour $4^s\ 17^d\ 24'\ 53''$ ... 1. 19. $57\frac{1}{4}$

## CALCUL DU LIEU DE LA LUNE.

| | |
|---|---|
| Moyen mouvem. de la Lune pour 1750 | $6^s\ 08^d\ 1[illegible]'\ 19''$ |
| Pour le 16 Novembre | 8. 16. 26. 47 |
| Pour $14^h\ 59'\ 37''$ | 0. 08. 15. $54\frac{1}{2}$ |
| Longitude moyenne de la Lune | 3. 02. 57. $00\frac{1}{2}$ |
| Premiere Equation | + 00. 08. $06\frac{1}{2}$ |
| Lieu de la Lune premièrement corrigé | 3. 03. 05. $07\frac{1}{6}$ |
| Seconde Equation | − 00. 03. 13 |
| Lieu de la Lune deuxièmement corrigé | 3. 03. 0[illegible]. $54\frac{1}{6}$ |
| Troisième Equation | + 00. 0[illegible]. $39\frac{1}{7}$ |
| Lieu de la Lune troisièmement corrigé | 3. 03. [illegible]. $33\frac{1}{6}$ |
| Equation du centre | + 06. 1[illegible]. $28\frac{1}{3}$ |
| Lieu de la Lune quatrièmement corrigé | 3. 09. [illegible]. $02\frac{1}{2}$ |
| Variation | + 00. 3[illegible]. $50\frac{1}{2}$ |
| Lieu de la Lune cinquièmement corrigé | 3. 09. [illegible]. $52\frac{1}{2}$ |
| Sixième Equation | − 00. 0[illegible]. 41 |
| Vrai lieu de la Lune | 3. 09. [illegible]. $11\frac{1}{2}$ |
| Réduction à l'Ecliptique | − 00. 0[illegible]. 09 |
| Longitude de la Lune | ♋ 09. [illegible]. $02\frac{1}{2}$ |
| Latitude de la Lune australe | 0. 01. 3[illegible]. 34 |
| Demi-diamètre horizontal de la Lune | 0. 00. 1[illegible]. $04\frac{1}{3}$ |
| Parallaxe horizontale de la Lune | 0. 00. 5[illegible]. $14\frac{1}{4}$ |

| | |
|---|---|
| Moyen mouv. de l'apogée de la Lune pour 1750 | $5^s\ 20^d\ 58'\ [illegible]''$ |
| Pour le 16 Novembre | 1. 03. 39. [illegible] |
| Pour $14^h\ 59'\ 37''$ | 0. 00. 04. [illegible] |
| Longitude moyenne de l'apogée de la Lune | 6. 26. 4[illegible]. [illegible] |
| Première Equation | − 00. 13. 4[illegible] |
| Lieu de l'apogée de la Lune premièrement corrigé | 6. 26. 28. [illegible] |
| Equation de l'apogée | + 09. 01. 3[illegible] |
| Vrai lieu de l'apogée de la Lune | 7. 05. 29. [illegible] |
| La plus grande d'entre les 2des équat. du moy. mouv. | $0^s\ 00^d\ 03'$ [illegible] |
| La plus grande variation | 0. 00. 36. [illegible] |
| Lieu du Soleil | $7^s\ 24^d\ 41'$ [illegible] |
| Apogée de la Lune premièrement corrigé | 6. [illegible]. 28. [illegible] |
| Argument annuel | 0. 28. 13. [illegible] |
| 2de équat. du moy. mouv. en suppos. la plus grande de 3' 45" | − 00. 03. [illegible] |

Ainsi 3' 45" : 3' 7" :: 3' 32" ½ : − 3' 13" Seconde équation vraie.
60' : 13' 10" :: 13' 23" !... R... $6^d$ 03' 23"  60' : 2' 6" :: 13' 23" !... R... $0^d$ 0[illegible]
8. 58. 14 ..... 7. 0[illegible]. [illegible]
Equat. de l'apog. ..... + 9. 01 37  La plus gr. éq. du centre ... 7. 08. [illegible]

| | |
|---|---|
| Lieu de la Lune troisièmement corrigé | $3^s\ 03^d\ 01'$ [illegible] |
| Apogée | − 7. 05. 29. [illegible] |
| Anomalie moyenne de la Lune | 7. 27. 32 [illegible] |

60' : [1' 39" / 3. 37] :: 32' 35" ! [1' 59" / 2. 08½] p. la 3e col. $6^d$ 06' 33" p. la 4e col. $6^d$ 4[illegible]
+ 01. 59 ..... + 0[illegible]
6. 08. 32 ..... 6. 44
35' 30" : 36' 10" ½ :: 8' 40" ! .... R. .... + 07. 56½ ..... 6. 08
Equation du centre ..... + 6. 16. 28⅓ Differ. ... 0. 36

| | |
|---|---|
| Lieu de la Lune quatrièmement corrigé | $03^s\ 09^d\ 19'$ [illegible] |
| Lieu du Soleil | 07. 24. 41. [illegible] |
| Distance de la Lune au Soleil | 07. 14. 37. [illegible] |

Pour 36' ..... 35' 59" ½ ; pour 37' ..... 36' 59" ½. Différence ..... [illegible]
Donc pour 36' 50" ½ Variation .... + 36. 50 ½

| | |
|---|---|
| Apogée de la Lune | $07^s\ 05^d\ 19'$ [illegible] |
| Apogée du Soleil | 03. 08. 36. [illegible] |
| Distance des Apogées | 03. 26. 33. [illegible] |
| Distance de la Lune au Soleil | 07. 14. 37. [illegible] |
| Somme des dist. de la Lune au Soleil & des apogées | 11. 11. 30. [illegible] |

| | |
|---|---|
| Moyen mouvement du Nœud rett. pour 1750 | $9^s\ 10^d\ 15'\ 00''$ |
| Pour le 16 Novemb... $16^d\ 56'\ 44''$ / Pour $14^h$ &c. ..... 00. 01. 59 } Somme à ôter. | 0. 16. 58. 43 |
| Longitude moyenne du Nœud | 8. 23. 16. 17 |
| Première Equation | + 00. 06. $31\frac{1}{2}$ |
| Lieu du Nœud premièrement corrigé | 8. 23. 22. $48\frac{1}{2}$ |
| Equation du Nœud | − 01. 14. $27\frac{1}{6}$ |
| Vrai lieu du Nœud | 8. 22. 08. $21\frac{1}{3}$ |
| Lieu du Soleil | $07^s\ 24^d\ 41'\ 45\frac{3}{4}$ |
| Lieu du Nœud premièrement corrigé | 08. 23. 22. $48\frac{1}{2}$ |
| Distance du Soleil au Nœud | 11. 01. 18. $56\frac{1}{4}$ |

60 : [1' 14" / 0. 13] :: 18' 56" ¼ ! [32" ½ / 4 ½]
$1^d$ 15' 00" ..... $5^d$ 13' 16"
− 00. 32 ½ ..... + 00. 04½
Equat. du Nœud − 1. 14. 27⅙ ..... 5. 13. 20½ Inclin. de l'orbite.

| | |
|---|---|
| Vrai lieu de la Lune | $3^s\ 09^d\ 55'\ 11''\frac{1}{2}$ |
| Lieu du Nœud | 8. 22. 08. $21\frac{1}{3}$ |
| Argument de la Latitude | 6. 17. 46. $56\frac{1}{6}$ |

R : sin. hyp. :: sin. incl. R. sin. $01^d\ 35'\ 34''$ Latitude australe.
$17^d\ 46'\ 50''$ ½ ..... $5^d\ 13'\ 20''$ ½
R : tang. hyp. :: cosin. inclin... ! R. tang. 17. 41. 41½ arc de l'Ecliptique.
17. 46. 50½ argum. de la Lait.
− 4. 09. Réduct. à l'Eclipt.

$6^d$ 00' : 6" :: $3^d$ 32' ½ ! 3" ½ ..... 16. 17 ..... 16. 19
− 03½ ..... − 03½
16. 13½ ..... 16. 15½
35d 30' : 21" :: 8' 40" ! ½ ..... + 00½ ..... 16. 13½
Demi-diamètre ..... 16. 14 Différence ... 00. 02
Correction ..... − 09⅔
Demi-diamètre corrigé ..... 16. 04⅓

$6^d$ 00' : [21" / 23] :: 3' 32" ½ ! [12" ½ / 13 ½] ..... 59. 01 ..... 59. 11
− 12½ ..... − 13½
58. 48½ ..... 58. 58½
35d 30' : 9" ½ :: 8' 40" ! ..... R. ..... 00. 02½ ..... 58. 48½
Parallaxe horizontale ..... 58. 50½ Differ. ... 00. 09½
Correction ..... − 36
Parallaxe horizont. corr. ..... 58. 14¼

LAKE ONTARIO

L. ERIE

UNIT

# MEMOIR

OF

# SAMUEL DE CHAMPLAIN.

## CHAPTER I.

HAMPLAIN was defcended from an anceftry whofe names are not recorded among the renowned families of France. He was the fon of Antoine de Champlain, a captain in the marine, and his wife Marguerite LeRoy. They lived in the little village of Brouage, in the ancient province of Saintonge. Of their fon Samuel, no contemporaneous record is known to exift indicating either the day or year of his birth. The period at which we find him engaged in active and refponfible duties, fuch as are ufually affigned to mature manhood, leads to the conjecture that he was born about

about the year 1567. Of his youth little is known. The forces that contributed to the formation of his character are moftly to be inferred from the abode of his early years, the occupations of thofe by whom he was furrounded, and the temper and fpirit of the times in which he lived.

Brouage is fituated in a low, marfhy region, on the fouthern bank of an inlet or arm of the fea, on the fouthweftern fhores of France, oppofite to that part of the Ifland of Oleron where it is feparated from the mainland only by a narrow channel. Although this little town can boaft a great antiquity, it never at any time had a large population. It is mentioned by local hiftorians as early as the middle of the eleventh century. It was a feigniory of the family of Pons. The village was founded by Jacques de Pons, after whofe proper name it was for a time called Jacopolis, but foon refumed its ancient appellation of Brouage.

An old chronicler of the fixteenth century informs us that in his time it was a port of great importance, and the theatre of a large foreign commerce. Its harbor, capable of receiving large fhips, was excellent, regarded, indeed, as the fineft in the kingdom of France.[1] It was a favorite idea of Charles VIII. to have at all times feveral war-fhips in this harbor, ready againft any fudden invafion of this part of the coaft.

At the period of Champlain's boyhood, the village of Brouage had two abforbing interefts. Firft, it had then recently

[1] The following from Marfhal de Monfluc refers to Brouage in 1568. Speaking of the Huguenots he fays : — " Or ils n'en pouvoient choifir un plus à leur advantage, que celui de la Rochelle, duquel dépend celui de Brouage, qui eft le plus beau port de mer de la France." *Commentaires*, Paris, 1760, Tom. III., p. 340.

cently become a military post of importance; and fecond, it
was the centre of a large manufacture of falt. To thefe
two interefts, the whole population gave their thoughts, their
energy, and their enterprife.

In the reign of Charles IX., a fhort time before or perhaps a little after the birth of Champlain, the town was
fortified, and diftinguifhed Italian engineers were employed
to defign and execute the work.[2] To prevent a fudden attack, it was furrounded by a capacious moat. At the four
angles formed by the moat were elevated ftruftures of earth
and wood planted upon piles, with baftions and projecting
angles, and the ufual devices of military architecture for the
attainment of ftrength and facility of defence.[3]

During the civil wars, ftretching over nearly forty years of
the laft half of the fixteenth century, with only brief and
fitful periods of peace, this little fortified town was a poft
ardently coveted by both of the contending parties. Situ-
ated on the fame coaft, and only a few miles from Rochelle,
the ftronghold of the Huguenots, it was obvioufly exceedingly important to them that it fhould be in their poffeffion,
both as the key to the commerce of the furrounding
country and from the very great annoyance which an
enemy holding it could offer to them in numberlefs ways.
Notwithftanding its ftrong defences, it was neverthelefs
taken and retaken feveral times during the ftruggles of that
period.

---

[2] "La Riviere Puitaillé qui en étoit
Gouverneur, fut chargé de faire travail-
ler aux fortifications. Belarmat, Be-
phano, Caftritio d'Urbin, & le Cavalier
Orlogio, tous Ingénieurs Italiens, pré-
fiderent aux travaux." — *Hiftoire La*

*Rochelle*, par Arcere, à la Rochelle, 1756,
Tom. I., p. 121.

[3] *Hiftoire de la Saintonge et de
l'Aunis*, 1152-1548, par M. D. Maffion,
Paris, 1838, Vol. II., p. 406.

period. It was furrendered to the Huguenots in 1570, but
was immediately reftored on the peace that prefently followed. The king of Navarre[4] took it by ftrategy in 1576,
placed a ftrong garrifon in it, repaired and ftrengthened its
fortifications; but the next year it was forced to furrender to
the royal army commanded by the duke of Mayenne.[5] In
1585, the Huguenots made another attempt to gain poffeffion
of the town. The Prince of Condé encamped with a ftrong
force on the road leading to Marennes, the only avenue to
Brouage by land, while the inhabitants of Rochelle co-oper-
ated by fending down a fleet which completely blocked up
the harbor.[6]  While the fiege was in fuccefsful progrefs, the
prince

[4] The King of Navarre "fent for
Monfieur *de Mirabeau* under colour of
treating with him concerning other bufi-
neffes, and forced him to deliver up
Brouage into his hands, a Fort of great
importance, as well for that it lies upon
the Coaft of the Ocean-sea, as becaufe
it abounds with fuch ftore of falt-pits,
which yeeld a great and conftant revenue; he made the Sieur de Montaut
Governour, and put into it a ftrong
Garrifon of his dependents, furnifhing
it with ammunition, and fortifying it
with exceeding diligence." — *His. Civ.
Warres of France,* by Henrico Caterino
Davila, London, 1647, p. 455.

[5] "The Duke of Mayenne, having
withoutdifficulty taken Thone-Charente,
and Marans, had laid fiege to Brouage, a
place, for fituation, ftrength, and the
profit of the falt-pits, of very great importance; when the Prince of Condé,
having tryed all poffible means to relieve
the befieged, the Hugonots after fome
difficulty were brought into fuch a condition, that about the end of Auguft
they delivered it up, faving only the

lives of the Souldiers and inhabitants,
which agreement the Duke punctually
obferved." — *His. Civ. Warres,* by
Davila, London, 1647, p. 472. See alfo
*Memoirs of Sully,* Phila., 1817, Vol. I.,
p. 69.
"*Le Jeudi* XXVIII *Mars.* Fut tenu
Confeil au Cabinet de la Royne mere
du Roy [pour] avifer ce que M. du
*Maine* avoit à faire, & j'ai mis en avant
l'enterprife de *Brouage.* — *Journal de
Henri III.,* Paris, 1744, Tom. III., p.
220.

[6] "The Prince of Condé refolved to
befiege Brouage, wherein was the Sieur
*de St. Luc,* one of the League, with no
contemptible number of infantry and
some other gentlemen of the Country.
The Rochellers confented to this Enterprife, both for their profit, and repu-
tation which redounded by it; and
having fent a great many Ships thither,
befieged the Fortrefs by Sea, whilft the
Prince having poffeffed that paffage
which is the only way to Brouage by
land, and having fhut up the Defendants
within the circuit of their walls, ftraight-
ned

prince unwifely drew off a part of his command for the relief of the caftle of Angiers;[7] and a month later the fiege was abandoned and the Huguenot forces were badly cut to pieces by de Saint Luc,[8] the military governor of Brouage, who purfued them in their retreat.

The next year, 1586, the town was again threatened by the Prince of Condé, who, having collected another army, was met by De Saint Luc near the ifland of Oleron, who fallied forth from Brouage with a ftrong force; and a conflict enfued, lafting the whole day, with equal lofs on both fides, but with no decifive refults.

Thus until 1589, when the King of Navarre, the leader of the Huguenots, entered into a truce with Henry III., from Champlain's birth through the whole period of his youth and until he entered upon his manhood, the little town within whofe walls he was reared was the fitful fcene of war and peace, of alarm and conflict.

But

ned the Siege very clofely on that fide." — *Davila*, p. 582. See alfo, *Hiftoire de Thou*, à Londres, 1734, Tom. IX., p. 383.

The blocking up the harbor at this time appears to have been more effective than convenient. Twenty boats or rafts filled with earth and ftone were funk with a purpofe of deftroying the harbor. De Saint Luc, the governor, fucceeded in removing only four or five. The entrance for veffels afterward remained difficult except at high tide. Subfequently Cardinal de Richelieu expended a hundred thoufand francs to remove the reft, but did not fucceed in removing one of them. — *Vide Hiftoire de La Rochelle*, par Arcere, Tom. I. p. 121.

[7] The Prince of Condé. "Leaving Monfieur de St. Mefmea with the In-

fantry and Artillery at the Siege of Brouage, and giving order that the Fleet fhould continue to block it up by fea, hee departed upon the eight of October to relieve the Caftle of Angiers with 800 Gentlemen and 1400 Harquebuziers on horfeback." — *Davila*, p. 583. See alfo *Memoirs of Sully*, Phila., 1817, Vol. I., p. 123; *Hiftoire de Thou*, à Londres, 1734, Tom. IX., p. 385.

[8] "*St. Luc* fallying out of Broüage, and following thofe that were fcattered feverall wayes, made a great flaughter of them in many places; whereupon the Commander, defpairing to rally the Army any more, got away as well as they could poffibly, to fecure their own ftrong holds." — *His. Civ. Warres of France*, by Henrico Caterino Davila, London, 1647, p. 588.

But in the intervals, when the waves of civil ſtrife ſettled into the calm of a temporary peace, the citizens returned with alacrity to their uſual employment, the manufacture of ſalt, which was the abſorbing article of commerce in their port.

This manufacture was carried on more extenſively in Saintonge than in any other part of France. The ſalt was obtained by ſubjecting water drawn from the ocean to ſolar evaporation. The low marſh-lands which were very exten- ſive about Brouage, on the ſouth towards Marennes and on the north towards Rochefort, were eminently adapted to this purpoſe. The whole of this vaſt region was cut up into ſalt baſins, generally in the form of parallelograms, excavated at different depths, the earth and rubbiſh ſcooped out and thrown on the ſides, forming a platform or path leading from baſin to baſin, the whole preſenting to the eye the appear- ance of a vaſt chefs-board. The argillaceous earth at the bottom of the pans was made hard to prevent the eſcape of the water by percolation. This was done in the larger ones by leading horſes over the ſurface, until, ſays an old chroni- cler, the baſins "would hold water as if they were braſs." The water was introduced from the ſea, through ſluices and ſieves of pierced planks, paſſing over broad ſurfaces in ſhal- low currents, furniſhing an opportunity for evaporation from the moment it left the ocean until it found its way into the numerous ſalt-baſins covering the whole expanſe of the marſhy plains. The water once in the baſins, the proceſs of evaporation was carried on by the ſun and the wind, aſſiſted by the workmen, who agitated the water to haſten the pro- ceſs. The firſt formation of ſalt was on the ſurface, having

a

a white, creamy appearance, exhaling an agreeable perfume
refembling that of violets. This was the fineft and moft
delicate falt, while that precipitated, or falling to the bottom
of the bafin, was of a darker hue.

When the cryftallization was completed, the falt was gathered up, drained, and piled in conical heaps on the platforms
or paths along the fides of the bafins. At the height of the
feafon, which began in May and ended in September, when
the whole marfh region was covered with countlefs white
cones of falt, it prefented an interefting picture, not unlike
the tented camp of a vaft army.

The falt was carried from the marfhes on pack-horfes,
equipped each with a white canvas bag, led by boys either to
the quay, where large veffels were lying, or to fmall barques
which could be brought at high tide, by natural or artificial
inlets, into the very heart of the marfh-fields.

When the period for removing the falt came, no time was
to be loft, as a fudden fall of rain might deftroy in an hour
the products of a month. A fmall quantity only could be
tranfported at a time, and confequently great numbers of
animals were employed, which were made to haften over the
finuous and angulated paths at their higheft fpeed. On
reaching the fhips, the burden was taken by men ftationed
for the purpofe, the boys mounted in hafte, and galloped
back for another.

The fcene prefented in the labyrinth of an extenfive falt-
marfh was lively and entertaining. The picturefque drefs
of the workmen, with their clean white frocks and linen
tights; the horfes in great numbers mantled in their fnowy
falt-bags, winding their way on the narrow platforms, moving
in

in all directions, turning now to the right hand and now to
the left, doubling almost numberlefs angles, here advancing
and again retreating, often going two leagues to make the
diftance of one, maintaining order in apparent confufion,
altogether prefented to the diftant obferver the afpect of a
grand equeftrian mafquerade.

The extent of the works and the labor and capital invefted
in them were doubtlefs large for that period. A contemporary of Champlain informs us that the wood employed in the
conftruction of the works, in the form of gigantic fluices,
bridges, beam-partitions, and fieves, was fo vaft in quantity
that, if it were deftroyed, the forefts of Guienne would not
fuffice to replace it. He alfo adds that no one who had feen
the falt works of Saintonge would eftimate the expenfe of
forming them lefs than that of building the city of Paris
itfelf.

The port of Brouage was the bufy mart from which
the falt of Saintonge was diftributed not only along the
coaft of France, but in London and Antwerp, and we know
not what other markets on the continent of Europe.[9]

The

<hr/>

[9] An old writer gives us fome idea of
the vaft quantities of falt exported from
France by the amount fent to a fingle
country.

"Important denique fexies mille vel
circiter centenarios falis, quorum finguli
conftant centenis modiis, ducentenas ut
minimum & vicenas quinas, vel & tri-
cenas, pro falis ipfius candore purita-
teque, libras pondo pendentibus. fena
igitur illa centenariorum millia, compu-
tatis in fingulos aureis nummis tricenis,
centum & octoginta referunt aureorum
millia." — *Belgicæ Defcriptio*, a Lud.
Gvicciardino, Amftelodami, 1652, p. 244.

TRANSLATION. — They import in fine
6000 centenarii of falt, each one of
which contains 100 bufhels, weighing
at leaft 225 or 230 pounds, according
to the purity and whitenefs of the falt;
therefore fix thoufand centenarii, com-
puting each at thirty golden nummi,
amount to 180,000 aurei.

It may not be eafy to determine the
value of this importation in money,
fince the value of gold is conftantly
changing, but the quantity imported
may be readily determined, which was
according to the above ftatement,
67,500 tons.

A

The early years of Champlain were of neceſſity intimately aſſociated with the ſtirring ſcenes thus preſented in this proſ-perous little ſeaport. As we know that he was a careful obſerver, endowed by nature with an active temperament and an unuſual degree of practical ſenſe, we are ſure that no event eſcaped his attention, and that no myſtery was per-mitted to go unſolved. The military and commercial enter-priſe of the place brought him into daily contact with men of the higheſt character in their departments. The ſalt-factors of Brouage were perſons of experience and activity, who knew their buſineſs, its methods, and the markets at home and abroad. The fortreſs was commanded by diſtin-guiſhed officers of the French army, and was a rendezvous of the young nobility ; like other ſimilar places, a training-ſchool for military command. In this aſſociation, whether near or remote, young Champlain, with his eagle eye and quick ear, was receiving leſſons and influences which were daily ſhaping his unfolding capacities, and gradually com-pacting and cryſtallizing them into the firmneſs and ſtrength of character which he ſo largely diſplayed in after years.

His education, ſuch as it was, was of courſe obtained dur-ing this period. He has himſelf given us no intimation of
                                                                         its

---

A treaty of April 30, 1527, between Francis I. of France and Henry VIII. of England, provided as follows : — "And, beſides, ſhould furniſh unto the ſaid *Henry*, as long as hee lived, yearly, of the Salt of *Broüage*, the value of fif-teene thouſand Crownes."—*Life and Raigne of Henry VIII.*, by Lord Her-bert of Cherbury, London, 1649, p. 206.

Saintonge continued for a long time to be the ſource of large exports of ſalt.

De Witt, writing about the year 1658, ſays they received in Holland of " ſalt, yearly, the lading of 500 or 600 ſhips, exported from Rochel, Maran, Brouage, the Iſland of Oleron, and Ree."—*Re-publick of Holland*, by John De Witt, London, 1702, p. 271. But it no longer holds the pre-eminence which it did three centuries ago. Saintonge long ſince yielded the palm to Brittany.

2

its character or extent. A careful examination of his numerous writings will, however, render it obvious that it was limited and rudimentary, fcarcely extending beyond the fundamental branches which were then regarded as neceffary in the ordinary tranfactions of bufinefs. As the refult of inftruction or affociation with educated men, he attained to a good general knowledge of the French language, but was never nicely accurate or eminently fkilful in its ufe. He evidently gave fome attention in his early years to the ftudy and practice of drawing. While the fpecimens of his work that have come down to us are marked by grave defects, he appears neverthelefs to have acquired facility and fome fkill in the art, which he made exceedingly ufeful in the illuftration of his difcoveries in the new world.

During Champlain's youth and the earlier years of his manhood, he appears to have been engaged in practical navigation. In his addrefs to the Queen [10] he fays, " this is the art which in my early years won my love, and has induced me to expofe myfelf almoft all my life to the impetuous waves of the ocean." That he began the practice of navigation at an early period may likewife be inferred from the fact that in 1599 he was put in command of a large French fhip of 500 tons, which had been chartered by the Spanifh authorities for a voyage to the Weft Indies, of which we fhall fpeak more particularly in the fequel. It is obvious that he could not have been intrufted with a command fo difficult and of fo great refponfibility without practical experience in navigation; and, as it will appear hereafter that he was in

the

[10] Vide *Œuvres de Champlain*, Quebec ed., Tom. III. p. v.

the army feveral years during the civil war, probably from
1592 to 1598, his experience in navigation muft have been
obtained anterior to that, in the years of his youth and early
manhood.

Brouage offered an excellent opportunity for fuch an employment. Its port was open to the commerce of foreign
nations, and a large number of veffels, as we have already
feen, was employed in the yearly diftribution of the falt of
Saintonge, not only in the feaport towns of France, but in
England and on the Continent. In thefe coafting expeditions, Champlain was acquiring fkill in navigation which was
to be of very great fervice to him in his future career, and
likewife gathering up rich ftores of experience, coming in
contaƈt with a great variety of men, obferving their manners
and cuftoms, and quickening and ftrengthening his natural
tafte for travel and adventure. It is not unlikely that he
was, at leaft during fome of thefe years, employed in the national marine, which was fully employed in guarding the
coaft againft foreign invafion, and in reftraining the power of
the Huguenots, who were firmly feated at Rochelle with a
fufficient naval force to give annoyance to their enemies
along the whole weftern coaft of France.

In 1592, or foon after that date, Champlain was appointed
quarter-mafter in the royal army in Brittany, difcharging the
office feveral years, until, by the peace of Vervins, in 1598, the
authority of Henry IV. was firmly eftablifhed throughout
the kingdom. This war in Brittany conftituted the clofing
fcene of that mighty ftruggle which had been agitating the
nation, wafting its refources and its beft blood for more
than half a century. It began in its incipient ftages as far
back

back as the decade following 1530, when the preaching of
Calvin in the Kingdom of Navarre began to make known
his tranfcendent power. The new faith, which was making
rapid ftrides in other countries, eafily awakened the warm
heart and active temperament of the French. The principle
of private judgment which lies at the foundation of Proteftant teaching, its fpontaneity as oppofed to a faith impofed
by authority, commended it efpecially to the learned and
thoughtful, while the fame principle awakened the quick and
impulfive nature of the maffes. The effort to put down the
movement by the extermination of thofe engaged in it,
proved not only unfuccefsful, but recoiled, as ufual in fuch
cafes, upon the hand that ftruck the blow. Confifcations, im-
prifonments, and the ftake daily increafed the number of
thofe which thefe fevere meafures were intended to dimin-
ifh. It was impoffible to mark its progrefs. When at intervals all was calm and placid on the furface, at the fame time,
down beneath, where the eye of the detective could not
penetrate, in the clofet of the fcholar and at the firefide of
the artifan and the peafant, the new gofpel, filently and without obfervation, was fpreading like an all-pervading leaven."

In 1562, the repreffed forces of the Huguenots could no
longer be reftrained, and, burfting forth, affumed the form
of

<hr />

[11] In 1558, it was eftimated that there
were already 400,000 perfons in France
who were declared adherents of the
Reformation.— *Ranke's Civil Wars in
France*, Vol. I., p. 234.

"Although our affemblies were moft
frequently held in the depth of midnight,
and our enemies very often heard us
paffing through the ftreet, yet fo it was,
that God bridled them in fuch manner
that we were preferved under His protection."— *Bernard Paliffy*, 1580. *Vide
Morlay's Life of Paliffy*, Vol. II., p.
274.

When Henry IV. befieged Paris, its
population was more than 200,000. —
*Malte-Brun.*

of organized civil war. With the exception of temporary lulls, originating in policy or exhauftion, there was no ceffation of arms until 1598. Although it is ufually and perhaps beft defcribed as a religious war, the ftruggle was not altogether between the Catholic and the Huguenot or Proteftant. There were many other elements that came in to give their coloring to the conteft, and efpecially to determine the courfe and policy of individuals.

The ultra-Catholic defired to maintain the old faith with all its ancient preftige and power, and to crufh out and exclude every other. With this party were found the court, certain ambitious and powerful families, and nearly all the officials of the church. In clofe alliance with it were the Roman Pontiff, the King of Spain, and the Catholic princes of Germany.

The Huguenots defired what is commonly known as liberty of confcience ; or, in other words, freedom to worfhip God according to their own views of the truth, without interference or reftriction. And in clofe alliance with them were the Queen of England and the Proteftant princes of Germany.

Perfonal motives, irrefpective of principle, united many perfons and families with either of thefe great parties which feemed moft likely to fubferve their private ambitions. The feudal fyftem was nearly extinct in form, but its fpirit was ftill alive. The nobles who had long held fway in fome of the provinces of France defired to hold them as diftinct and feparate governments, and to tranfmit them as an inheritance to their children. This motive often determined their political affociation.

During

During moſt of the period of this long civil war, Catherine de Médicis [15] was either regent or in the exerciſe of a controlling influence in the government of France. She was a woman of commanding perſon and extraordinary ability, ſkilful in intrigue, without conſcience and without perſonal religion. She heſitated at no crime, however black, if through it ſhe could attain the objects of her ambition. Neither of her three ſons, Francis, Charles, and Henry, who came ſucceſſively to the throne, left any legal heir to ſucceed him. The ſucceſſion became, therefore, at an early period, a queſtion of great intereſt. If not the potent cauſe, it was neverthelefs intimately connected with moſt of the blood-ſhed of that bloody period.

A ſolemn league was entered into by a large number of the ultra-Catholic nobles to ſecure two avowed objects, the ſucceſſion of a Catholic prince to the throne, and the utter extermination of the Huguenots. Henry, King of Navarre, afterwards Henry IV. of France, admitted to be the legal heir to the throne, was a Proteſtant, and therefore by the decree of the League difqualified to ſucceed. Around his ſtandard, the Huguenots rallied in great numbers. With him were aſſociated the princes of Condé, of royal blood, and many other diſtinguiſhed nobles. They contended for the double purpofe of ſecuring the throne to its rightful heir and of emancipating and eſtabliſhing the Proteſtant faith.

But there was another claſs, acting indeed with one or the

other

15 "Catherine de Médicis was of a large and, at the ſame time, firm and powerful figure; her countenance had an olive tint, and her prominent eyes and curled lip reminded the ſpectator of her great uncle, Leo X."— *Civil Wars in France,* by Leopold Ranke, London, 1852, p. 28.

other of thefe two great parties, neverthelefs influenced by very different motives. It was compofed of moderate Catholics, who cared little for the political fchemes and civil power of the Roman Pontiff, who dreaded the encroachments of the King of Spain, who were firmly patriotic and defired the aggrandizement and glory of France.

The ultra-Catholic party was, for a long period, by far the moft numerous and the more powerful; but the Huguenots were fufficiently ftrong to keep up the ftruggle with varying fuccefs for nearly forty years.

After the alliance of Henry of Navarre with Henry III. againft the League, the moderate Catholics and the Huguenots were united and fought together under the royal ftandard until the clofe of the war in 1598.

Champlain was perfonally engaged in the war in Brittany for feveral years. This province on the weftern coaft of France, conftituting a tongue of land jutting out as it were into the fea, ifolated and remote from the great centres of the war, was among the laft to furrender to the arms of Henry IV. The Huguenots had made but little progrefs within its borders. The Duke de Mercœur [18] had been its governor for fixteen years, and had bent all his energies to
separate

---

[18] Philippe Emanuel de Lorraine, Duc de Mercœur, born at Nomény, September 9, 1558, was the fon of Nicolas, Count de Vaudemont, by his fecond wife, Jeanne de Savoy, and was half-brother of Queen Louife, the wife of Henry III. He was made governor of Brittany in 1582. He embraced the party of the League before the death of Henry III., entered into an alliance with Philip II., and gave the Spaniards poffeffion of the port of Blavet in 1591. He made his fubmiffion to Henry IV. in 1598, on which occafion his only daughter Françoife, probably the richeft heirefs in the kingdom, was contracted in marriage to Céfar, Duc de Vendôme, the illegitimate fon of Henry IV. by Gabrielle d'Eftrées, the Duchefs de Beaufort. The Duc de Mercœur died at Nuremburg, February 19, 1602. — *Vide Birch's Memoirs of Queen Elizabeth,* Vol. I., p. 82; *Davila's His. Civil Warres of France,* p. 1476.

feparate it from France, organize it into a diftinct kingdom, and tranfmit its fceptre to his own family.

Champlain informs us that he was quarter-mafter in the army of the king under Marfhal d'Aumont, de Saint Luc, and Marshal de Briffac, diftinguifhed officers of the French army, who had been fucceffively in command in that province for the purpofe of reducing it into obedience to Henry IV.

Marfhal d'Aumont¹⁴ took command of the army in Brittany in 1592. He was then feventy years of age, an able and patriotic officer, a moderate Catholic, and an uncompromifing foe of the League. He had expreffed his fympathy for Henry IV. a long time before the death of Henry III., and when that event occurred he immediately efpoufed the caufe of the new monarch, and was at once appointed to the command

¹⁴ Jean d'Aumont, born in 1522, a Marfhal of France who ferved under fix kings, Francis I., Henry II., Francis II., Charles IX., Henry III., and Henry IV. He diftinguifhed himfelf at the battles of Dreux, Saint-Denis, Montcontour, and in the famous fiege of Rochelle in 1573. After the death of Henry III., he was the firft to recognize Henry IV., whom he ferved with the fame zeal as he had his five predeceffors. He took part in the brilliant battle of Arques in 1589. In the following year, he fo diftinguifhed himfelf at Ivry that Henry IV., inviting him to fup with him after this memorable battle, addreffed to him thefe flattering words, "Il eft jufte que vous foyez du feftin, après m'avoir fi bien fervi à mes noces." At the fiege of the Château de Camper, in Upper Brittany, he received a mufket fhot which fractured his arm, and died of the wound on the 19th of Auguft, 1595, at the age of feventy-three years. "Ce grand capitaine qui avoit fi bien merité du Roi et de la nation, emporta dans le tombeau les regrets des Officiers & des foldats, qui pleurerent amérement la perte de leur Général. La Bretagne qui le regardoit comme fon pere, le Roi, tout le Royaume enfin, furent extrêmement touchez de fa mort. Malgré la haine mutuelle des factions qui divifoient la France, il étoit fi eftimé dans les deux partis, que f'il fe fût agi de trouver un chevalier François fans reproche, tel que nos peres en ont autrefois eu, tout le monde auroit jetté les yeux fur d'Aumont." — *Hiftoire Univerfelle de Jacque-Augufte de Thou*, à Londres, 1734, Tom. XII., p. 446. *Vide* alfo, *Larouffe; Camden's His. Queen Elizabeth*, London, 1675, pp. 486, 487; *Memoirs of Sully*, Philadelphia, 1817, pp. 122, 210; *Œuvres de Brantôme*, Tom. IV., pp. 46–49; *Histoire de Bretagne*, par M. Daru, Paris, 1826, Vol. III. p. 319; *Freer's His. Henry IV.*, Vol. II., p. 70.

command of one of the three great divifions of the French army. He received a wound at the fiege of the Château de Camper, in Brittany, of which he died on the 19th of Auguft, 1595.

De Saint Luc, already in the fervice in Brittany, as lieutenant-general under D'Aumont, continued, after the death of that officer, in fole command.[15] He raifed the fiege of the Château de Camper after the death of his fuperior, and proceeded to capture feveral other pofts, marching through the lower part of the province, repreffing the licenfe of the foldiery, and introducing order and difcipline. On the 5th of September, 1596, he was appointed grand-mafter of the artillery of France, which terminated his fpecial fervice in Brittany.

The king immediately appointed in his place Marfhal de Briffac,[16] an officer of broad experience, who added other great

[15] François d'Efpinay de Saint-Luc, fometimes called *Le Brave Saint Luc*, was born in 1554, and was killed at the battle of Amiens on the 8th of September, 1597. He was early appointed governor of Saintonge, and of the Fortrefs of Brouage, which he fuccefsfully defended in 1585 againft the attack of the King of Navarre and the Prince de Condé. He affifted at the battle of Coutras in 1587. He ferved as a lieutenant-general in Brittany from 1592 to 1596. In 1594, he planned with Briffac, his brother-in-law, then governor of Paris for the League, for the furrender of Paris to Henry IV. For this he was offered the baton of a Marfhal of France by the king, which he modeftly declined, and begged that it might be given to Briffac. In 1578, through the influence or authority of Henry III., he married the

heirefs, Jeanne de Coffe-Briffac, fifter of Charles de Coffe-Briffac, mentioned in note 16, *poftea*, a lady of no perfonal attractions, but of excellent underftanding and character. — *Vide Courcelles' Hiftoire Généalogique des Pairs de France*, Vol. II.; *Birch's Memoirs of Queen Elizabeth*, Vol. I., pp. 163, 191; *Freer's Henry III.*, p. 162; *De Mezeray's His. France*, 1683, p. 861.

[16] Charles de Coffe-Briffac, a Marfhal of France and governor of Angiers. He was a member of the League as early as 1585. He conceived the idea of making France a republic after the model of ancient Rome. He laid his views before the chief Leaguers but none of them approved his plan. He delivered up Paris, of which he was governor, to Henry IV. in 1594, for which he received the Marfhal's baton. He died in 1621, at

3

great qualities to thofe of an able foldier. No diftinguifhed battles fignalized the remaining months of the civil war in this province. The exhaufted refources and faltering courage of the people could no longer be fuftained by the flatteries or promifes of the Duke de Mercœur. Wherever the fquadrons of the marfhal made their appearance the flag of truce was raifed, and town, city, and fortrefs vied with each other in their hafte to bring their enfigns and lay them at his feet.

On the feventh of June, 1598, the peace of Vervins was publifhed in Paris, and the kingdom of France was a unit, with the general fatisfaction of all parties, under the able, wife, and catholic fovereign, Henry the Fourth.[17]

CHAPTER II.

at the fiege of Saint Jean d'Angely.— *Vide Davila*, pp. 538, 584, 585 ; *Sully*, Philadelphia, 1817, Vol. I., p. 420; *Brantôme*, Vol. III., p. 84; *His. Collections*, London, 1598, p. 35 ; *De Thou*, a Londres, 1724, Tome XII., p. 449.

[17] "By the Articles of this Treaty the king was to reftore the County of *Charolois* to the king of *Spain*, to be by him held of the Crown of *France*; who in exchange reftor'd the towns of *Calice, Ardres, Montbulin, Dourlens, la Capelle,* and *le Catelet* in *Picardy*, and *Blavet* in

*Britanny:* which Articles were Ratifi'd and Sign'd by his Majefty the eleventh of June [1598] ; who in his gayety of humour, at fo happy a conclufion, told the Duke of *Efpernon, That with one dafh of his Pen he had done greater things, than he could of a long time have perform'd with the beft Swords of his Kingdom." — *Life of the Duke of Efpernon*, London, 1670, p. 203 ; *Hiftoire du Roy Henry le Grand*, par Prefixe, Paris, 1681, p. 243.

### CHAPTER II.

Quarter-master. — Visit to West Indies, South America, Mexico. — His Report. — Suggests a Ship Canal. — Voyage of 1603. — Earlier Voyages. — Cartier, De la Roque, Marquis de la Roche, Sieur de Chauvin, De Chastes. — Preliminary Voyage. — Return to France. — Death of de Chastes. — Sieur de Monts obtains a Charter, and prepares for an Expedition to Canada.

HE fervice of Champlain as quarter-mafter in the war in Brittany commenced probably with the appointment of Marfhal d'Aumont to the command of the army in 1592, and, if we are right in this conjecture, it covered a period of not far from fix years. The activity of the army, and the difficulty of obtaining fupplies in the general deftitution of the province, impofed upon him conftant and perplexing duty. But in the midft of his embarraffments he was gathering up valuable experience, not only relating to the conduct of war, but to the tranfactions of bufinefs under a great variety of forms. He was brought into clofe and intimate relations with men of character, ftanding, and influence. The knowledge, difcipline, and felf-control of which he was daily becoming mafter were unconfcioufly fitting him for a career, humble though it might feem in its feveral ftages, but neverthelefs noble and potent in its relations to other generations.

At the clofe of the war, the army which it had called into exiftence was difbanded, the foldiers departed to their homes, the office of quarter-mafter was of neceffity vacated, and Champlain was left without employment.

Cafting

Cafting about for fome new occupation, following his in-
ftinctive love of travel and adventure, he conceived the idea
of attempting an exploration of the Spanifh Weft Indies,
with the purpofe of bringing back a report that should be
ufeful to France. But this was an enterprife not eafy either
to inaugurate or carry out. The colonial eftablifhments of
Spain were at that time hermetically fealed againft all intercourfe with foreign nations. Armed fhips, like watch-dogs,
were ever on the alert, and foreign merchantmen entered
their ports only at the peril of confifcation. It was neceffary for Spain to fend out annually a fleet, under a convoy
of fhips of war, for the tranfportation of merchandife and
fupplies for the colonies, returning laden with cargoes of
almoft pricelefs value. Champlain, fertile in expedient, propofed to himfelf to vifit Spain, and there form fuch acquaintances and obtain fuch influence as would fecure to him in
fome way a paffage to the Indies in this annual expedition.

The Spanifh forces, allies of the League in the late war, had
not yet departed from the coaft of France. He haftened to
the port of Blavet,[18] where they were about to embark, and
learned to his furprife and gratification that feveral French
fhips had been chartered, and that his uncle, a diftinguifhed
French mariner, commonly known as the *Provençal Cappitaine*, had received orders from Marfhal de Briffac to conduct
the fleet, on which the garrifon of Blavet was embarked, to
Cadiz in Spain. Champlain eafily arranged to accompany

his

[18] Blavet was fituated at the mouth of
the River Blavet, on the fouthern coaft
of Brittany. Its occupation had been
granted to the Spanifh by the Duke de
Mercœur during the civil war, and, with
other places held by the Spanifh, was
furrendered by the treaty of Vervins, in
June, 1598. It was rebuilt and fortified
by Louis XIII., and is now known as
Port Louis.

his uncle, who was in command of the " St. Julian," a ftrong, well-built fhip of five hundred tons.

Having arrived at Cadiz, and the object of the voyage having been accomplifhed, the French fhips were difmiffed, with the exception of the " St. Julian," which was retained, with the Provincial Captain, who had accepted the office of pilot-general for that year, in the fervice of the King of Spain.

After lingering a month at Cadiz, they proceeded to St. Lucar de Barameda, where Champlain remained three months, agreeably occupied in making obfervations and drawings of both city and country, including a vifit to Seville, fome fifty miles in the interior.

In the mean time, the fleet for the annual vifit to the Weft Indies, to which we have already alluded, was fitting out at Saint Lucar, and about to fail under the command of Don Francifco Colombo, who, attracted by the fize and good failing qualities of the " Saint Julian," chartered her for the voyage. The fervices of the pilot-general were required in another direction, and, with the approbation of Colombo, he gave the command of the " Saint Julian " to Champlain. Nothing could have been more gratifying than this appointment, which affured to Champlain a vifit to the more important Spanifh colonies under the moft favorable circumftances.

He accordingly fet fail with the fleet, which left Saint Lucar at the beginning of January, 1599.

Paffing the Canaries, in two months and fix days they fighted the little ifland of Defeada,[19] the *veftibule* of the

great

---

[19] *Defeada*, fignifying in Spanifh the defired land.

great Caribbean archipelago, touched at Guadaloupe, wound
their way among the group called the Virgins, turning to
the fouth made for Margarita,[20] then famous for its pearl
fifheries, and from thence failed to St. Juan de Porto-rico.
Here the fleet was divided into three fquadrons. One was
to go to Porto-bello, on the Ifthmus of Panama, another to
the coaft of South America, then called Terra Firma, and
the third to Mexico, then known as New Spain. This latter
fquadron, to which Champlain was attached, coafted along
the northern fhore of the ifland of Saint Domingo, otherwife Hifpaniola, touching at Porto Platte, Mancenilla, Mofquitoes, Monte Chrifto, and Saint Nicholas. Skirting the
fouthern coaft of Cuba, reconnoitring the Caymans,[21] they
at length caft anchor in the harbor of San Juan d'Ulloa, the
ifland fortrefs near Vera Cruz. While here, Champlain
made an inland journey to the City of Mexico, where he
remained a month. He alfo failed in a *patache*, or advice-
boat, to Porto-bello, when, after a month, he returned again
                                                          to

[20] *Margarita*, a Spanifh word from the Greek μαργαρίτης, fignifying a pearl. The following account by an eye-witnefs will not be uninterefting: " Efpecially it yieldeth ftore of pearls, thofe gems which the Latin writers call *Uniones*, becaufe *nulli duo reperiuntur difcreti*, they always are found to grow in couples. In this Ifland there are many rich Mer- chants, who have thirty, forty, fifty *Blackmore* flaves only to fifh out of the fea about the rocks thefe pearls. . . . They are let down in bafkets into the Sea, and fo long continue under the water, until by pulling the rope by which they are let down, they make their fign to be taken up. . . . From *Margarita* are all the Pearls fent to be refined and bored to *Carthagena*, where is a fair and goodly ftreet of no other fhops then of thefe Pearl dreffers. Commonly in the month of *July* there is a fhip or two at moft ready in the Ifland to carry the King's revenue, and the Merchant's pearls to *Carthagena*. One of thefe fhips is valued commonly at three fcore thoufand or four fcore thoufand ducats and fometimes more, and therefore are reafonable well manned; for that the *Spaniards* much fear our *Englifh* and the *Holland* fhips."—*Vide New Survey of the Weft Indies*, by Thomas Gage, London, 1677, p. 174.
[21] *Caymans*, Crocodiles.

to San Juan d'Ulloa. The fquadron then failed for Havana, from which place Champlain was commiffioned to
vifit, on public bufinefs, Cartagena, within the prefent limits
of New Grenada, on the coaft of South America. The
whole *armada* was finally collected together at Havana, and
from thence took its departure for Spain, paffing through
the channel of Bahama, or Gulf of Florida, fighting Ber-
muda and the Azores, reaching Saint Lucar early in March,
1601, after an abfence from that port of two years and two
months."

On Champlain's return to France, he prepared an elaborate report of his obfervations and difcoveries, luminous
with fixty-two illuftrations fketched by his own hand. As it
was his avowed purpofe in making the voyage to procure
information that fhould be valuable to his government, he
undoubtedly communicated it in fome form to Henry IV.
The document remained in manufcript two hundred and
fifty-feven years, when it was firft printed at London in an
Englifh tranflation by the Hakluyt Society, in 1859. It is
an exceedingly interefting and valuable tract, containing a
lucid defcription of the peculiarities, manners, and cuftoms
of the people, the foil, mountains, and rivers, the trees, fruits,
and plants, the animals, birds, and fifhes, the rich mines found
at different points, with frequent allufions to the fyftem of
colonial management, together with the character and fources
of the vaft wealth which thefe fettlements were annually
yielding to the Spanifh crown.
The

<sub>™ For an interefting account of the English corfairs, see *Notes on Giovanni da Verrazano*, by J. C. Brevoort, New York, 1874, p. 101.</sub>

The reader of this little treatife will not fail to fee the drift and tendency of Champlain's mind and character un-folded on nearly every page. His indomitable perfeverance, his careful obfervation, his honeft purpofe and amiable fpirit are at all times apparent. Although a Frenchman, a foreigner, and an entire ftranger in the Spanifh fleet, he had won the confidence of the commander fo completely, that he was allowed by fpecial permiffion to vifit the City of Mexico, the Ifthmus of Panama, and the coaft of South America, all of which were prominent and important centres of intereft, but neverthelefs lying beyond the circuit made by the fquadron to which he was attached.

For the moft part, Champlain's narrative of what he faw and of what he learned from others is given in fimple terms, without inference or comment.

His views are, however, clearly apparent in his defcription of the Spanifh method of converting the Indians by the Inquifition, reducing them to flavery or the horrors of a cruel death, together with the retaliation practifed by their furviving comrades, refulting in a milder method. This treatment of the poor favages by their more favage mafters Champlain illuftrates by a graphic drawing, in which two ftolid Spaniards are guarding half a dozen poor wretches who are burning for their faith. In another drawing he reprefents a miferable victim receiving, under the eye and direction of the prieft, the blows of an uplifted baton, as a penalty for not attending church.

Champlain's forecaft and fertility of mind may be clearly feen in his fuggeftion that a ship-canal acrofs the Ifthmus of Panama would be a work of great practical utility, faving, in the

the voyage to the Pacific fide of the Ifthmus, a diftance of more than fifteen hundred leagues.[23]

As it was the policy of Spain to withhold as much as poffible all knowledge of her colonial fyftem and wealth in the Weft Indies, we may add, that there is probably no work extant, on this fubject, written at that period, fo full, impartial, and truthful as this tract by Champlain. It was undoubtedly written out from notes and fketches made on the fpot

[23] At the time that Champlain was at the ifthmus, in 1599–1601, the gold and filver of Peru were brought to Panama, then tranfported on mules a diftance of about four leagues to a river, known as the Rio Chagres, whence they were conveyed by water firft to Chagres, and thence along the coaft to Porto-bello, and there fhipped to Spain.

Champlain refers to a fhip-canal in the following words : "One might judge, if the territory four leagues in extent lying between Panama and this river were cut through, he could pafs from the fouth fea to that on the other fide, and thus fhorten the route by more than fifteen hundred leagues. From Panama to the Straits of Magellan would conftitute an ifland, and from Panama to New Foundland another, fo that the whole of America would be in two iflands." — *Vide Brief Difcovrs des Chofes Plvs Remarqvables*, par Sammvel Champlain de Brovage, 1599, Quebec ed., Vol. I. p. 41. This project of a fhip canal acrofs the ifthmus thus fuggefted by Champlain two hundred and eighty years ago is now attracting the public attention both in this country and in Europe. Several fchemes are on foot for bringing it to pafs, and it will undoubtedly be accomplifhed, if it fhall be found after the moft careful and thorough inveftigation to be within the fcope of

human power, and to offer adequate commercial advantages.

Some of the difficulties to be overcome are fuggefted by Mr. Marfh in the following excerpt :—

"The moft coloffal project of canalization ever fuggefted, whether we confider the phyfical difficulties of its execution, the magnitude and importance of the waters propofed to be united, or the diftance which would be faved in navigation, is that of a channel between the Gulf of Mexico and the Pacific, acrofs the Ifthmus of Darien. I do not now fpeak of a lock-canal, by way of the Lake of Nicaragua, or any other route, — for fuch a work would not differ effentially from other canals and would fcarcely poffefs a geographical character, —but of an open cut between the two feas. The late furvey by Captain Selfridge, fhowing that the loweft point on the dividing ridge is 763 feet above the fea-level, muft be confidered as determining in the negative the queftion of the poffibility of fuch a cut, by any means now at the control of man ; and both the fanguine expectations of benefits, and the dreary fuggeftions of danger from the realization of this great dream, may now be difmiffed as equally chimerical." — *Vide The Earth as Modified by Human Action*, by George P. Marfh, New York, 1874, p. 612.

4

fpot, and probably occupied the early part of the two years that followed his return from this expedition, during which period we are not aware that he entered upon any other important enterprife.[24]

This tour among the Spanifh colonies, and the defcription which Champlain gave of them, information fo much defired and yet fo difficult to obtain, appear to have made a ftrong and favorable impreffion upon the mind of Henry IV., whose quick comprehenfion of the character of men was one of the great qualities of this diftinguifhed fovereign. He clearly faw that Champlain's character was made up of thofe elements which are indifpenfable in the fervants of the executive will. He accordingly affigned him a penfion to enable him to refide near his perfon, and probably at the fame time honored him with a place within the charmed circle of the nobility.[25]

While Champlain was refiding at court, rejoicing doubtlefs in his new honors and full of the marvels of his recent travels, he formed the acquaintance, or perhaps renewed an old one, with Commander de Chaftes,[26] for many years governor

[24] A tranflation of Champlain's Voyage to the Weft Indies and Mexico was made by Alice Wilmere, edited by Norton Shaw, and publifhed by the Hakluyt Society, London, 1859.

[25] No pofitive evidence is known to exift as to the time when Champlain was ennobled. It feems moft likely to have been in acknowledgment of his valuable report made to Henry IV. after his vifit to the Weft Indies.

[26] Amyar de Chaftes died on the 13th of May, 1603, greatly refpected and beloved by his fellow-citizens. He was charged by his government with many important and refponfible duties. In 1583, he was fent by Henry III., or rather by Catherine de Médicis, to the Azores with a military force to fuftain the claims of Antonio, the Prior of Crato, to the throne of Portugal. He was a warm friend and fupporter of Henry IV., and took an active part in the battles of Ivry and Arques. He commanded the French fleet on the coafts of Brittany; and, during the long ftruggle of this monarch with internal enemies and external foes, he was in frequent communication

ernor of Dieppe, who had given a long life to the fervice of
his country, both by fea" and by land, and was a warm and
attached friend of Henry IV. The enthufiafm of the young
voyager and the long experience of the old commander made
their interviews mutually inftructive and entertaining. De
Chaftes had obferved and ftudied with great intereft the recent efforts at colonization on the coaft of North America.
His zeal had been kindled and his ardor deepened doubtlefs
by the glowing recitals of his young friend. It was eafy for
him to believe that France, as well as Spain, might gather in
the golden fruits of colonization. The territory claimed by
France was farther to the north, in climate and in fources of
wealth widely different, and would require a different management. He had determined, therefore, to fend out an
expedition for the purpofe of obtaining more definite information than he already poffeffed, with the view to furrender fubfequently his government of Dieppe, take up his
abode in the new world, and there dedicate his remaining
years to the fervice of God and his king. He accordingly
obtained

cation with the Englifh to fecure their
co-operation, particularly againft the
Spanifh. He accompanied the Duke
de Boullon, the diftinguifhed Huguenot
nobleman, to England, to be prefent and
witnefs the oath of Queen Elizabeth to
the treaty made with France.

On this occafion he received a valuable jewel as a prefent from the Englifh
queen. He afterwards directed the ceremonies and entertainment of the Earl of
Shrewfbury, who was deputed to receive
the ratification of the before-mentioned
treaty by Henry IV. *Vide Buft's His.
Spain and Portugal,* London, 1833, p.
129 *et paffim; Denis' His. Portugal,*

Paris, 1846, p. 296; *Freer's Life of
Henry IV.,* Vol. I. p. 121, *et paffim;
Memoirs of Sully,* Philadelphia, 1817,
Vol. I. p. 204; *Birch's Memoirs Queen
Elizabeth,* London, 1754, Vol. II. pp.
121, 145, 151, 154, 155; *Affelini MSS.
Chron.,* cited by Shaw in *Nar. Voyage
to Weft Ind. and Mexico,* Hakluyt Soc.,
1859, p. xv.

" "Au même tems les nouvelles
vinrent. . . . . . . que le Commandeur
de Chaftes dreffoit une grande Armée de
Mer en Bretagne."— *Journal de Henri
III.* (1586), Paris, 1744, Tom. III. p.
279.

obtained a commiffion from the king, affociating with himfelf
fome of the principal merchants of Rouen and other cities,
and made preparations for defpatching a pioneer fleet to reconnoitre and fix upon a proper place for fettlement, and to
determine what equipment would be neceffary for the convenience and comfort of the colony. He fecured the fervices
of Pont Gravé,[28] a diftinguifhed merchant and Canadian fur-
trader, to conduct the expedition. Having laid his views
open fully to Champlain, he invited him alfo to join the exploring party, as he defired the opinion and advice of fo
careful an obferver as to a proper plan of future operations.

No propofition could have been more agreeable to Champlain than this, and he expreffed himfelf quite ready for the
enterprife, provided De Chaftes would fecure the confent of
the king, to whom he was under very great obligations.
De Chaftes readily obtained the defired permiffion, coupled,
however, with an order from the king to Champlain to bring
back to him a faithful report of the voyage. Leaving Paris,
Champlain haftened to Honfleur, armed with a letter of in-
ftructions from M. de Gefures, the fecretary of the king, to
Pont Gravé, directing him to receive Champlain and afford
him every facility for feeing and exploring the country which
they were about to vifit. They failed for the fhores of the
New World on the 15th of March, 1603.

The reader fhould here obferve that anterior to this date no
colonial fettlement had been made on the northern coafts of
America.

[28] Du Pont Gravé was a merchant of
St. Malo. He had been affociated with
Chauvin in the Canada trade, and continued to vifit the St. Lawrence for this
purpofe almoft yearly for thirty years. He was greatly refpected by Champlain,
and was clofely affociated with him till
1629. After the Englifh captured Quebec, he appears to have retired, forced
to do fo by the infirmities of age.

America. Thefe regions had, however, been frequented by European fifhermen at a very early period, certainly within the decade after its difcovery by John Cabot in 1497. But the Bafques, Bretons, and Normans,[29] who vifited thefe coafts, were intent upon their employment, and confequently brought home only meagre information of the country from whofe fhores they yearly bore away rich cargoes of fifh.

The firft voyage made by the French for the purpofe of difcovery in our northern waters of which we have any authentic record was by Jacques Cartier in 1534, and another was made for the fame purpofe by this diftinguifhed navigator in 1535. In the former, he coafted along the fhores of Newfoundland, entered and gave its prefent name to the Bay of Chaleur, and at Gafpé took formal poffeffion of the country in the name of the king. In the fecond, he afcended the St. Lawrence as far as Montreal, then an Indian village known by the aborigines as Hochelaga, fituated on an ifland at the bafe of an eminence which they named *Mont-Royal,* from which the prefent commercial metropolis of the Dominion derives its name. After a winter of great fuffering, which they paffed on the St. Charles, near Quebec, and the death of many of his company, Cartier returned to France early in the fummer of 1536. In 1541, he made a third voyage, under the patronage of François de la Roque, Lord de Roberval, a nobleman of Picardy. He failed up the St. Lawrence,

---

[29] Jean Parmentier, of Dieppe, author of the *Difcorfo d'un gran capitano* in Ramufio, Vol. III., p. 423, wrote in the year 1539, and he fays the Bretons and Normans were in our northern waters thirty-five years before, which would be in 1504. *Vide* Mr. Parkman's learned note and citations in *Pioneers of France in the New World,* pp. 171, 172. The above is doubtlefs the authority on which the early writers, such as Pierre Biard, Champlain, and others, make the year 1504 the period when the French voyages for fifhing commenced.

rence, anchoring probably at the mouth of the river Cap Rouge, about four leagues above Quebec, where he built a fort which he named *Charlefbourg-Royal.* Here he paffed another dreary and diſheartening winter, and returned to France in the ſpring of 1542. His patron, De Roberval, who had failed to fulfil his intention to accompany him the preceding year, met him at St. John, Newfoundland. In vain Roberval urged and commanded him to retrace his courſe ; but the refolute old navigator had too recent an experience and faw too clearly the inevitable obſtacles to fuccefs in their undertaking to be diverted from his purpoſe. Roberval proceeded up the Saint Lawrence, apparently to the fort juſt abandoned by Cartier, which he repaired and occupied the next winter, naming it *Roy-François;*[10] but the diſaſters which followed, the ſicknefs and death of many of his company, foon forced him, likewiſe, to abandon the enterpriſe and return to France.

Of these voyages, Cartier, or rather his pilot-general, has left full and elaborate reports, giving intereſting and detailed accounts of the mode of life among the aborigines, and of the character and products of the country.

The entire want of fuccefs in all theſe attempts, and the abforbing and waſting civil wars in France, paralyzed the zeal and put to reſt all afpirations for colonial adventure for more than half a century.

But in 1598, when peace again began to dawn upon the nation, the fpirit of colonization revived, and the Marquis de la Roche, a nobleman of Brittany, obtained a royal commiſſion

[10] *Vide Voyage of Iohn Alphonſe of Xanctoigne,* Hakluyt, Vol. III., p. 293.

miffion with extraordinary and exclufive powers of government and trade, identical with thofe granted to Roberval
nearly fixty years before.  Having fitted out a veffel and
placed on board forty convicts gathered out of the prifons of
France, he embarked for the northern coafts of America.
The firft land he made was Sable Ifland, a moft forlorn fand-
heap rifing out of the Atlantic Ocean, fome thirty leagues
foutheaft of Cape Breton.   Here he left thefe wretched criminals to be the ftrength and hope, the bone and finew of the
little kingdom which, in his fancy, he pictured to himfelf
rifing under his foftering care in the New World.   While
reconnoitring the mainland, probably fome part of Nova
Scotia, for the purpofe of felecting a fuitable location for his
intended fettlement, a furious gale fwept him from the coaft,
and, either from neceffity or inclination, he returned to
France, leaving his hopeful colonifts to a fate hardly furpaffed by that of Selkirk himfelf, and at the fame time dif-
miffing the bright vifions that had fo long haunted his mind,
of perfonal aggrandizement at the head of a colonial eftablifhment.
   The next year, 1599, Sieur de Saint Chauvin, of Normandy, a captain in the royal marine, at the fuggeftion of
Pont Gravé, of Saint Malo, an experienced fur-trader, to
whom we have already referred, and who had made feveral
voyages to the northweft anterior to this, obtained a commiffion fufficiently comprehenfive, amply providing for a colonial fettlement and the propagation of the Chriftian faith,
with, indeed, all the privileges accorded by that of the Marquis de la Roche.   But the chief and prefent object which
Chauvin and Pont Gravé hoped to attain was the monopoly
                                                         of

of the fur trade, which they had good reafon to believe they could at that time conduct with fuccefs. Under this commiffion, an expedition was accordingly fitted out and failed for Tadouffac. Succefsful in its main object, with a full cargo of valuable furs, they returned to France in the autumn, leaving, however, fixteen men, fome of whom perifhed during the winter, while the reft were refcued from the fame fate by the charity of the Indians. In the year 1600, Chauvin made another voyage, which was equally remunerative, and a third had been projected on a much broader fcale, when his death intervened and prevented its execution.

The death of Sieur de Chauvin appears to have vacated his commiffion, at leaft practically, opening the way for another, which was obtained by the Commander de Chaftes, whofe expedition, accompanied by Champlain, as we have already feen, left Honfleur on the 15th of March, 1603. It confifted of two barques of twelve or fifteen tons, one commanded by Pont Gravé, and the other by Sieur Prevert, of Saint Malo, and was probably accompanied by one or more advice-boats. They took with them two Indians who had been in France fome time, doubtlefs brought over by De Chauvin on his laft voyage. With favoring winds, they foon reached the banks of Newfoundland, fighted Cape Ray, the northern point of the Ifland of Cape Breton, Anticofti and Gaspé, coafting along the fouthern fide of the river Saint Lawrence as far as the Bic, where, croffing over to the northern fhore, they anchored in the harbor of Tadouffac. After reconnoitring the Saguenay twelve or fifteen leagues, leaving their veffels at Tadouffac, where an active fur trade was in progrefs with the Indians, they proceeded up the St. Lawrence

Lawrence in a light boat, paſſed Quebec, the Three Rivers, Lake St. Peter, the Richelieu, which they called the river of the Iroquois, making an excurſion up this ſtream five or ſix leagues, and then, continuing their courſe, paſſing Montreal, they finally caſt anchor on the northern ſide, at the foot of the Falls of St. Louis, not being able to proceed further in their boat.

Having previouſly conſtructed a ſkiff for the purpoſe, Pont Gravé and Champlain, with five ſailors and two Indians with a canoe, attempted to paſs the falls. But after a long and perſevering trial, exploring the ſhores on foot for ſome miles, they found any further progreſs quite impoſſible with their preſent equipment. They accordingly abandoned the undertaking and ſet out on their return to Tadouſſac. They made ſhort ſtops at various points, enabling Champlain to purſue his inveſtigations with thoroughneſs and deliberation. He interrogated the Indians as to the courſe and extent of the St. Lawrence, as well as that of the other large rivers, the location of the lakes and falls, and the outlines and general features of the country, making rude drawings or maps to illuſtrate what the Indians found difficult otherwiſe to explain.[81]

The ſavages alſo exhibited to them ſpecimens of native copper, which they repreſented as having been obtained from the diſtant north, doubtleſs from the neighborhood of Lake Superior. On reaching Tadouſſac, they made another excurſion in one of the barques as far as Gaſpé, obſerving the rivers,

[81] Compare the reſult of theſe inquiries as ſtated by Champlain, p. 252 of this vol. and *New Voyages,* by Baron La Hontan, 1684, ed. 1735, Vol. I. p. 30.

rivers, bays, and coves along the route. When they had completed their trade with the Indians and had fecured from them a valuable collection of furs, they commenced their return voyage to France, touching at feveral important points, and obtaining from the natives fome general hints in regard to the exiftence of certain mines about the head waters of the Bay of Fundy.

Before leaving, one of the Sagamores placed his fon in charge of Pont Gravé, that he might fee the wonders of France, thus exhibiting a commendable appreciation of the advantages of foreign travel. They alfo obtained the gift of an Iroquois woman, who had been taken in war, and was foon to be immolated as one of the victims at a cannibal feaft. Befides thefe, they took with them alfo four other natives, a man from the coaft of La Cadie, and a woman and two boys from Canada.

The two little barques left Gafpé on the 24th of Auguft; on the 5th of September they were at the fifhing ftations on the Grand Banks, and on the 20th of the fame month arrived at Havre de Grâce, having been abfent fix months and fix days.

Champlain received on his arrival the painful intelligence that the Commander de Chaftes, his friend and patron, under whofe aufpices the late expedition had been conducted, had died on the 13th of May preceding. This event was a perfonal grief as well as a ferious calamity to him, as it deprived him of an intimate and valued friend, and caft a cloud over the bright vifions that floated before him of difcoveries and colonies in the New World. He loft no time in repairing to the court, where he laid before his fovereign, Henry IV.,

Henry IV., a map conftructed by his own hand of the regions which he had juft vifited, together with a very particular narrative of the voyage.

This "petit difcours," as Champlain calls it, is a clear, compact, well-drawn paper, containing an account of the character and products of the country, its trees, plants, fruits, and vines, with a defcription of the native inhabitants, their mode of living, their clothing, food and its preparation, their banquets, religion, and method of burying their dead, with many other interefting particulars relating to their habits and cuftoms.

Henry IV. manifefted a deep intereft in Champlain's narrative. He liftened to its recital with great apparent fatiffaction, and by way of encouragement promifed not to abandon the undertaking, but to continue to beftow upon it his royal favor and patronage.

There chanced at this time to be refiding at court, a Huguenot gentleman who had been a faithful adherent of Henry IV. in the late war, Pierre du Guaft, Sieur de Monts, gentleman ordinary to the king's chamber, and governor of Pons in Saintonge. This nobleman had made a trip for pleafure or recreation to Canada with De Chauvin, feveral years before, and had learned fomething of the country, and efpecially of the advantages of the fur trade with the Indians. He was quite ready, on the death of De Chaftes, to take up the enterprife which, by this event, had been brought to a fudden and difaftrous termination. He immediately devifed a fcheme for the eftablifhment of a colony under the patronage of a company to be compofed of merchants of Rouen, Rochelle, and of other places, their contributions for covering

ing the expenfe of the enterprife to be fupplemented, if not rendered entirely unneceffary, by a trade in furs and peltry to be conducted by the company.

In lefs than two months after the return of the laft expe- dition, De Monts had obtained from Henry IV., though contrary to the advice of his moft influential minifter,[*] a char- ter conftituting him the king's lieutenant in La Cadie, with all neceffary and defirable powers for a colonial fettlement. The grant included the whole territory lying between the 40th and 46th degrees of north latitude.  Its fouthern boundary was on a parallel of Philadelphia, while its north- ern was on a line extended due weft from the moft eafterly point of the Ifland of Cape Breton, cutting New Brunfwick on a parallel near Fredericton, and Canada near the junc- tion of the river Richelieu and the St. Lawrence.  It will be obferved that the parts of New France at that time beft known were not included in this grant, viz., Lake St. Peter, Three Rivers, Quebec, Tadouffac, Gafpé, and the Bay Cha- leur.  Thefe were points of great importance, and had doubtlefs been left out of the charter by an overfight arifing from an almoft total want of a definite geographical knowl- edge of our northern coaft.  Juftly apprehending that the places above mentioned might not be included within the limits of his grant, De Monts obtained, the next month, an extenfion of the bounds of his exclufive right of trade, fo that

---

[*] The Duke of Sully's difapproba- tion is expreffed in the following words : " The colony, that was fent to Canada this year, was among the num- ber of thofe things that had not my ap- probation ; there was no kind of riches to be expected from all thofe countries of the new world, which are beyond the fortieth degree of latitude.  His majefty gave the conduct of this expedition to the Sieur du Mont."—*Memoirs of Sully,* Philadelphia, 1817, Vol. III. p. 185.

that it fhould comprehend the whole region of the gulf and river of St. Lawrence.[33]

The following winter, 1603–4, was devoted by De Monts to organizing his company, the collection of a fuitable band of colonifts, and the neceffary preparations for the voyage. His commiffion authorized him to feize any idlers in the city or country, or even convicts condemned to tranfportation, to make up the bone and finew of the colony.  To what extent he reforted to this method of filling his ranks, we know not.  Early in April he had gathered together about a hundred and twenty artifans of all trades, laborers, and foldiers, who were embarked upon two fhips, one of 120 tons, under the direction of Sieur de Pont Gravé, commanded, however, by Captain Morel, of Honfleur ; another of 150 tons, on which De Monts himfelf embarked with feveral noblemen and gentlemen, having Captain Timothée, of Havre de Grâce, as commander.

De Monts extended to Champlain an invitation to join the expedition, which he readily accepted, but, neverthelefs, on the condition, as in the previous voyage, of the king's affent, which was freely granted, neverthelefs with the command that he fhould prepare a faithful report of his obfervations and difcoveries.

CHAPTER III.

---

[33] " Frequenter, negocier, et communiquer durant ledit temps de dix ans, depuis le Cap de Raze jufques au quarantiéme degré, comprenant toute la côte de la Cadie, terre et Cap Breton, Bayes de Sainct-Cler, de Chaleur, Ile Percée, Gachepé, Chinfchedec, Mefamichi, Lefquemin, Tadouffac, et la riviere de Canada, tant d'un côté que d'autre, et toutes les Bayes et rivieres qui entrent au dedans defdites côtes."— Extract of Commiffion. *Hiftoire de la Nouvelle-France*, par Lefcarbot, Paris, 1866, Vol. II. p. 416.

## CHAPTER III.

DE MONTS LEAVES FOR LA CADIE — THE COASTS OF NOVA SCOTIA. — THE
BAY OF FUNDY. — SEARCH FOR COPPER MINE. — CHAMPLAIN EXPLORES
THE PENOBSCOT. — DE MONTS'S ISLAND. — SUFFERINGS OF THE COLONY.
— EXPLORATION OF THE COAST AS FAR AS NAUSET, ON CAPE COD.

E MONTS, with Champlain and the other noblemen, left Havre de Grâce on the 7th April,
1604, while Pont Gravé, with the other veffel,
followed three days later, to rendezvous at Canfeau.

Taking a more foutherly courfe than he had originally
intended, De Monts came in fight of La Hève on the 8th of
May, and on the 12th entered Liverpool harbor, where he
found Captain Roffignol, of Havre de Grâce, carrying on a
contraband trade in furs with the Indians, whom he arrefted,
and confifcated his veffel.

The next day they anchored at Port Mouton, where they
lingered three or four weeks, awaiting news from Pont
Gravé, who had in the mean time arrived at Canfeau, the
rendezvous agreed upon before leaving France. Pont Gravé
had there difcovered feveral Bafque fhips engaged in the fur-
trade. Taking poffeffion of them, he fent their mafters to
De Monts. The fhips were fubfequently confifcated and
fent to Rochelle.

Captain Fouques was defpatched to Canfeau in the veffel
which had been taken from Roffignol, to bring forward the
fupplies which had been brought over by Pont Gravé.

Having tranffhipped the provifions intended for the colony,
Pont Gravé

Pont Gravé proceeded through the Straits of Canfeau up
the St. Lawrence, to trade with the Indians, upon the profits
of which the company relied largely for replenifhing their
treafury.

In the mean time Champlain was fent in a barque of eight
tons, with the fecretary Sieur Ralleau, Mr. Simon, the miner,
and ten men, to reconnoitre the coaft towards the weft.
Sailing along the fhore, touching at numerous points, doubling Cape Sable, he entered the Bay of Fundy, and after
exploring St. Mary's Bay, and difcovering feveral mines of
both filver and iron, returned to Port Mouton and made to
De Monts a minute and careful report.

De Monts immediately weighed anchor and failed for the
Bay of St. Mary, where he left his veffel, and, with Champlain, the miner, and fome others, proceeded to explore the
Bay of Fundy.  They entered and examined Annapolis
harbor, coafted along the weftern fhores of Nova Scotia,
touching at the Bay of Mines, paffing over to New Brunfwick, fkirting its whole foutheaftern coaft, entering the harbor of St. John, and finally penetrating Paffamaquoddy Bay
as far as the mouth of the river St. Croix, and fixed upon
De Monts's Ifland [34] as the feat of their colony.  The veffel
at

[34] *De Monts's Ifland.*  Of this ifland
Champlain fays: "This place was named
by Sieur De Monts the Ifland of St.
Croix."—*Vide* Vol. II. p. 32, note 86.
St. Croix has now for a long time been
applied as the name of the river in which
this ifland is found.  The French denominated this ftream the River of the
Etechemins, after the name of the tribe
of favages inhabiting its fhores.  *Vide*
Vol. II. p. 31.  It continued to be fo
called for a long time.  Denys fpeaks
of it under this name in 1672.  "Depuis
la riviere de Pentagoüet, jufques à celle
de faint Jean, il peut y avoir quarante à
quarante cinq lieuës ; la premiere riviere
que l'on rencontre le long de la cofte, eft
celle des Etechemins, qui porte le nom
du pays, depuis Bafton jufques au Port
royal, dont les Sauvages qui habitent
toute cette étenduë, portent auffi le
mefme nom." — *Defcription Geogra-
phique et Hiftorique des Coftes de
L'Ameriqve Septentrionale*, par Nicholas Denys, Paris, 1672, p. 29, *et verfo*.

at St. Mary's with the colonifts was ordered to join them, and immediately active meafures were taken for laying out gardens, erecting dwellings and ftorehoufes, and all the neceffary preparations for the coming winter. Champlain was commiffioned to defign and lay out the town, if fo it could be called.

When the work was fomewhat advanced, he was fent in a barque of five or fix tons, manned with nine failors, to fearch for a mine of pure copper, which an Indian named Meffamoüet had affured them he could point out to them on the coaft towards the river St. John. Some twenty-five miles from the river St. Croix, they found a mine yielding eighteen per cent, as eftimated by the miner; but they did not difcover any pure copper, as they had hoped.

On the laft day of Auguft, 1604, the veffel which had brought out the colony, together with that which had been taken from Roffignol, took their departure for the fhores of France. In it failed Poutrincourt, Ralleau the fecretary of De Monts, and Captain Roffignol.

From the moment of his arrival on the coaft of America, Champlain employed his leifure hours in making fketches and drawings of the moft important rivers, harbors, and Indian fettlements which they had vifited.

While the little colony at De Monts's Ifland was active in getting its appointments arranged and fettled, De Monts wifely determined, though he could not accompany it himfelf, neverthelefs to fend out an expedition during the mild days of autumn, to explore the region ftill further to the fouth, then called by the Indians Norumbegue. Greatly to the fatisfaction of Champlain, he was perfonally charged with this

this important expedition.  He fet out on the 2d of September, in a barque of feventeen or eighteen tons, with twelve failors and two Indian guides.  The inevitable fogs of that region detained them nearly a fortnight before they were able to leave the banks of Paffamaquoddy.  Paffing along the rugged fhores of Maine, with its endlefs chain of iflands rifing one after another into view, which they called the Ranges, they at length came to the ancient Pemetiq, lying clofe in to the fhore, having the appearance at fea of feven or eight mountains drawn together and fpringing from the fame bafe.  This Champlain named *Monts Déferts*, which we have anglicized into Mount Defert,[15] an appellation which has furvived the viciffitudes of two hundred and feventy-five years, and now that the ifland, with its falubrious air and cool fhades, its bold and picturefque fcenery, is attracting thoufands from the great cities during the heats of fummer, the name is likely to abide far down into a diftant and indefinite future.

Leaving Mount Defert, winding their way among numerous iflands, taking a northerly direction, they foon entered the Penobfcot,[16] known by the early navigators as the river Norumbegue.

[15] Champlain had, by his own explorations and by confulting the Indians, obtained a very full and accurate knowledge of this ifland at his firft vifit, on the 5th of September, 1604, when he named it *Monts-déferts*, which we preferve in the English form, MOUNT DESERT.  He obferved that the diftance acrofs the channel to the mainland on the north fide was lefs than a hundred paces.  The rocky and barren fummits of this clufter of little mountains obvioufly induced him to give to the ifland its appropriate and defcriptive name.  *Vide* Vol. II. p. 39.  Dr. Edward Ballard derives the Indian name of this ifland, *Pemetiq*, from *pemé'te*, floping, and *ki*, land.  He adds that it probably denoted a fingle locality which was taken by Biard's company as the name of the whole ifland.  *Vide Report of U. S. Coaft Survey* for 1868, p. 253.

[16] *Penobfcot* is a corruption of the Abnaki *pa⁎nawoa⁎bfkik*.  A nearly exact tranflation is "at the fall of the rock," or "at the defcending rock."  *Vide Trumball's*

6

Norumbegue. They proceeded up the river as far as the
mouth of an affluent now known as the Kendufkeag,[17] which
was then called, or rather the place where it made a junction
with the Penobfcot was called by the natives, *Kadefquit*, fituated at the head of tide-water, near the prefent fite of the
city of Bangor. The falls above the city intercepted their
further progrefs. The river-banks about the harbor were
fringed with a luxurious growth of foreft trees. On one
fide, lofty pines reared their gray trunks, forming a natural
palifade along the fhore. On the other, maffive oaks alone
were to be feen, lifting their fturdy branches to the fkies,
gathered into clumps or ftretching out into long lines, as
if a landfcape gardener had planted them to pleafe the eye
and gratify the tafte. An exploration revealed the whole
furrounding region clothed in a fimilar wild and primitive
beauty.

After a leifurely furvey of the country, they returned to
the mouth of the river. Contrary to what might have been
expected, Champlain found fcarcely any inhabitants dwelling
on the borders of the Penobfcot. Here and there they faw
a few deferted wigwams, which were the only marks of human occupation. At the mouth of the river, on the borders
of

*Trumball's Ind. Geog. Names*, Collections Conn. His. Society, Vol. II. p. 19.
This name was originally given probably
to fome part of the river to which its
meaning was particularly applicable.
This may have been at the mouth of the
river a Fort Point, a rocky elevation not
lefs than eighty feet in height. Or it
may have been the "fall of water coming
down a flope of feven or eight feet," as
Champlain exprefles it, a fhort diftance
above the fite of the prefent city of Bangor. That this name was firft obtained
by thofe who only vifited the mouth of
the river would feem to favor the former
fuppofition.

[17] Dr. Edward Ballard fuppofes the
original name of this ftream, *Kadefquit*,
to be derived from *kaht*, a Micmac word
for *eel*, denoting *eel ftream*, now cor-
rupted into *Kendufkeag*. The prefent
fite of the city of Bangor is where Biard
intended to eftablifh his miffion in 1613,
but he was finally induced to fix it at
Mount Defert. —*Vide Relations des Jéfuites*, Quebec ed., Vol. I. p. 44.

of Penobſcot Bay, the native inhabitants were numerous. They were of a friendly diſpoſition, and gave their viſitors a cordial welcome, readily entered into negotiations for the ſale of beaver-ſkins, and the two parties mutually agreed to maintain a friendly intercourſe in the future.

Having obtained from the Indians ſome valuable informa- tion as to the ſource of the Penobſcot, and obſerved their mode of life, which did not differ from that which they had ſeen ſtill further eaſt, Champlain departed on the 20th of September, directing his courſe towards the Kennebec. But, encountering bad weather, he found it neceſſary to take ſhelter under the lee of the iſland of Monhegan.

After failing three or four leagues farther, finding that his proviſions would not warrant the continuance of the voyage, he determined, on the 23d of September, to return to the ſettle- ment at Saint Croix, or what is now known as De Monts's Iſland, where they arrived on the 2d day of October, 1604.

De Monts's Iſland, having an area of not more than ſix or ſeven acres, is ſituated in the river Saint Croix, midway be- tween its oppoſite ſhores, directly upon the dividing line between the townſhips of Calais and Robinſton in the State of Maine. At the northern end of the iſland, the buildings of the ſettlement were cluſtered together in the form of a quadrangle with an open court in the centre. Firſt came the magazine and lodgings of the ſoldiers, then the manſion of the governor, De Monts, ſurmounted by the colors of France. Houſes for Champlain and the other gentlemen,[28] for the curé, the artiſans and workmen, filled up and

[28] The other gentlemen whoſe names we have learned were Meſſieurs d'Orville, Champdoré, Beaumont, la Motte Bou- rioli, Fougeray or Foulgeré de Vitré, Geneſtou,

and completed the quadrangle. Below the houſes, gardens were laid out for the ſeveral gentlemen, and at the ſouthern extremity of the iſland cannon were mounted for protection againſt a ſudden aſſault.

In the ample foreſts of Maine or New Brunſwick, rich in oak and maple and pine, abounding in deer, partridge, and other wild game, watered by cryſtal fountains ſpringing from every acre of the ſoil, we naturally picture for our coloniſts a winter of robuſt health, phyſical comfort, and ſocial enjoy-ment. The little iſland which they had choſen was indeed a charming ſpot in a ſummer's day, but we can hardly com-prehend in what view it could have been regarded as ſuitable for a colonial plantation. In ſpace it was wholly inade-quate; it was deſtitute of wood and freſh water, and its ſoil was ſandy and unproductive. In fixing the location of their ſettlement and in the conſtruction of their houſes, it is obvi-ous that they had entirely miſapprehended the character of the climate. While the latitude was nearly the ſame, the temperature was far more rigorous than that of the ſunny France which they had left. The ſnow began to fall on the 6th of October. On the 3d of December the ice was ſeen floating on the ſurface of the water. As the ſeaſon ad-vanced, and the tide came and went, huge floes of ice, day after day, ſwept by the iſland, rendering it impracticable to navigate the river or paſs over to the mainland. They were therefore impriſoned in their own home. Thus cut off from the game with which the neighboring foreſts abounded, they were compelled to ſubſiſt almoſt excluſively upon ſalted meats.

Geneſtou, Sourin, and Boulay. The orthography of the names, as they are mentioned from time to time, is vari-ous.

meats. Nearly all the foreft trees on the ifland had been ufed in the conftruction of their houfes, and they had confequently but a meagre fupply of fuel to refift the chilling winds and penetrating frofts. For frefh water, their only reliance was upon melted fnow and ice. Their ftore-houfe had not been furnifhed with a cellar, and the froft left nothing untouched; even cider was difpenfed in folid blocks. To crown the gloom and wretchednefs of their fituation, the colony was vifited with difeafe of a virulent and fatal character. As the malady was beyond the knowledge, fo it baffled the fkill of the furgeons. They called it *mal de la terre.* Of the feventy-nine perfons, compofing the whole number of the colony, thirty-five died, and twenty others were brought to the verge of the grave. In May, having been liberated from the baleful influence of their winter prifon and revived by the genial warmth of the vernal fun and by the frefh meats obtained from the favages, the difeafe abated, and the furvivors gradually regained their ftrength.

Difheartened by the bitter experiences of the winter, the governor, having fully determined to abandon his prefent eftablifhment, ordered two boats to be conftructed, one of fifteen and the other of feven tons, in which to tranfport his colony to Gafpé, in cafe he received no fupplies from France, with the hope of obtaining a paffage home in fome of the fifhing veffels on that coaft. But from this difagreeable alternative he was happily relieved. On the 15th of June, 1605, Pont Gravé arrived, to the great joy of the little colony, with all needed fupplies. The purpofe of returning to France was at once abandoned, and, as no time was to be loft, on the 18th of the fame month, De Monts, Champlain,

feveral

feveral gentlemen, twenty failors, two Indians, Panounias and his wife, fet fail for the purpofe of difcovering a more eligible fite for his colony fomewhere on the fhores of the prefent New England.   Paffing flowly along the coaft, with which Champlain was already familiar, and confequently without extenfive explorations, they at length reached the waters of the Kennebec,[39] where the furvey of the previous year had terminated and that of the prefent was about to begin.

On the 5th of July, they entered the Kennebec, and, bearing to the right, paffed through Back River,[40] grazing their barque on the rocks in the narrow channel, and then fweeping down round the fouthern point of Jerremifquam Ifland, or Weftport, they afcended along its eaftern fhores till they came near the prefent fite of Wifcaffet, from whence they returned on the weftern fide of the ifland, through Monfeag Bay, and threading the narrow paffage between Arrowfick and Woolwich, called the Upper Hell-gate, and again entering the Kennebec, they finally reached Merrymeeting Bay. Lingering here but a fhort time, they returned through the Sagadahock, or lower Kennebec, to the mouth of the river.

This exploration did not yield to the voyagers any very interefting or important refults.   Several friendly interviews were held with the favages at different points along the route.   Near the head waters of the Sheepfcot, probably in Wifcaffet Bay, they had an interview, an interefting and joyous

[39] *Kennebec.* Biard, in the *Relation de la Nouvelle France, Relations des Jéfuites,* Quebec ed., Vol. I. p. 35, writes it *Quinibequi,* and Champlain writes it *Quinibequy* and *Quinebequi;* hence Mr. Trumball infers that it is probably equivalent in meaning to *quin-ni-pi-ohke.* meaning "long water place," derived from the Abnaki, *K͞oo né-be-ki.* — *Vide Ind. Geog. Names,* Col. Conn. His. Soc. Vol. II. p. 15.
[40] *Vide* Vol. II. note 110.

ous meeting, with the chief Manthoumerme and his twenty-five or thirty followers, with whom they exchanged tokens of friendſhip. Along the ſhores of the Sheepſcot their attention was attraƈted by ſeveral pleaſant ſtreams and fine expanſes of meadow; but the ſoil obſerved on this expedition generally, and eſpecially on the Sagadahock,⁴¹ or lower Kennebec, was rough and barren, and offered, in the judgment of De Monts and Champlain, no eligible ſite for a new ſettlement.

Proceeding, therefore, on their voyage, they ſtruck direƈtly acroſs Caſco Bay, not attempting, in their ignorance, to enter the fine harbor of Portland.

On the 9th of July, they made the bay that ſtretches from Cape Elizabeth to Fletcher's Neck, and anchored under the lee of Stratton Iſland, direƈtly in ſight of Old Orchard Beach, now a famous watering place during the ſummer months.

The ſavages having ſeen the little French barque approaching in the diſtance, had built fires to attraƈt its attention, and came down upon the ſhore at Prout's Neck, formerly known as Black Point, in large numbers, indicating their friendlineſs by lively demonſtrations of joy. From this anchorage, while awaiting the influx of the tide to enable them to paſs over the bar and enter a river which they ſaw flowing into the bay, De Monts paid a viſit to Richmond's Iſland,

⁴¹ *Sagadahock.* This name is particularly applied to the lower part of the Kennebec. It is from the Abnaki, *ſaᵘghedeʹaki,* "land at the mouth." — *Vide Indian Geographical Names,* by J. H. Trumball, Col. Conn. His. Society, Vol. II. p. 30. Dr. Edward Ballard derives it from *ſanktai-i-wi,* to finiſh, and *onk,* a locative, "the finiſhing place," which means the mouth of a river. — *Vide Report of U. S. Coaſt Survey,* 1868, p. 258.

Ifland, about four miles diftant, with which he was greatly
delighted, as he found it richly ftudded with oak and hickory,
whofe bending branches were wreathed with luxuriant grape-
vines loaded with green clufters of unripe fruit. In honor of
the god of wine, they gave to the ifland the claffic name of
Bacchus.⁴² At full tide they paffed over the bar and caft
anchor within the channel of the Saco.

The Indians whom they found here were called Almouchiquois, and differed in many refpects from any which they
had feen before, from the Sourequois of Nova Scotia and
the Etechemins of the northern part of Maine and New
Brunfwick. They fpoke a different language, and, unlike
their neighbors on the eaft, did not fubfist mainly by the
chafe, but upon the products of the foil, fupplemented by
fifh, which were plentiful and of excellent quality, and which
they took with facility about the mouth of the river. De
Monts and Champlain made an excurfion upon the fhore,
where their eyes were refrefhed by fields of waving corn,
and gardens of fquafhes, beans, and pumpkins, which were
then burfting into flower.⁴³ Here they saw in cultivation
the

⁴² *Bacchus Ifland.* This was Richmond's Ifland, as we have ftated in Vol.
II. note 123. It will be admitted that
the Bacchus Ifland of Champlain was
either Richmond's Ifland or one of thofe
in the bay of the Saco. Champlain does
not give a fpecific name to any of the
iflands in the bay, as may be feen by
referring to the explanations of his map
of the bay, Vol. II. p. 65. If one of
them had been Bacchus Ifland, he would
not have failed to refer to it, according
to his uniform cuftom, under that name.
Hence it is certain that his Bacchus
Ifland was not one of thofe figured on
his local map of the bay of the Saco.
By reference to the large map of 1632,
it will be feen that Bacchus Ifland is
reprefented by the number 50, which is
placed over againft the largeft ifland in
the neighborhood and that fartheft to the
eaft, which, of courfe, muft be Richmond's Ifland. It is, however, proper to
ftate that thefe reference figures are not
in general fo carefully placed as to enable
us to rely upon them in fixing a locality,
particularly if unfupported by other evidence. But in this cafe other evidence
is not wanting.
⁴³ *Vide* Vol. II. pp. 64-67.

the rank narcotic *petun*, or tobacco," juft beginning to
fpread out its broad velvet leaves to the fun, the fole luxury
of favage life. The forefts were thinly wooded, but were
neverthelefs rich in primitive oak, in lofty afh and elm, and
in the more humble and fturdy beech. As on Richmond's
Ifland fo here, along the bank of the river they found grapes
in luxurious growth, from which the failors bufied themfelves
in making verjuice, a delicious beverage in the meridian
heats of a July fun. The natives were gentle and amiable,
graceful in figure, agile in movement, and exhibited unufual
tafte, dreffing their hair in a variety of twifts and braids,
intertwined with ornamental feathers.

Champlain obferved their method of cultivating Indian
corn, which the experience of two hundred and feventy-five
years has in no effential point improved or even changed.
They planted three or four feeds in hills three feet apart,
and heaped the earth about them, and kept the foil clear of
weeds. Such is the method of the fuccefsful New England
farmer to-day. The experience of the favage had taught
him how many individuals of the rank plant could occupy
prolifically a given area, how the foil muft be gathered about
the roots to fuftain the heavy ftock, and that there muft be
no rival near it to draw away the nutriment on which the
voracious plant feeds and grows. Civilization has invented
implements to facilitate the proceffes of culture, but the obfervation of the favage had led him to a knowledge of all
that is abfolutely neceffary to enfure a prolific harveft.

After lingering two days at Saco, our explorers proceeded
on

" *Nicotiana ruftica. Vide* Vol. II. by Charles Pickering, M.D. Bofton,
note 130. *Chronological His. Plants,* 1879. p. 741, *et paffim.*

on their voyage. When they had advanced not more than twenty miles, driven by a fierce wind, they were forced to caſt anchor near the ſalt marſhes of Wells. Having been driven by Cape Porpoiſe, on the ſubſidence of the wind, they returned to it, reconnoitred its harbor and adjacent iſlands, together with Little River, a few miles ſtill further to the eaſt. The ſhores were lined all along with nut-trees and grape-vines. The iſlands about Cape Porpoiſe were matted all over with wild currants, ſo that the eye could ſcarcely diſcern any thing elſe. Attracted doubtleſs by this fruit, clouds of wild pigeons had aſſembled there, and were having a midſummer's feſtival, fearleſs of the treacherous ſnare or the hunter's deadly aim. Large numbers of them were taken, which added a coveted luxury to the not over-ſtocked larder of the little French barque.

On the 15th of July, De Monts and his party left Cape Porpoiſe, keeping in and following cloſely the ſinuoſities of the ſhore. They ſaw no ſavages during the day, nor any evidences of any, except a riſing ſmoke, which they approached, but found to be a lone beacon, without any ſurroundings of human life. Thoſe who had kindled the fire had doubtleſs concealed themſelves, or had fled in diſmay. Poſſibly they had never ſeen a ſhip under ſail. The fiſhermen who frequented our northern coaſt rarely came into theſe waters, and the little craft of our voyagers, moving without oars or any apparent human aid, ſeemed doubtleſs to them a monſter gliding upon the wings of the wind. At the ſetting of the ſun, they were near the flat and ſandy coaſt, now known as Wallace's Sands. They ſought in vain for a roadſtead where they might anchor ſafely for the night. When they were
oppoſite

oppofite to Little Boar's Head, with the Ifles of Shoals directly eaft of them, and the reflected rays of the fun were
ftill throwing their light upon the waters, they faw in the
diftance the dim outline of Cape Anne, whither they directed their courfe, and, before morning, came to anchor
near its eaftern extremity, in fixteen fathoms of water. Near
them were the three well-known iflands at the apex of the
cape, covered with foreft-trees, and the woodlefs clufter of
rocks, now called the Savages, a little further from the
fhore.

The next morning five or fix Indians timidly approached
them in a canoe, and then retired and fet up a dance on the
fhore, as a token of friendly greeting. Armed with crayon
and drawing-paper, Champlain was defpatched to feek from
the natives fome important geographical information. Dif-
penfing knives and bifcuit as a friendly invitation, the favages gathered about him, affured by their gifts, when he
proceeded to impart to them their firft leffon in topographical drawing. He pictured to them the bay on the north
fide of Cape Anne, which he had juft traverfed, and fignifying to them that he defired to know the courfe of the fhore
on the fouth, they immediately gave him an example of their
apt fcholarfhip by drawing with the fame crayon an accurate
outline of Maffachufetts Bay, and finifhed up Champlain's
own fketch by introducing the Merrimac River, which, not
having been feen, owing to the prefence of Plum Ifland,
which ftretches like a curtain before its mouth, he had
omitted to portray. The intelligent natives volunteered a
bit of hiftory. By placing fix pebbles at equal diftances,
they intimated that Maffachufetts Bay was occupied by fix
tribes,

tribes, and governed by as many chiefs.[45] He learned from
them, likewife, that the inhabitants of this region fubfifted
by agriculture, as did thofe at the mouth of the Saco, and
that they were very numerous.

Leaving Cape Anne on Saturday, the 16th of July, De
Monts entered Maffachufetts Bay, failed into Bofton harbor,
and anchored on the weftern fide of Noddle's Ifland, now better
known as Eaft Bofton. In paffing into the bay, they obferved
large patches of cleared land, and many fields of waving
corn both upon the iflands and the mainland. The water
and the iflands, the open fields and lofty foreft-trees, prefented fine contrafts, and rendered the fcenery attractive and
beautiful. Here for the firft time Champlain obferved the
log canoe. It was a clumfy though ferviceable boat in ftill
waters, neverthelefs unftable and dangerous in unfkilful
hands. They faw, iffuing into the bay, a large river, coming
from the weft, which they named River du Guaft, in honor
of Pierre du Guaft, Sieur de Monts, the patentee of La
Cadie, and the patron and director of this expedition. This
was Charles River, feen, evidently juft at its confluence with
the Myftic.[46]

On Sunday, the 17th of July, 1605, they left Bofton harbor, threading their way among the iflands, paffing leifurely
along

[45] Daniel Gookin, who wrote in 1674, fpeaks of the following fubdivifions among the Maffachufetts Indians: "Their chief fachem held dominion over many other petty governours; as thofe of Weechagafkas, Neponfitt, Punkapaog, Nonantam, Nafhaway, and fome of the Nipmuck people." — *Vide Gookin's His. Col.*

[46] *Vide* Vol. II. note 159. *Mufhau-* *womuk*, which we have converted into *Shawmut*, means, "where there is going-by-boat." The French, if they heard the name and learned its meaning, could hardly have failed to fee the appropriatenefs of it as applied by the aborigines to Bofton harbor. — *Vide Trumball* in Connecticut Hiftorical Society's Collections, Vol. II. p. 5.

along the fouth fhore, rounding Point Allerton on the peninfula of Nantafket, gliding along near Cohaffet and Scitu-
ate, and finally caft anchor at Brant Point, upon the fouthern
borders of Marfhfield.  When they left the harbor of Bofton,
the iflands and mainland were fwarming with the native population.  The Indians were, naturally enough, intenfely interefted in this vifit of the little French barque.  It may
have been the firft that had ever made its appearance in the
bay.  Its fize was many times greater than any water-craft
of their own.  Spreading its white wings and gliding filently
away without oarfmen, it filled them with furprife and admiration.  The whole population was aftir.  The cornfields and
fifhing ftations were deferted.  Every canoe was manned,
and a flotilla of their tiny craft came to attend, honor, and
fpeed the parting guefts, experiencing, doubtlefs, a fenfe of
relief that they were going, and filled with a painful curiofity
to know the meaning of this myfterious vifit.

Having paffed the night at Brant Point, they had not advanced more than two leagues along a fandy fhore dotted
with wigwams and gardens, when they were forced to enter
a fmall harbor, to await a more favoring wind.  The Indians
flocked about them, greeted them with cordiality, and invited them to enter the little river which flows into the
harbor, but this they were unable to do, as the tide was
low and the depth infufficient.  Champlain's attention was
attra&ed by feveral canoes in the bay, which had juft completed their morning's work in fifhing for cod.  The fifh
were taken with a primitive hook and line, apparently in
a manner not very different from that of the prefent day.
The line was made of a filament of bark ftripped from the
                                                        trunk

trunk of a tree; the hook was of wood, having a fharp
bone, forming a barb, lafhed to it with a cord of a graffy
fibre, a kind of wild hemp, growing fpontaneoufly in that
region.   Champlain landed, diftributed trinkets among the
natives, examined and fketched an outline of the place,
which identifies it as Plymouth harbor, which Captain John
Smith vifited in 1614, and where the May Flower, ftill fix
years later, landed the firft permanent colony planted upon
New England foil.

After a day at Plymouth, the little barque weighed anchor,
fwept down Cape Cod Bay, approaching near to the reefs of
Billingfgate, defcribing a complete femicircle, and finally,
with fome difficulty, doubled the cape, whofe white fands
they had feen in the diftance glittering in the funlight, and
which they appropriately named *Cap Blanc*.  This cape,
however, had been vifited three years before by Bartholomew
Gofnold, and named Cape Cod, which appellation it has retained to the prefent time.  Paffing down on the outfide
of the cape fome diftance, they came to anchor, fent explorers on fhore, who, afcending one of the lofty fand-
banks[47] which may ftill be feen there filently refifting the
winds and the waves, difcovered, further to the fouth, what is
now known as Naufet harbor, entirely furrounded by Indian
cabins.   The next day, the 20th of July, 1605, they effected
                                                          an

[47] It was probably on this very bluff, from which was feen Naufet harbor on the 19th of July, 1605, that, after the lapfe of two hundred and feventy-four years, on the 17th of November, 1879, the citizens of the United States, with the flags of America, France, and England gracefully waving over their heads, addreffed their congratulations by tele-graph to the citizens of France, at Breft, on the communication between the two countries, that day completed, through fubmarine wires, under the aufpices of the "Compagnie Françaife du Télé-graphe de Paris à New York."

an entrance without much difficulty. The bay was fpacious, being nine or ten miles in circumference. Along the borders, there were, here and there, cultivated patches, interfperfed with dwellings of the natives. The wigwam was cone-fhaped, heavily thatched with reeds, having an orifice at the apex for the emiffion of fmoke. In the fields were growing Indian corn, Brazilian beans, pumpkins, radifhes, and tobacco; and in the woods were oak and hickory and red cedar. During their ftay in the harbor they encountered an eafterly ftorm, which continued four days, fo raw and chilling that they were glad to hug their winter cloaks about them on the 22d of July. The natives were friendly and cordial, and entered freely into converfation with Champlain; but, as the language of each party was not underftood by the other, the information he obtained from them was moftly by figns, and confequently too general to be hiftorically interefting or important.

The firft and only act of hoftility by the natives which De Monts and his party had thus far experienced in their explorations on the entire coaft occurred in this harbor. Several of the men had gone afhore to obtain frefh water. Some of the Indians conceived an uncontrollable defire to capture the copper veffels which they faw in their hands. While one of the men was ftooping to dip water from a fpring, one of the favages darted upon him and fnatched the coveted veffel from his hand. An encounter followed, and, amid fhowers of arrows and blows, the poor failor was brutally murdered. The victorious Indian, fleet as the reindeer, efcaped with his companions, bearing his prize with him into the depths of the foreft. The natives on the fhore,
who

who had hitherto fhown the greateft friendlinefs, foon came
to De Monts, and by figns difowned any participation in
the act, and affured him that the guilty parties belonged far
in the interior.   Whether this was the truth or a piece of
adroit diplomacy, it was neverthelefs accepted by De Monts,
fince punifhment could only be adminiftered at the rifk of
caufing the innocent to fuffer inftead of the guilty.

The young failor whofe earthly career was thus fuddenly
terminated, whofe name even has not come down to us, was
doubtlcfs the firft European, if we except Thorvald, the
Northman, whofe mortal remains flumber in the foil of
Maffachufetts.

As this voyage of difcovery had been planned and provifioned for only fix weeks, and more than five had already
elapfed, on the 25th of July DeMonts and his party left
Naufett harbor, to join the colony ftill lingering at St.
Croix.   In paffing the bar, they came near being wrecked,
and confequently gave to the harbor the fignificant appellation of *Port de Mallebarre*, a name which has not been loft,
but neverthelefs, like the fhifting fands of that region, has
floated away from its original moorings, and now adheres to
the fandy cape of Monomoy.

On their return voyage, they made a brief ftop at Saco, and
likewife at the mouth of the Kennebec.   At the latter point
they had an interview with the fachem, Anaffou, who informed them that a fhip had been there, and that the men
on board her had feized, under color of friendfhip, and killed
five favages belonging to that river.   From the defcription
given by Anaffou, Champlain was convinced that the fhip
was Englifh, and fubfequent events render it quite certain
that

that it was the "Archangel," fitted out by the Earl of South-
ampton and Lord Arundel of Wardour, and commanded by
Captain George Weymouth. The defign of the expedition
was to fix upon an eligible fite for a colonial plantation, and,
in purfuance of this purpofe, Weymouth anchored off Monhegan on the 28th of May, 1605, *new ftyle*, and, after fpend-
ing a month in explorations of the region contiguous, left
for England on the 26th of June.[48] He had feized and carried away five of the natives, having concealed them in the
hold of his fhip, and Anaffou, under the circumftances, naturally fuppofed they had been killed. The ftatement of the
fachem, that the natives captured belonged to the river
where Champlain then was, namely, the Kennebec, goes far
to prove that Weymouth's explorations were in the Kennebec, or at leaft in the network of waters then comprehended
under that appellation, and not in the Penobfcot or in any
other river farther eaft, as fome hiftorical writers have fuppofed.

It would appear that while the French were carefully fur-
veying the coafts of New England, in order to fix upon an
eligible fite for a permanent colonial fettlement, the Englifh
were likewife upon the ground, engaged in a fimilar inveftigation for the fame purpofe. From this period onward, for
more than a century and a half, there was a perpetual conflict and ftruggle for territorial poffeffion on the northern
coaft of America, between thefe two great nations, fometimes active and violent, and at others fubfiding into a femi-
flumber, but never ceafing until every acre of foil belonging
to

[48] *Vide* Vol. II. p. 91, note 176.

8

to the French had been transferred to the Englifh by a folemn international compact.

On this exploration, Champlain noticed along the coaft
from Kennebec to Cape Cod, and defcribed feveral objects in
natural hiftory unknown in Europe, fuch as the horfe-foot
crab,[49] the black fkimmer, and the wild turkey, the latter two
of which have long fince ceafed to vifit this region.

## CHAPTER IV.

ARRIVAL OF SUPPLIES AND REMOVAL TO PORT ROYAL. — DE MONTS RE-
TURNS TO FRANCE. — SEARCH FOR MINES. — WINTER. — SCURVY. — LATE
ARRIVAL OF SUPPLIES AND EXPLORATIONS ON THE COAST OF MASSA-
CHUSETTS. — GLOCESTER HARBOR, STAY AT CHATHAM AND ATTACK OF
THE SAVAGES. — WOOD'S HOLL. — RETURN TO ANNAPOLIS BASIN.

N the 8th of Auguft, the exploring party reached
St. Croix. During their abfence, Pont Gravé
had arrived from France with additional men
and provifions for the colony. As no fatisfactory fite had been found by De Monts in his
recent tour along the coaft, it was determined to remove the
colony temporarily to Port Royal, fituated within the bay
now known as Annapolis Bafin. The buildings at St. Croix,
with

[49] The Horfefoot-crab, *Limulus poly-phemus.* Champlain gives the Indian name, *figuenoc.* Hariot faw, while at Roanoke Ifland, in 1585, and defcribed the fame cruftacean under the name of *feekanauk.* The Indian word is ob-vioufly the fame, the differing French and Englifh orthography reprefenting the fame found. It thus appears that this fhell-fifh was at that time known by the aborigines under the fame name for at leaft a thoufand miles along the Atlantic coaft, from the Kennebec, in Maine, to Roanoke Ifland, in North Carolina. *Vide Hariot's Briefe and True Report of the New Found Land of Virginia,* Hakluyt, Vol. III. p. 334. See alfo Vol. II. of this work, notes 171, 172, 173, for fome account of the black fkimmer and the wild turkey.

with the exception of the ftore-houfe, were taken down and
tranfported to the bay. Champlain and Pont Gravé were
fent forward to felect a place for the fettlement, which was
fixed on the north fide of the bafin, directly oppofite to Goat
Ifland, near or upon the prefent fite of Lower Granville.
The fituation was protected from the piercing and dreaded
winds of the northweft by a lofty range of hills,[50] while it was
elevated and commanded a charming view of the placid bay
in front. The dwellings which they erected were arranged
in the form of a quadrangle with an open court in the centre,
as at St. Croix, while gardens and pleafure-grounds were laid
out by Champlain in the immediate vicinity.

When the work of the new fettlement was well advanced,
De Monts, having appointed Pont Gravé as his lieutenant,
departed for France, where he hoped to obtain additional
privileges from the government in his enterprife of planting
a colony in the New World. Champlain preferred to remain, with the purpofe of executing more fully his office as
geographer to the king, by making difcoveries on the Atlantic coaft ftill further to the fouth.

From the beginning, the patentee had cherifhed the defire
of difcovering valuable mines fomewhere on his domains,
whofe wealth, as well as that of the fur-trade, might defray
fome part of the heavy expenfes involved in his colonial enterprife. While feveral inveftigations for this purpofe had
proved abortive, it was hoped that greater fuccefs would be
attained by fearches along the upper part of the Bay of
Fundy. Before the approach of winter, therefore, Champlain

[50] On Lefcarbot's map of 1609, this elevation is denominated *Mont de la
Roque.* *Vide* alfo Vol. II. note 180.

plain and the miner, Mafter Jaques, a Sclavonian, made a tour
to St. John, where they obtained the fervices of the Indian
chief, Secondon, to accompany them and point out the place
where copper ore had been difcovered at the Bay of Mines.
The fearch, thorough as was practicable under the circumftances, was, in the main, unfuccefsful; the few fpecimens
which they found were meagre and infignificant.

The winter at Port Royal was by no means fo fevere as
the preceding one at St. Croix. The Indians brought in
wild game from the forefts. The colony had no want of
fuel and pure water. But experience, bitter as it had been,
did not yield to them the fruit of practical wifdom. They
referred their fufferings to the climate, but took too little
pains to protect themfelves againft its rugged power. Their
dwellings, haftily thrown together, were cold and damp,
arifing from the green, unfeafoned wood of which they were
doubtlefs in part conftructed, and from the ftanding rain-
water with which their foundations were at all times inun-
dated, which was neither diverted by embankments nor
drawn away by drainage. The dreaded *mal de la terre*, or
fcurvy, as might have been anticipated, made its appearance
in the early part of the feafon, caufing the death of twelve
out of the forty-five comprifing their whole number, while
others were proftrated by this painful, repulfive, and depreff-
ing difeafe.

The purpofe of making further difcoveries on the fouthern
coaft, warmly cherifhed by Champlain, and entering fully
into the plans of De Monts, had not been forgotten. Three
times during the early part of the fummer they had equipped
their barque, made up their party, and left Port Royal for
this

this undertaking, and as many times had been driven back by the violence of the winds and the waves.

In the mean time, the fupplies which had been promifed and expected from France had not arrived. This naturally gave to Pont Gravé, the lieutenant, great anxiety, as without them it was clearly inexpedient to venture upon another winter in the wilds of La Cadie. It had been ftipulated by De Monts, the patentee, that if fuccors did not arrive before the middle of July, Pont Gravé fhould make arrangements for the return of the colony by the fifhing veffels to be found at the Grand Banks. Accordingly, on the 17th of that month, Pont Gravé fet fail with the little colony in two barques, and proceeded towards Cape Breton, to feek a paffage home. But De Monts had not been remifs in his duty. He had, after many difficulties and delays, defpatched a veffel of a hundred and fifty tons, called the "Jonas," with fifty men and ample provifions for the approaching winter. While Pont Gravé with his two barques and his retreating colony had run into Yarmouth Bay for repairs, the "Jonas" paffed him unobferved, and anchored in the bafin before the deferted fettlement of Port Royal. An advice-boat had, however, been wifely defpatched by the "Jonas" to reconnoitre the inlets along the fhore, which fortunately intercepted the departing colony near Cape Sable, and, elated with frefh news from home, they joyfully returned to the quarters they had fo recently abandoned.

In addition to a confiderable number of artifans and laborers for the colony, the "Jonas" had brought out Sieur De Poutrincourt, to remain as lieutenant of La Cadie, and likewife Marc Lefcarbot, a young attorney of Paris, who had
already

already made fome fcholarly attainments, and who fubfe-quently diftinguifhed himfelf as an author, efpecially by the publication of a hiftory of New France.

De Poutrincourt immediately addreffed himfelf to putting all things in order at Port Royal, where it was obvioufly expedient for the colony to remain, at leaft for the winter. As foon as the " Jonas " had been unladen, Pont Gravé and moft of thofe who had fhared his recent hardfhips, departed in her for the fhores of France. When the tenements had been cleanfed, refitted, and refurnifhed, and their provifions had been fafely ftored, De Poutrincourt, by way of experi-ment, to teft the charaćter of the climate and the capability of the foil, defpatched a fquad of gardeners and farmers five miles up the river, to the grounds now occupied by the village of Annapolis,[51] where the foil was open, clear of foreft trees, and eafy of cultivation. They planted a great variety of feeds, wheat, rye, hemp, flax, and of garden efculents, which grew with extraordinary luxuriance, but, as the feafon was too late for any of them to ripen, the experiment failed either as a teft of the foil or the climate.

On a former vifit in 1604, De Poutrincourt had conceived a great admiration for Annapolis bafin, its protećted fituation, its fine fcenery, and its rich foil. He had a ftrong defire to bring his family there and make it his permanent abode. With this defign, he had requefted and received from De Monts a perfonal grant of this region, which had alfo been confirmed to him [52] by Henry IV. But De Monts wifhed to

plant

[51] Lefcarbot locates Poutrincourt's fort on the fame fpot which he called *Mariefort*, the fite of the prefent village of Annapolis.

[52] " Doncques l'an 1607, tous les François eftans reuenus (ainfi qu'a efté dićt) le Sieur de Potrincourt pre-fenta à feu d'immortelle memorie Henry le Grand la donnation à luy faićte

plant his La Cadian colony in a milder and more genial climate. He had therefore enjoined upon De Poutrincourt, as
his lieutenant, on leaving France, to continue the explorations
for the felection of a fite ftill farther to the fouth. Accordingly, on the 5th of September, 1606, De Poutrincourt left
Annapolis Bafin, which the French called Port Royal, in a
barque of eighteen tons, to fulfil this injunction.

It was Champlain's opinion that they ought to fail directly
for Naufet harbor, on Cape Cod, and commence their explorations where their fearch had terminated the preceding
year, and thus advance into a new region, which had not
already been furveyed. But other counfels prevailed, and a
large part of the time which could be fpared for this inveftigation was exhaufted before they reached the harbor of
Naufet. They made a brief vifit to the ifland of St. Croix,
in which De Monts had wintered in 1604–5, touched alfo at
Saco, where the Indians had already completed their harveft,
and the grapes at Bacchus Ifland were ripe and lufcious.
Thence failing directly to Cape Anne, where, finding no fafe
roadftead, they paffed round to Gloucefter harbor, which they
found fpacious, well protected, with good depth of water,
and which, for its great excellence and attractive fcenery,
they named *Beauport*, or the beautiful harbor. Here they
remained feveral days. It was a native fettlement, comprifing two hundred favages, who were cultivators of the foil,
which was prolific in corn, beans, melons, pumpkins, tobacco,
and grapes. The harbor was environed with fine foreft
trees, as hickory, oak, afh, cyprefs, and faffafras. Within
the

faicte par le fieur de Monts, reque- dicte Requefte," &c. *Relations des*
rant humblement Sa Majefté de la ra- *Jéfuites*, 1611, Quebec ed., Vol. I. p.
tifier. Le Roy eut pour agreable la 25. *Vide* Vol. II. of this work, p. 37.

the town there were feveral patches of cultivated land, which
the Indians were gradually augmenting by felling the trees,
burning the wood, and after a few years, aided by the natural
procefs of decay, eradicating the ftumps. The French were
kindly received and entertained with generous hofpitality.
Grapes juft gathered from the vines, and fquafhes of feveral
varieties, the trailing bean ftill well known in New England,
and the Jerufalem artichoke crifp from the unexhaufted foil,
were prefented as offerings of welcome to their guefts. While
thefe gifts were doubtlefs tokens of a genuine friendlinefs fo
far as the favages were capable of that virtue, the lurking fpirit
of deceit and treachery which had been inherited and foftered
by their habits and mode of life, could not be reftrained.

The French barque was lying at anchor a fhort diftance
northeaft of Ten Pound Ifland. Its boat was undergoing
repairs on a peninfula near by, now known as Rocky Neck,
and the failors were wafhing their linen juft at the point
where the peninfula is united to the mainland. While Champlain was walking on this caufeway, he obferved about fifty
favages, completely armed, cautioufly fcreening themfelves
behind a clump of bufhes on the edge of Smith's Cove. As
foon as they were aware that they were feen, they came forth,
concealing their weapons as much as poffible, and began to
dance in token of a friendly greeting. But when they difcovered De Poutrincourt in the wood near by, who had
approached unobferved, with eight armed mufketeers to dif-
perfe them in cafe of an attack, they immediately took to
flight, and, fcattering in all directions, made no further hoftile demonftrations.[53] This ferio-comic incident did not interfere

[53] This fcene is well reprefented on Champlain's map of *Beauport* or Gloucefter Harbor. *Vide* Vol. II. p. 114.

terfere with the interchange of friendly offices between the two parties, and when the voyagers were about to leave, the favages urged them with great earneftnefs to remain longer, affuring them that two thoufand of their friends would pay them a vifit the very next day. This invitation was, however, not heeded. In Champlain's opinion it was a *rufe* contrived only to furnifh a frefh opportunity to attack and overpower them.

On the 30th of September, they left the harbor of Gloucefter, and, during the following night, failing in a foutherly direction, paffing Brant Point, they found themfelves in the lower part of Cape Cod Bay. When the fun rofe, a low, fandy fhore ftretched before them. Sending their boat forward to a place where the fhore feemed more elevated, they found deeper water and a harbor, into which they entered in five or fix fathoms. They were welcomed by three Indian canoes. They found oyfters in fuch quantities in this bay, and of fuch excellent quality, that they named it *Le Port aux Huiſtres,*[14] or Oyfter Harbor. After a few hours, they weighed anchor, and directing their courfe north, a quarter northeaft, with a favoring wind, foon doubled Cape Cod. The next day, the 2d of October, they arrived off Naufet. De Poutrincourt, Champlain, and others entered the harbor in a fmall boat, where they were greeted by a hundred and fifty favages with finging and dancing, according to their ufual cuftom. After a brief vifit, they returned to the barque and continued their courfe along the fandy fhore. When near the heel of the cape, off Chatham, they found themfelves imperilled among breakers and fand-banks, fo dangerous as
to

14 *Le Port aux Huiſtres,* Barnſtable Harbor. *Vide* Vol. II. Note 208.

9

to render it inexpedient to attempt to land, even with a fmall boat. The favages were obferving them from the fhore, and foon manned a canoe, and came to them with finging and demonftrations of joy. From them, they learned that lower down a harbor would be found, where their barque might ride in fafety. Proceeding, therefore, in the fame direction, after many difficulties, they fucceeded in rounding the peninfula of Monomoy, and finally, in the gray of the evening, caft anchor in the offing near Chatham, now known as Old Stage Harbor. The next day they entered, paffing between Harding's Beach Point and Morris Ifland, in two fathoms of water, and anchored in Stage Harbor. This harbor is about a mile long and half a mile wide, and at its weftern extremity is connected by tide-water with Oyfter Pond, and with Mill Cove on the eaft by Mitchell's River. Mooring their barque between thefe two arms of the harbor, towards the wefterly end, the explorers remained there about three weeks. It was the centre of an Indian fettlement, containing five or fix hundred perfons. Although it was now well into October, the natives of both fexes were entirely naked, with the exception of a flight band about the loins. They fubfifted upon fifh and the products of the foil. Indian corn was their ftaple. It was fecured in the autumn in bags made of braided grafs, and buried in the fand-banks, and withdrawn as it was needed during the winter. The favages were of fine figure and of olive complexion. They adorned themfelves with an embroidery fkilfully interwoven with feathers and beads, and dreffed their hair in a variety of braids, like thofe at Saco. Their dwellings were conical in fhape, covered with thatch of rufhes and corn-hufks, and furrounded

by

by cultivated fields. Each cabin contained one or two beds, a kind of matting, two or three inches in thickneſs, ſpread upon a platform on which was a layer of elaſtic ſtaves, and the whole raiſed a foot from the ground. On theſe they ſecured refreſhing repoſe. Their chiefs neither exerciſed nor claimed any ſuperior authority, except in time of war. At all other times and in all other matters complete equality reigned throughout the tribe.

The ſtay at Chatham was neceſſarily prolonged in baking bread to ſerve the remainder of the voyage, and in repairing their barque, whoſe rudder had been badly ſhattered in the rough paſſage round the cape. For theſe purpoſes, a bakery and a forge were ſet up on ſhore, and a tent pitched for the convenience and protection of the workmen. While theſe works were in progreſs, De Poutrincourt, Champlain, and others made frequent excurſions into the interior, always with a guard of armed men, ſometimes making a circuit of twelve or fifteen miles. The explorers were faſcinated with all they ſaw. The aroma of the autumnal foreſt and the balmy air of October ſtimulated their ſenſes. The nut-trees were loaded with ripe fruit, and the rich cluſters of grapes were hanging temptingly upon the vines. Wild game was plentiful and delicious. The fiſh of the bay were sweet, delicate, and of many varieties. Nature, unaided by art, had thus ſupplied ſo many human wants that Champlain gravely put upon record his opinion that this would be a moſt excellent place in which to lay the foundations of a commonwealth, if the harbor were deeper and better protected at its mouth.

After the voyagers had been in Chatham eight or nine days,

to render it inexpedient to attempt to land, even with a fmall
boat. The favages were obferving them from the fhore, and
foon manned a canoe, and came to them with finging and
demonftrations of joy. From them, they learned that lower
down a harbor would be found, where their barque might
ride in fafety. Proceeding, therefore, in the fame direction,
after many difficulties, they fucceeded in rounding the peninfula of Monomoy, and finally, in the gray of the evening,
caft anchor in the offing near Chatham, now known as Old
Stage Harbor. The next day they entered, paffing between
Harding's Beach Point and Morris Ifland, in two fathoms of
water, and anchored in Stage Harbor. This harbor is about
a mile long and half a mile wide, and at its weftern extremity is connected by tide-water with Oyfter Pond, and with
Mill Cove on the eaft by Mitchell's River. Mooring their
barque between thefe two arms of the harbor, towards the
wefterly end, the explorers remained there about three weeks.
It was the centre of an Indian fettlement, containing five or
fix hundred perfons. Although it was now well into October, the natives of both fexes were entirely naked, with the
exception of a flight band about the loins. They fubfifted
upon fifh and the products of the foil. Indian corn was
their ftaple. It was fecured in the autumn in bags made of
braided grafs, and buried in the fand-banks, and withdrawn
as it was needed during the winter. The favages were of
fine figure and of olive complexion. They adorned themfelves with an embroidery fkilfully interwoven with feathers
and beads, and dreffed their hair in a variety of braids, like
thofe at Saco. Their dwellings were conical in fhape, covered with thatch of rufhes and corn-hufks, and furrounded

by

by cultivated fields.  Each cabin contained one or two beds, a kind of matting, two or three inches in thicknefs, fpread upon a platform on which was a layer of elaftic ftaves, and the whole raifed a foot from the ground.  On thefe they fecured refrefhing repofe.  Their chiefs neither exercifed nor claimed any fuperior authority, except in time of war. At all other times and in all other matters complete equality reigned throughout the tribe.

The ftay at Chatham was neceffarily prolonged in baking bread to ferve the remainder of the voyage, and in repairing their barque, whofe rudder had been badly fhattered in the rough paffage round the cape.  For thefe purpofes, a bakery and a forge were fet up on fhore, and a tent pitched for the convenience and protection of the workmen.  While thefe works were in progrefs, De Poutrincourt, Champlain, and others made frequent excurfions into the interior, always with a guard of armed men, fometimes making a circuit of twelve or fifteen miles.  The explorers were fafcinated with all they faw.  The aroma of the autumnal foreft and the balmy air of October ftimulated their fenfes.  The nut-trees were loaded with ripe fruit, and the rich clufters of grapes were hanging temptingly upon the vines.  Wild game was plentiful and delicious.  The fifh of the bay were sweet, delicate, and of many varieties.  Nature, unaided by art, had thus fupplied fo many human wants that Champlain gravely put upon record his opinion that this would be a most excellent place in which to lay the foundations of a commonwealth, if the harbor were deeper and better protected at its mouth.

After the voyagers had been in Chatham eight or nine
days,

days, the Indians, tempted by the implements which they faw about the forge and bakery, conceived the idea of taking forcible poffeffion of them, in order to appropriate them to their own ufe. As a preparation for this, and particularly to put themfelves in a favorable condition in cafe of an attack or reprifal, they were feen removing their women, children, and effects into the forefts, and even taking down their cabins. De Poutrincourt, obferving this, gave orders to the workmen to pafs their nights no longer on fhore, but to go on board the barque to affure their perfonal fafety. This command, however, was not obeyed. The next morning, at break of day, four hundred favages, creeping foftly over a hill in the rear, furrounded the tent, and poured fuch a volley of arrows upon the defencelefs workmen that efcape was impoffible. Three of them were killed upon the fpot ; a fourth was mortally and a fifth badly wounded. The alarm was given by the fentinel on the barque. De Poutrincourt, Champlain, and the reft, aroufed from their flumbers, rufhed half-clad into the fhip's boat, and haftened to the refcue. As foon as they touched the fhore, the favages, fleet as the greyhound, efcaped to the wood. Purfuit, under the circumftances, was not to be made ; and, if it had been, would have ended in their utter deftruction. Freed from immediate danger, they collected the dead and gave them Chriftian burial near the foot of a crofs, which had been erected the day before. While the fervice of prayer and fong was offered, the favages in the diftance mocked them with derifive attitudes and hideous howls. Three hours after the French had retired to their barque, the mifcreants returned, tore down the crofs, difinterred the dead, and carried off the

garments

garments in which they had been laid to reft. They were immediately driven off by the French, the crofs was reftored to its place, and the dead reinterred.

Before leaving Chatham, fome anxiety was felt in regard to their fafety in leaving the harbor, as the little barque had fcarcely been able to weather the rough feas of Monomoy on their inward voyage. A boat had been fent out in fearch of a fafer and a better roadway, which, creeping along by the fhore fixteen or eighteen miles, returned, announcing three fathoms of water, and neither bars nor reefs. On the 16th of October they gave their canvas to the breeze, and failed out of Stage Harbor, which they had named *Port Fortuné*,[55] an appellation probably fuggefted by their narrow efcape in entering and by the bloody tragedy to which we have juft referred. Having gone eighteen or twenty miles, they fighted the ifland of Martha's Vineyard lying low in the diftance before them, which they called *La Soupçonneufe*, the fufpicious one, as they had feveral times been in doubt whether it were not a part of the mainland. A contrary wind forced them to return to their anchorage in Stage Harbor. On the 20th they fet out again, and continued their courfe in a fouthwefterly direction until they reached the entrance of Vineyard Sound. The rapid current of tide water flowing from Buzzard's Bay into the found through the rocky channel

---

[55] *Port Fortuné.* In giving this name there was doubtlefs an allufion to the goddefs FORTUNA of the ancients, whofe office it was to difpenfe riches and poverty, pleafures and pains, bleffings and calamities. They had experienced good and evil at her fickle hand. They had entered the harbor in peril and fear, but neverthelefs in fafety. They had fuffered by the attack of the favages, but fortunately had efcaped utter annihilation, which they might well have feared. It had been to them eminently the port of hazard or chance. *Vide* Vol. II. Note 231. *La Soupçonneufe Vide* Vol. II, Note 227.

nel between Nonameffet and Wood's Holl, they took to be a
river coming from the mainland, and named it *Rivière de
Champlain*.

This point, in front of Wood's Holl, is the fouthern limit
of the French explorations on the coaft of New England,
reached by them on the 20th of October, 1606.

Encountering a ftrong wind, approaching a gale, they
were again forced to return to Stage Harbor, where they
lingered two or three days, awaiting favoring winds for their
return to the colony at the bay of Annapolis.

We regret to add that, while they were thus detained,
under the very fhadow of the crofs they had recently
erected, the emblem of a faith that teaches love and forgive-
nefs, they decoyed, under the guife of friendfhip, feveral of
the poor favages into their power, and inhumanly butchered
them in cold blood. This deed was perpetrated on the bafe
principle of *lex talionis*, and yet they did not know, much
lefs were they able to prove, that their victims were guilty or
took any part in the late affray. No form of trial was obferved, no witneffes teftified, and no judge adjudicated. It
was a fimple murder, for which we are fure any Chriftian's
cheek would mantle with fhame who fhould offer for it any
defence or apology.

When this piece of barbarity had been completed, the
little French barque made its final exit from Stage Harbor,
paffed fuccefsfully round the fhoals of Monomoy, and anchored near Naufet, where they remained a day or two, leaving on the 28th of October, and failing directly to Ifle
Haute in Penobfcot Bay. They made brief ftops at fome
of the iflands at the mouth of the St. Croix, and at the
                                                              Grand

Grand Manan, and arrived at Annapolis Bafin on the 14th of November, after an exceedingly rough paffage and many hair-breadth efcapes.

## CHAPTER V.

RECEPTION OF THE EXPLORERS AT ANNAPOLIS BASIN. — A DREARY WINTER RELIEVED BY THE ORDER OF BON TEMPS. — NEWS FROM FRANCE. — BIRTH OF A PRINCE. — RUIN OF DE MONTS'S COMPANY. — TWO EXCURSIONS AND DEPARTURE FOR FRANCE. — CHAMPLAIN'S EXPLORATIONS COMPARED. — DE MONTS'S NEW CHARTER FOR ONE YEAR AND CHAMPLAIN'S RETURN IN 1608 TO NEW FRANCE AND THE FOUNDING OF QUEBEC. — CONSPIRACY OF DU VAL AND HIS EXECUTION.

ITH the voyage which we have defcribed in the laft chapter, Champlain terminated his explorations on the coaft of New England. He never afterward ftepped upon her foil. But he has left us, nevertheless, an invaluable record of the character, manners, and cuftoms of the aborigines as he faw them all along from the eaftern borders of Maine to the Vineyard Sound, and carefully ftudied them during the period of three confecutive years. Of the value of thefe explorations we need not here fpeak at length. We fhall refer to them again in the fequel.

The return of the explorers was hailed with joy by the colonifts at Annapolis Bafin. To give *éclat* to the occafion, Lefcarbot compofed a poem in French, which he recited at the head of a proceffion which marched with gay reprefentations to the water's edge, to receive their returning friends. Over the gateway of the quadrangle formed by their dwell-

ings,

ings, dignified by them as their fort, were the arms of France, wreathed in laurel, together with the motto of the king: —

DVO PROTEGIT VNVS.

Under this, the arms of De Monts were difplayed, overlaid with evergreen, and bearing the following infcription: —

DABIT DEVS HIS QVOQVE FINEM.

Then came the arms of Poutrincourt, crowned alfo with garlands, and infcribed: —

IN VIA VIRTVTI NVLLA EST VIA.

When the excitement of the return had paffed, the little fettlement fubfided into its ufual routine. The leifure of the winter was devoted to various objects bearing upon the future profperity of the colony. Among others, a corn mill was erected at a fall on Allen River, four or five miles from the fettlement, a little eaft of the prefent fite of Annapolis. A road was commenced through the foreft leading from Lower Granville towards the mouth of the bay. Two fmall barques were built, to be in readinefs in anticipation of a failure to receive fuccors the next fummer, and new buildings were erected for the accommodation of a larger number of colonifts. Still, there was much unoccupied time, and, fhut out as they were from the ufual affociations of civilized life, it was hardly poffible that the winter fhould not feem long and dreary, efpecially to the gentlemen.

To break up the monotony and add variety to the dull routine of their life, Champlain contrived what he called L'ORDRE DE BON TEMPS, or The Rule of Mirth, which was introduced and carried out with fpirit and fuccefs. The fifteen gentlemen who fat at the table of De Poutrincourt, the governor,

ernor, comprifing the whole number of the order, took turns
in performing the duties of fteward and caterer, each holding
the office for a fingle day.  With a laudable ambition, the
Grand Mafter for the time being laid the foreft and the fea
under contribution, and the table was conftantly furnifhed with
the moft delicate and well feafoned game, and the fweeteft as
well as the choiceft varieties of fish.  The frequent change
of office and the ingenuity difplayed, offered at every repaft,
either in the viands or mode of cooking, fomething new and
tempting to the appetite.  At each meal, a ceremony becoming the dignity of the order was ftrictly obferved.  At
a given fignal, the whole company marched into the dining-
hall, the Grand Mafter at the head, with his napkin over his
fhoulder, his ftaff of office in his hand, and the glittering
collar of the order about his neck, while the other members
bore each in his hand a difh loaded and fmoking with fome
part of the delicious repaft.  A ceremony of a fomewhat
fimilar character was obferved at the bringing in of the
fruit.  At the clofe of the day, when the laft meal had been
ferved, and grace had been faid, the mafter formally completed his official duty by placing the collar of the order
upon the neck of his fucceffor, at the fame time prefenting
to him a cup of wine, in which the two drank to each other's health and happinefs.  Thefe ceremonies were generally
witneffed by thirty or forty favages, men, women, boys, and
girls, who gazed in refpectful admiration, not to fay awe,
upon this exhibition of European civilization.  When Membertou,[96] the venerable chief of the tribe, or other fagamores
were

*66 Membertou.* See Pierre Biard's account of his death in 1611. *Relations des Jéfuites.* Quebec ed., Vol. I. p. 32.

were prefent, they were invited to a feat at the table, while bread was gratuitoufly diftributed to the reft.

When the winter had paffed, which proved to be an exceedingly mild one, all was aftir in the little colony. The preparation of the foil, both in the gardens and in the larger fields, for the fpring fowing, created an agreeable excitement and healthy activity.

On the 24th May, in the midft of thefe agricultural enterprifes, a boat arrived in the bay, in charge of a young man from St. Malo, named Chevalier, who had come out in command of the "Jonas," which he had left at Canfeau engaged in fifhing for the purpofe of making up a return cargo of that commodity. Chevalier brought two items of intelligence of great intereft to the colonifts, but differing widely in their character. The one was the birth of a French prince, the Duke of Orleans; the other, that the company of De Monts had been broken up, his monopoly of the fur-trade withdrawn, and his colony ordered to return to France. The birth of a prince demanded expreffions of joy, and the event was loyally celebrated by bonfires and a *Te Deum.* It was, however, giving a fong when they would gladly have hung their harps upon the willows.

While the fcheme of De Monts's colonial enterprife was defective, containing in itfelf a principle which muft fooner or later work its ruin, the difappointment occafioned by its fudden termination was none the lefs painful and humiliating. The monopoly on which it was bafed could only be maintained by a degree of feverity and apparent injuftice, which always creates enemies and engenders ftrife. The feizure and confifcation of feveral fhips with their valuable cargoes

on

on the fhores of Nova Scotia, had awakened a perfonal hof-
tility in influential circles in France, and the fufferers were
able, in turn, to ftrike back a damaging blow upon the
author of their loffes. They eafily and perhaps juftly reprefented that the monopoly of the fur-trade fecured to De
Monts was fapping the national commerce and diverting to
perfonal emolument revenues that properly belonged to the
ftate. To an impoverifhed fovereign with an empty treafury this appeal was irrefiftible. The facrednefs of the king's
commiffion and the lofs to the patentee of the property already embarked in the enterprife had no weight in the
royal fcales. De Monts's privilege was revoked, with the
tantalizing falvo of fix thoufand livres in remuneration, to
be collected at his own expenfe from unproductive fources.

Under thefe circumftances, no money for the payment of
the workmen or provifions for the coming winter had been
fent out, and De Poutrincourt, with great reluctance, proceeded to break up the eftablifhment. The goods and
utenfils, as well as fpecimens of the grain which they had
raifed, were to be carefully packed and fent round to the
harbor of Canfeau, to be fhipped by the "Jonas," together
with the whole body of the colonifts, as foon as fhe fhould
have received her cargo of fifh.

While thefe preparations were in progrefs, two excurfions
were made ; one towards the weft, and another northeafterly
towards the head of the Bay of Fundy. Lefcarbot accompanied the former, paffing feveral days at St. John and the
ifland of St. Croix, which was the wefterly limit of his explorations and perfonal knowledge of the American coaft.
The other excurfion was conducted by De Poutrincourt,
accompanied

accompanied by Champlain, the object of which was to fearch for ores of the precious metals, a fpecies of wealth earneftly coveted and overvalued at the court of France. They failed along the northern fhores of Nova Scotia, entered Mines Channel, and anchored off Cape Fendu, now Anglicifed into the uneuphonious name of Cape Split. De Poutrincourt landed on this headland, and afcended a fteep and lofty fummit which is not lefs than four hundred feet in height. Mofs feveral feet in thicknefs, the growth of centuries, had gathered upon it, and, when he ftood upon the pinnacle, it yielded and trembled like gelatine under his feet. He found himfelf in a critical fituation. From this giddy and unftable height he had neither the fkill or courage to return. After much anxiety, he was at length refcued by fome of his more nimble failors, who managed to put a hawfer over the fummit, by means of which he fafely defcended. They named it *Cap de Poutrincourt.*

They proceeded as far as the head of the Bafin of Mines, but their fearch for mineral wealth was fruitlefs, beyond a few meagre fpecimens of copper. Their labors were chiefly rewarded by the difcovery of a mofs-covered crofs in the laft ftages of decay, the relic of fifhermen, or other Chriftian mariners, who had, years before, been upon the coaft.

The exploring parties having returned to Port Royal, to their fettlement in what is now known as Annapolis Bafin, the bulk of the colonifts departed in three barques for Canfeau, on the 30th of July, while De Poutrincourt and Champlain, with a complement of failors, remained fome days longer, that they might take with them fpecimens of wheat ftill in the field and not yet entirely ripe.

On

On the 11th of Auguft they likewife bade adieu to Port Royal amid the tears of the affembled favages, with whom they had lived in friendfhip, and who were difappointed and grieved at their departure. In paffing round the peninfula of Nova Scotia in their little fhallop, it was neceffary to keep clofe in upon the fhore, which enabled Champlain, who had not before been upon the coaft eaft of La Hève, to make a careful furvey from that point to Canfeau, the refults of which are fully ftated in his notes, and delineated on his map of 1613.

On the 3d of September, the "Jonas," bearing away the little French colony, failed out of the harbor of Canfeau, and, directing its courfe towards the fhores of France, arrived at Saint Malo on the 1ft of October, 1607.

Champlain's explorations on what may be ftrictly called the Atlantic coaft of North America were now completed. He had landed at La Hève in Nova Scotia on the 8th of May, 1604, and had confequently been in the country three years and nearly four months. During this period he had carefully examined the whole fhore from Canfeau, the eaftern limit of Nova Scotia, to the Vineyard Sound on the fouthern boundaries of Maffachufetts. This was the moft ample, accurate, and careful furvey of this region which was made during the whole period from the difcovery of the continent in 1497 down to the eftablifhment of the Englifh colony at Plymouth in 1620. A numerous train of navigators had paffed along the coaft of New England: Sebaftian Cabot, Eftévan Gomez, Jean Alfonfe, André Thevet, John Hawkins, Bartholomew Gofnold, Martin Pring, George Weymouth, Henry Hudfon, John Smith, and the reft, but the

knowledge

knowledge of the coaſt which we obtain from them is exceedingly meagre and unſatisfactory, eſpecially as compared with that contained in the full, ſpecific, and detailed deſcriptions, maps, and drawings left us by this diſtinguiſhed pioneer in the ſtudy and illuſtration of the geography of the New England coaſt.[97]

The

[97] Had the diſtinguiſhed navigators who early viſited the coaſts of North America illuſtrated their narratives by drawings and maps, it would have added greatly to their value. Capt. John Smith's map, though neceſſarily indefinite and general, is indiſpenſable to the ſatisfactory ſtudy of his ſtill more indefinite "Deſcription of New England." It is, perhaps, a ſufficient apology for the vagueneſs of Smith's ſtatements, and therefore it ought to be borne in mind, that his work was originally written, probably, from memory, at leaſt for the moſt part, while he was a priſoner on board a French man-of-war in 1615. This may be inferred from the following ſtatement of Smith himſelf. In ſpeaking of the movement of the French fleet, he ſays: "Still we ſpent our time about the Iles neere *Fyall*: where to keepe my perplexed thoughts from too much meditation of my miſerable eſtate, I writ this diſcourſe." *Vide Deſcription of New England* by Capt. John Smith, London. 1616.

While the deſcriptions of our coaſt left by Champlain are invaluable to the hiſtorian and cannot well be overeſtimated, the proceſs of making theſe ſurveys, with his profound love of ſuch explorations and adventures, muſt have given him great perſonal ſatisfaction and enjoyment. It would be difficult to find any region of ſimilar extent that could offer, on a ſummer's excurſion, ſo much beauty to his eager and critical eye as this. The following deſcription of the Gulf of Maine, which comprehends the major part of the field ſurveyed by Champlain, that lying between the headlands of Cape Sable and Cape Cod, gives an excellent idea of the infinite variety and the unexpected and marvellous beauties that are ever revealing themſelves to the voyager as he paſſes along our coaſt:—

"This ſhoreland is alſo remarkable, being ſo battered and frayed by ſea and ſtorm, and worn perhaps by arctic currents and glacier beds, that its natural front of ſome 250 miles is multiplied to an extent of not leſs than 2,500 miles of ſalt-water line; while at an average diſtance of about three miles from the mainland, ſtretches a chain of outpoſts conſiſting of more than three hundred iſlands, fragments of the main, ſtriking in their diverſity on the weſt; low, wooded and graſſy to the water's edge, and riſing eaſtward through bolder types to the crowns and cliffs of Mount Deſert and Quoddy Head, an advancing ſeries from beauty to ſublimity; and behind all theſe are deep baſins and broad river-mouths, affording convenient and ſpacious harbors, in many of which the navies of nations might ſafely ride at anchor. . . . Eſpecially attractive was the region between the Piſcataqua and Penobſcot, in its marvellous beauty of ſhore and ſea, of iſland and inlet, of bay and river and harbor, ſurpaſſing any other equally extenſive portion of the Atlantic coaſt, and compared

The winter of 1607-8 Champlain paffed in France, where he was pleafantly occupied in focial recreations which were efpecially agreeable to him after an abfence of more than three years, and in recounting to eager lifteners his experiences in the New World. He took an early opportunity to lay before Monfieur de Monts the refults of the explorations which he had made in La Cadie fince the departure of the latter from Annapolis Bafin in the autumn of 1605, illuftrating his narrative by maps and drawings which he had prepared of the bays and harbors on the coaft of Nova Scotia, New Brunfwick, and New England.

While moft men would have been difheartened by the oppofition which he encountered, the mind of De Monts was, neverthelefs, rekindled by the recitals of Champlain with frefh zeal in the enterprife which he had undertaken. The vifion of building up a vaft territorial eftablifhment, contemplated by his charter of 1604, with his own perfonal aggrandizement and that of his family, had undoubtedly vanifhed. But he clung, neverthelefs, with extraordinary tenacity to his original purpofe of planting a colony in the New World. This he refolved to do in the face of many obftacles, and notwithftanding the withdrawment of the royal protection and bounty. The generous heart of Henry IV. was by no means infenfible to the merits of his faithful fubject, and, on his folicitation, he granted to him letters-patent for the exclufive right of trade in America, but for the fpace only of a fingle year. With this fmall boon from the royal hand, De Monts haftened to fit out two veffels for the expedition. One

pared by travellers earlieft and lateft, with the famed archipelago of the Ægean." *Vide Maine, Her Place in* *Hiftory*, by Jofhua L. Chamberlain, LL.D., Prefident of Bowdoin College, Augufta, 1877, pp. 4-5.

One was to be commanded by Pont Gravé, who was to devote his undivided attention to trade with the Indians for
furs and peltry ; the other was to convey men and material
for a colonial plantation.

Champlain, whofe energy, zeal, and prudence had impreffed themfelves upon the mind of De Monts, was appointed lieutenant of the expedition, and intrufted with the
civil adminiftration, having a fufficient number of men for
all needed defence againft favage intruders, Bafque fifher
men, or interloping fur-traders.

On the 13th of April, 1608, Champlain left the port of
Honfleur, and arrived at the harbor of Tadouffac on the 3d
of June. Here he found Pont Gravé, who had preceded
him by a few days in the voyage, in trouble with a Bafque
fur-trader. The latter had perfifted in carrying on his traffic,
notwithftanding the royal commiffion to the contrary, and
had fucceeded in difabling Pont Gravé, who had but little
power of refiftance, killing one of his men, ferioufly wound-
ing Pont Gravé himfelf, as well as feveral others, and had
forcibly taken poffeffion of his whole armament.

When Champlain had made full inquiries into all the circumftances, he faw clearly that the difficulty muft be com-
promifed; that the exercife of force in overcoming the
intruding Bafque would effeétually break up his plans for
the year, and bring utter and final ruin upon his undertaking.
He wifely decided to pocket the infult, and let juftice flumber for the prefent. He confequently required the Bafque,
who began to fee more clearly the illegality of his courfe, to
enter into a written agreement with Pont Gravé that neither
fhould interfere with the other while they remained in the
country,

country, and that they fhould leave their differences to be fettled in the courts on their return to France.

Having thus poured oil upon the troubled waters, Champlain proceeded to carry out his plans for the location and eftablifhment of his colony. The difficult navigation of the St. Lawrence above Tadouffac was well known to him. The dangers of its numberlefs rocks, fand-bars, and fluctuating channels had been made familiar to him by the voyage of 1603. He determined, therefore, to leave his veffel in the harbor of Tadouffac, and conftruct a fmall barque of twelve or fourteen tons, in which to afcend the river and fix upon a place of fettlement.

While the work was in progrefs, Champlain reconnoitred the neighborhood, collecting much geographical information from the Indians relating to Lake St. John and a traditionary falt fea far to the north, exploring the Saguenay for fome diftance, of which he has given us a defcription fo accurate and fo carefully drawn that it needs little revifion after the lapfe of two hundred and feventy years.

On the laft of June, the barque was completed, and Champlain, with a complement of men and material, took his departure. As he glided along in his little craft, he was exhilarated by the fragrance of the atmofphere, the bright coloring of the foliage, the bold, picturefque fcenery that conftantly revealed itfelf on both fides of the river. The lofty mountains, the expanding valleys, the luxuriant forefts, the bold headlands, the enchanting little bays and inlets, and the numerous tributaries burfting into the broad waters of the St. Lawrence, were all carefully examined and noted in his journal. The expedition feemed more like a holiday

11                                                        excurfion

excurfion than the grave prelude to the founding of a city to be renowned in the hiftory of the continent.

On the fourth day, they approached the fite of the prefent city of Quebec. The expanfe of the river had hitherto been from eight to thirteen miles. Here a lofty headland, approaching from the interior, advances upon the river and forces it into a narrow channel of three-fourths of a mile in width. The river St. Charles, a fmall ftream flowing from the northweft, uniting here with the St. Lawrence, forms a bafin below the promontory, fpreading out two miles in one direction and four in another. The rocky headland, jutting out upon the river, rifes up nearly perpendicularly, and to a height of three hundred and forty-five feet, commanding from its fummit a view of water, foreft and mountain of furpaffing grandeur and beauty. A narrow belt of fertile land formed by the crumbling *débris* of ages, ftretches along between the water's edge and the bafe of the precipice, and was then covered with a luxurious growth of nut-trees. The magnificent bafin below, the protecting wall of the headland in the rear, the deep water of the river in front, rendered this fpot peculiarly attractive. Here on this narrow plateau, Champlain refolved to place his fettlement, and forthwith began the work of felling trees, excavating cellars, and conftructing houfes.

On the 3d day of July, 1608, Champlain laid the foundation of Quebec. The name which he gave to it had been applied to it by the favages long before. It is derived from the Algonquin word *quebio*, or *quebec*, fignifying a *narrowing*, and was defcriptive of the form which the river takes at that place, to which we have already referred.

A

A few days after their arrival, an event occurred of exciting interest to Champlain and his little colony. One of their number, Jean du Val, an abandoned wretch, who poffeffed a large fhare of that ftrange magnetic power which fome men have over the minds of others, had fo fkilfully practifed upon the credulity of his comrades that he had drawn them all into a fcheme which, afide from its atrocity, was weak and ill-contrived at every point. It was nothing lefs than a plan to affaffinate Champlain, feize the property belonging to the expedition, and fell it to the Bafque fur-traders at Tadouffac, under the hallucination that they fhould be enriched by the pillage. They had even entered into a folemn compact, and whoever revealed the fecret was to be vifited by inftant death. Their purpofe was to feize Champlain in an unguarded moment and ftrangle him, or to fhoot him in the confufion of a falfe alarm to be raifed in the night by themfelves. But before the plan was fully ripe for execution, a barque unexpectedly arrived from Tadouffac with an inftalment of utenfils and provifions for the colony. One of the men, Antoine Natel, who had entered into the confpiracy with reluctance, and had been reftrained from a difclofure by fear, fummoned courage to reveal the plot to the pilot of the boat, firft fecuring from him the affurance that he fhould be fhielded from the vengeance of his fellow-confpirators. The fecret was forthwith made known to Champlain, who, by a ftroke of fineffe, placed himfelf beyond danger before he flept. At his fuggeftion, the four leading fpirits of the plot were invited by one of the failors to a focial repaft on the barque, at which two bottles of wine which he pretended had been given him at Tadouffac were to be uncorked. In the midft

of

of the feftivities, the " four worthy heads of the confpiracy," as Champlain fatirically calls them, were fuddenly clapped into irons. It was now late in the evening, but Champlain never-thelefs fummoned all the reft of the men into his prefence, and offered them a full pardon, on condition that they would difclofe the whole fcheme and the motives which had induced them to engage in it. This they were eager to do, as they now began to comprehend the dangerous compact into which they had entered, and the peril which threatened their own lives. Thefe preliminary inveftigations rendered it obvious to Champlain that grave confequences muft follow, and he therefore proceeded with great caution.

The next day, he took the depofitions of the pardoned men, carefully reducing them to writing. He then departed for Tadouffac, taking the four confpirators with him. On confultation, he decided to leave them there, where they could be more fafely guarded until Pont Gravé and the principal men of the expedition could return with them to Quebec, where he propofed to give them a more public and formal trial. This was accordingly done. The prifoners were duly confronted with the witneffes. They denied nothing, but freely admitted their guilt. With the advice and concurrence of Pont Gravé, the pilot, furgeon, mate, boatfwain, and others, Champlain condemned the four con-fpirators to be hung; three of them, however, to be fent home for a confirmation or revifion of their fentence by the authorities in France, while the fentence of Jean Du Val, the arch-plotter of the malicious fcheme, was duly executed in their prefence, with all the folemn forms and ceremonies ufual on fuch occafions. Agreeably to a cuftom of that

period,

period, the ghaftly head of Du Val was elevated on the higheft pinnacle of the fort at Quebec, looking down and uttering its filent warning to the bufy colonifts below; the grim fignal to all beholders, that "the way of the tranfgreffor is hard."

The cataftrophe, had not the plot been nipped in the bud, would have been fure to take place. The final purpofe of the confpirators might not have been realized; it muft have been defeated at a later ftage; but the hand of Du Val, prompted by a malignant nature, was nerved to ftrike a fatal blow, and the life of Champlain would have been facrificed at the opening of the tragic fcene.

The punifhment of Du Val, in its chara&ter and degree, was not only agreeable to the civil policy of the age, but was neceffary for the prote&tion of life and the maintenance of order and difcipline in the colony. A confpiracy on land, under the prefent circumftances, was as dangerous as a mutiny at fea; and the calm, careful, and dignified procedure of Champlain in firmly vifiting upon the criminal a fevere though merited punifhment, reveals the wifdom, prudence, and humanity which were prominent elements in his mental and moral conftitution.

CHAPTER VI.

## CHAPTER VI.

ERECTION OF BUILDINGS AT QUEBEC. — THE SCURVY AND THE STARVING SAVAGES. — DISCOVERY OF LAKE CHAMPLAIN, AND THE BATTLE AT TICONDEROGA. — CRUELTIES INFLICTED ON PRISONERS OF WAR, AND THE FESTIVAL AFTER VICTORY. — CHAMPLAIN'S RETURN TO FRANCE AND HIS INTERVIEW WITH HENRY IV. — VOYAGE TO NEW FRANCE AND PLANS OF DISCOVERY. — BATTLE WITH THE IROQUOIS NEAR THE MOUTH OF THE RICHELIEU. — REPAIR OF BUILDINGS AT QUEBEC. — NEWS OF THE ASSASSINATION OF HENRY IV. — CHAMPLAIN'S RETURN TO FRANCE AND HIS CONTRACT OF MARRIAGE. — VOYAGE TO QUEBEC IN 1611.

N the 18th of September, 1608, Pont Gravé, having obtained his cargo of furs and peltry, failed for France.

The autumn was fully occupied by Champlain and his little band of colonifts in completing the buildings and in making fuch other provifions as were needed againft the rigors of the approaching winter. From the foreft trees beams were hewed into fhape with the axe, boards and plank were cut from the green wood with the faw, walls were reared from the rough ftones gathered at the bafe of the cliff, and plots of land were cleared near the fettlement, where wheat and rye were fown and grapevines planted, which fuccefsfully tefted the good qualities of the foil and climate.

Three lodging-houfes were erected on the northweft angle formed by the junction of the prefent ftreets St. Peter and Sous le Fort, near or on the fite of the Church of Notre Dame. Adjoining, was a ftore-houfe. The whole was furrounded by a moat fifteen feet wide and fix feet deep, thus

giving

giving the fettlement the character of a fort ; a wife precau-
tion againft a fudden attack of the treacherous favages.[18]

At length the funny days of autumn were gone, and the
winter, with its fierce winds and its penetrating frofts and
deep banks of fnow, was upon them. Little occupation
could be furnifhed for the twenty-eight men that compofed
the colony. Their idlenefs foon brought a defpondency that
hung like a pall upon their fpirits. In February, difeafe
made its approach. It had not been expected. Every defence within their knowledge had been provided againft it.
Their houfes were clofely fealed and warm ; their clothing
was abundant ; their food nutritious and plenty. But a diet
too exclufively of falt meat had, notwithftanding, in the opinion of Champlain, and we may add the want, probably, of
exercife and the prefence of bad air, induced the *mal de la
terre* or fcurvy, and it made fearful havoc with his men.
Twenty, five out of each feven of their whole number,
had been carried to their graves before the middle of April,
and half of the remaining eight had been attacked by the
loathfome fcourge.

While the mind of Champlain was oppreffed by the fuffering and death that were at all times prefent in their abode,
his fympathies were ftill further taxed by the condition of the
favages, who gathered in great numbers about the fettlement, in the moft abject mifery and in the laft ftages of
ftarvation. As Champlain could only furnifh them, from his
limited ftores, temporary and partial relief, it was the more
painful to fee them flowly dragging their feeble frames about
in

[18] The fituation of Quebec and an    may be feen by reference to Vol II. pp.
engraved reprefentation of the buildings    175, 183.

in the fnow, gathering up and devouring with avidity dif-
carded meat in which the procefs of decompofition was far
advanced, and which was already too potent with the ftench
of decay to be approached by his men.

Beyond the ravages of difeafe [59] and the ftarving Indians,
Champlain adds nothing more to complete the gloomy picture of his firft winter in Quebec.  The gales of wind that
fwept round the wall of precipice that protected them in the
rear, the drifts of fnow that were piled up in frefh inftal-
ments with every ftorm about their dwelling, the biting froft,
more piercing and benumbing than they had ever experienced before, the unceafing groans of the fick within, the
femi-weekly proceffion bearing one after another of their
diminifhing numbers to the grave, the myftery that hung
over the difeafe, and the impotency of all remedies, we know
were prominent features in the picture.  But the imagination feeks in vain for more than a fingle circumftance that
could throw upon it a beam of modifying and foftening light,
and that was the prefence of the brave Champlain, who bore
all without a murmur, and, we may be fure, without a throb
of unmanly fear or a fenfation of cowardly difcontent.

But the winter, as all winters do, at length melted reluc-
tantly away, and the fpring came with its verdure and its
new life.  The fpirits of the little remnant of a colony began to revive.  Eight of the twenty-eight with which the
winter began were ftill furviving.  Four had efcaped attack,
and four were rejoicing convalefcents.

On the 5th of June, news came that Pont Gravé had arrived from France, and was then at Tadouffac, whither
                                                    Champlain

[59] Scurvy, or *mal de la terre.* — *Vide* Vol. II. note 105.

Champlain immediately repaired to confer with him, and particularly to make arrangements at the earlieſt poſſible moment for an exploring expedition into the interior, an undertaking which De Monts had enjoined upon him, and which was not only agreeable to his own wiſhes, but was a kind of enterpriſe which had been a paſſion with him from his youth.

In anticipation of a tour of exploration during the approaching ſummer, Champlain had already aſcertained from the Indians that, lying far to the ſouthweſt, was an extenſive lake, famous among the ſavages, containing many fair iſlands, and ſurrounded by a beautiful and productive country. Having expreſſed a deſire to viſit this region, the Indians readily offered to act as guides, provided, neverthelefs, that he would aid them in a warlike raid upon their enemies, the Iroquois, the tribe known to us as the Mohawks, whoſe homes were beyond the lake in queſtion. Champlain without heſitation acceded to the condition exacted, but with little appreciation, as we confidently believe, of the bitter conſequences that were deſtined to follow the alliance thus inaugurated; from which, in after years, it was inexpedient, if not impoſſible, to recede.

Having fitted out a ſhallop, Champlain left Quebec on his tour of exploration on the 18th of June, 1609, with eleven men, together with a party of Montagnais, a tribe of Indians who, in their hunting and fiſhing excurſions, roamed over an indefinite region on the north ſide of the St. Lawrence, but whoſe headquarters were at Tadouſſac. After aſcending the St. Lawrence about ſixty miles, he came upon an encampment of two hundred or three hundred ſavages,

Hurons

12

Hurons [60] and Algonquins, the former dwelling on the borders of the lake of the fame name, the latter on the upper
waters of the Ottawa. They had learned fomething of the
French from a fon of one of their chiefs, who had been at
Quebec the preceding autumn, and were now on their
way to enter into an alliance with the French againft the
Iroquois. After formal negotiations and a return to Quebec to vifit the French fettlement and witnefs the effect of
their firearms, of which they had heard and which greatly
excited their curiofity, and after the ufual ceremonies of feafting and dancing, the whole party proceeded up the river
until they reached the mouth of the Richelieu. Here they
remained two days, as guefts of the Indians, feafting upon
fifh, venifon, and water-fowl.

While thefe feftivities were in progrefs, a difagreement
arofe among the favages, and the bulk of them, including
the women, returned to their homes. Sixty warriors, however, fome from each of the three allied tribes, proceeded up
the Richelieu with Champlain. At the Falls of Chambly,
finding it impoffible for the fhallop to pafs them, he directed
the pilot to return with it to Quebec, leaving only two men
from the crew to accompany him on the remainder of the
expedition. From this point, Champlain and his two brave
companions entrufted themfelves to the birch canoe of the
favages. For a fhort diftance, the canoes, twenty-four in all,
were

[60] *Hurons.* "The word Huron comes
from the French, who feeing thefe Indians with the hair cut very fhort, and
ftanding up in a ftrange fafhion, giving
them a fearful air, cried out, the firft
time they faw them, *Quelle hures!*
what boars' heads! and fo got to call
them Hurons." — *Charlevoix's His.
New France,* Shea's Trans. Vol. II. p.
71. *Vide Relations des Jéfuites,* Quebec ed. Vol. I. 1639, p. 51; alfo note
321, Vol. II. of this work, for brief
notice of the Algonquins and other
tribes.

were tranfported by land. The fall and rapids, extending as far as St. John, were at length paffed. They then proceeded up the river, and, entering the lake which now bears the name of Champlain, crept along the weftern bank, advancing after the firft few days only in the night, hiding themfelves during the day in the thickets on the fhore to avoid the obfervation of their enemies, whom they were now liable at any moment to meet.

On the evening of the 29th of July, at about ten o'clock, when the allies were gliding noifeleffly along in reftrained filence, as they approached the little cape that juts out into the lake at Ticonderoga, near where Fort Carillon was afterwards erected by the French, and where its ruins are ftill to be feen,⁶¹ they difcovered a flotilla of heavy canoes, of oaken bark, containing not far from two hundred Iroquois warriors, armed and impatient for conflict. A furor and frenzy as of fo many enraged tigers inftantly feized both parties. Champlain and his allies withdrew a fhort diftance, an arrow's range from the fhore, faftening their canoes by poles to keep them together, while the Iroquois haftened to the water's edge, drew up their canoes fide by fide, and began to fell trees and conftruct a barricade, which they were well able to accomplifh with marvellous facility and fkill. Two boats were fent out to inquire if the Iroquois defired to fight, to which they replied that they wanted nothing fo much, and, as

---

⁶¹ For the identification of the fite of this battle, fee Vol. II. p. 223, note 348. It is eminently hiftorical ground. Near it Fort Carrillon was erected by the French in 1756. Here Abercrombie was defeated by Montcalm in 1758. Lord Amherft captured the fort in 1759. Again it was taken from the Englifh by the patriot Ethan Allen in 1775. It was evacuated by St. Clair when environed by Burgoyne in 1777, and now for a complete century it has been vifited by the tourift as a ruin memorable for its many hiftorical affociations.

as it was now dark, at funrife the next morning they would give them battle. The whole night was fpent by both parties in loud and tumultuous boafting, berating each other in the roundeft terms which their favage vocabulary could furnifh, infultingly charging each other with cowardice and weaknefs, and declaring that they would prove the truth of their affertions to their utter ruin the next morning.

When the fun began to gild the diftant mountain-tops, the combatants were ready for the fray. Champlain and his two companions, each lying low in feparate canoes of the Montagnais, put on, as beft they could, the light armor in ufe at that period, and, taking the fhort hand-gun, or arquebus, went on fhore, concealing themfelves as much as poffible from the enemy. As foon as all had landed, the two parties haftily approached each other, moving with a firm and determined tread. The allies, who had become fully aware of the deadly character of the hand-gun and were anxious to fee an exhibition of its myfterious power, promptly opened their ranks, and Champlain marched forward in front, until he was within thirty paces of the Iroquois. When they faw him, attracted by his pale face and ftrange armor, they halted and gazed at him in a calm bewilderment for fome feconds. Three Iroquois chiefs, tall and athletic, ftood in front, and could be eafily diftinguifhed by the lofty plumes that waved above their heads. They began at once to make ready for a difcharge of arrows. At the fame inftant, Champlain, perceiving this movement, levelled his piece, which had been loaded with four balls, and two chiefs fell dead, and another favage was mortally wounded by the fame fhot. At this, the allies raifed a fhout rivalling thunder in its ftunning effect. From
both

both fides the whizzing arrows filled the air. The two French arquebufiers, from their ambufcade in the thicket, immediately attacked in flank, pouring a deadly fire upon the enemy's right. The explofion of the firearms, altogether new to the Iroquois, the fatal effects that inftantly followed, their chiefs lying dead at their feet and others faft falling, threw them into a tumultuous panic. They at once abandoned every thing, arms, provifions, boats, and camp, and without any impediment, the naked favages fled through the foreft with the fleetnefs of the terrified deer. Champlain and his allies purfued them a mile and a half, or to the firft fall in the little ftream that connects Lake Champlain [60] and Lake George.[61]  The victory was complete.  The allies gathered

[60] This lake, difcovered and explored by Champlain, is ninety miles in length. Through its centre runs the boundary line between the State of New York and that of Vermont.  From its difcovery to the prefent time it has appropriately borne the honored name of Champlain.  For its Indian name, *Caniaderiguarûnte*, fee Vol. II. note 349. According to Mr. Shea the Mohawk name of Lake Champlain is *Caniatagaronte*. — *Vide Shea's Charlevoix*, Vol. II. p. 18.

Lake Champlain and the Hudfon River were both difcovered the fame year, and were feverally named after the diftinguifhed navigators by whom they were explored.  Champlain completed his explorations at Ticonderoga, on the 30th of July, 1609, and Hudfon reached the higheft point made by him on the river, near Albany. on the 22d of September of the fame year. — *Vide* Vol. II. p. 219. Alfo *The Third Voyage of Mafter Henry Hudfon*, written by Robert Ivet of Lime-houfe. *Collections of New York His. Society*, Vol. I. p. 140.

[61] *Lake George*.  The Jefuit Father, Ifaac Jogues, having been fummoned in 1646 to vifit the Mohawks, to attend to the formalities of ratifying a treaty of peace which had been concluded with them, paffing by canoe up the Richelieu, through Lake Champlain, and arriving at the end of Lake George on the 29th of May, the eve of Corpus Chrifti, a feftival celebrated by the Roman Church on the Thurfday after Trinity Sunday, in honor of the Holy Euchariſt or the Lord's Supper, named this lake LAC DU SAINT SACREMENT. The following is from the Jefuit Relation of 1646 by Pere Hierofme Lalemant. Ils arriuèrent la veille du S. Sacrement au bout du lac qui eſt ioint au grand lac de Champlain.  Les Iroquois le nomment Andiatarocté, comme qui diroit, là où le lac fe ferme.  Le Pere le nomma le lac du S. Sacrement. — *Relations des Jéfuites*, Quebec ed. Vol. II. 1646, p. 15.

Two important facts are here made perfectly plain ; viz. that the original Indian name of the lake was *Andiatarocté*. and

gathered at the fcene of conflict, danced and fang in triumph, collected and appropriated the abandoned armor, feafted on the provifions left by the Iroquois, and, within three hours, with ten or twelve prifoners, were failing down the lake on their homeward voyage.

After they had rowed about eight leagues, according to Champlain's eftimate, they encamped for the night. A prevailing characteriftic of the favages on the eaftern coaft, in the early hiftory of America, was the barbarous cruelties which they inflicted upon their prifoners of war.[64] They did not depart from their ufual cuftom in the prefent inftance. Having kindled a fire, they felected a victim, and proceeded to excoriate his back with red-hot burning brands, and to apply live coals to the ends of his fingers, where they would

and that the French named it *Lac du Saint Sacrement* becaufe they arrived on its fhores on the eve of the feftival celebrated in honor of the Eucharift or the Lord's Supper. Notwithftanding this very plain ftatement, it has been affirmed without any hiftorical foundation whatever, that the original Indian name of this lake was *Horican*, and that the Jefuit miffionaries, having felected it for the typical purification of baptifm on account of its limpid waters, named it *Lac du Saint Sacrement*. This perverfion of hiftory originated in the extraordinary declaration of Mr. James Fenimore Cooper, in his novel entitled "The Laft of the Mohicans," in which thefe two erroneous ftatements are given as veritable hiftory. This new difcovery by Cooper was heralded by the public journals, fcholars were deceived, and the bold impofition was fo fuccefsful that it was even introduced into a meritorious poem in which the Horican of the ancient tribes and the baptifmal waters of the limpid lake are handled with fkill and effect. Twenty-five years after the writing of his novel, Mr. Cooper's confcience began ferioufly to trouble him, and he publicly confeffed, in a preface to " The Laft of the Mohicans," that the name Horican had been firft applied to the lake by himfelf, and without any hiftorical authority. He is filent as to the reafon he had affigned for the French name of the lake, which was probably an affumption growing out of his ignorance of its meaning. — *Vide The Laft of The Mohicans*, by J. Fenimore Cooper, Gregory's ed., New York, 1864, pp. ix-x and 12.

[64] " There are certain general cuftoms which mark the California Indians, as, the non-ufe of torture on prifoners of war," &c. — *Vide The Tribes of California*, by Stephen Powers, in *Contributions to North American Ethnology*, Vol. III. e. p. 15. *Tribes of Wafhington and Oregon*, by George Gibbs, *idem*, Vol. I. p. 192.

would give the moft exquifite pain. They tore out his finger-nails, and, with fharp flivers of wood, piercced his wrifts and rudely forced out the quivering finews. They flayed off the fkin from the top of his head,[65] and poured upon the bleeding wound a ftream of boiling melted gum. Champlain remonftrated in vain. The piteous cries of the poor, tormented victim excited his unavailing compaffion, and he turned away in anger and difguft. At length, when thefe inhuman tortures had been carried as far as they defired, Champlain was permitted, at his earneft requeft, with a mufket-fhot to put an end to his fufferings. But this was not the termination of the horrid performance. The dead victim was hacked in pieces, his heart fevered into parts, and the furviving prifoners were ordered to eat it. This was too revolting to their nature, degraded as it was; they were forced, however, to take it into their mouths, but they would do no more, and their guard of more compaffionate Algonquins allowed them to caft it into the lake.

This exhibition of favage cruelty was not extraordinary, but according to their ufual cuftom. It was equalled, and, if poffible, even furpaffed, in the treatment of captives generally

65 " It has been erroneoufly afferted that the practice of fcalping did not prevail among the Indians before the advent of Europeans. In 1535, Cartier faw five fcalps at Quebec, dried and ftretched on hoops. In 1564, Laudonnière faw them among the Indians of Florida. The Algonquins of New England and Nova Scotia were accuftomed to cut off and carry away the head, which they afterwards fcalped. Thofe of Canada, it feems, fometimes fcalped the dead bodies on the field. The Algonquin practice of carrying off heads as trophies is mentioned by Lalemant, Roger Williams, Lefcarbot, and Champlain." — *Vide Pioneers of France in the New World*, by Francis Parkman, Boston, 1874, p. 322. The practice of the tribes on the Pacific coaft is different. " In war they do not take fcalps, but decapitate the flain and bring in the heads as trophies." — *Contributions to Am. Ethnology*, by Stephen Powers, Wafhington, 1877, Vol. III. pp. 21, 221. *Vide* Vol. I. p. 192. The Yuki are an exception. Vol. III. p. 129.

generally, and efpecially of the Jefuit miffionaries in after years.[66]

When the party arrived at the Falls of Chambly, the Hurons and Algonquins left the river, in order to reach their homes by a fhorter way, tranfporting their canoes and effects over land to the St. Lawrence near Montreal, while the reft continued their journey down the Richelieu and the St. Lawrence to Tadouffac, where their families were encamped, waiting to join in the ufual ceremonies and rejoicings after a great victory.

When the returning warriors approached Tadouffac, they hung aloft on the prow of their canoes the fcalped heads of thofe whom they had flain, decorated with beads which they had begged from the French for this purpofe, and with a favage grace prefented thefe ghaftly trophies to their wives and daughters, who, laying afide their garments, eagerly fwam out to obtain the precious mementoes, which they hung about their necks and bore rejoicing to the fhore, where they further teftified their fatisfaction by dancing and finging.

After a few days, Champlain repaired to Quebec, and early in September decided to return with Pont Gravé to France. All arrangements were fpeedily made for that purpofe. Fifteen men were left to pafs the winter at Quebec, in charge of Captain Pierre Chavin of Dieppe. On the 5th of September they failed from Tadouffac, and, lingering fome days at Ifle Percé, arrived at Honfleur on the 13th of October, 1609.

Champlain

[66] For an account of the fufferings of *Hiftory of Catholic Miffions*, by John Brébeuf, Lalemant, and Jogues, fee Gilmary Shea, pp. 188, 189, 217.

Champlain haftened immediately to Fontainebleau, to make a detailed report of his proceedings to Sieur de Monts, who was there in official attendance upon the king.[67] On this occafion he fought an audience alfo with Henry IV., who had been his friend and patron from the time of his firft voyage to Canada in 1603. In addition to the new difcoveries and obfervations which he detailed to him, he exhibited a belt curioufly wrought and inlaid with porcupine-quills, the work of the favages, which efpecially drew forth the king's admiration. He alfo prefented two fpecimens of the fcarlet tanager, *Pyranga rubra*, a bird of great brilliancy of plumage and peculiar to this continent, and likewife the head of a gar-pike, a fifh of fingular charaderiftics, then known only in the waters of Lake Champlain.[68]

At this time De Monts was urgently feeking a renewal of his commiffion for the monopoly of the fur-trade. In this Champlain was deeply interefted. But to this monopoly a powerful oppofition arofe, and all efforts at renewal proved utterly fruitlefs. De Monts did not, however, abandon the enterprife on which he had entered. Renewing his engagements with the merchants of Rouen with whom he had already been affociated, he refolved to fend out in the early fpring, as a private enterprife and without any fpecial privileges or monopoly, two veffels with the neceffary equipments for ftrengthening his colony at Quebec and for carrying on trade as ufual with the Indians.

Champlain was again appointed lieutenant, charged with the

[67] He was gentleman in ordinary to the king's chamber. " Gentil-homme ordinaire de nôftre Chambre." — *Vide Commiffion du Roy au Sieur de Monts, Hiftoire de la Nouvelle France,* par Marc Lefcarbot, Paris, 1612, p. 432.
[68] Called by the Indians *chaoufarou.* For a full account of this cruftacean vide Vol. II. note 343.

the government and management of the colony, with the
expectation of paffing the next winter at Quebec, while Pont
Gravé, as he had been before, was fpecially entrufted with
the commercial department of the expedition.

They embarked at Honfleur, but were detained in the
Englifh Channel by bad weather for fome days. In the
mean time Champlain was taken ferioufly ill, the veffel
needed additional ballaft, and returned to port, and they did
not finally put to fea till the 8th of April. They arrived at
Tadouffac on the 26th of the fame month, in the year 1610,
and, two days later, failed for Quebec, where they found the
commander, Captain Chavin, and the little colony all in excellent health.

The eftablifhment at Quebec, it is to be remembered, was
now a private enterprife. It exifted by no chartered rights,
it was protected by no exclufive authority. There was confequently little encouragement for its enlargement beyond
what was neceffary as a bafe of commercial operations. The
limited cares of the colony left, therefore, to Champlain, a
larger fcope for the exercife of his indomitable defire for exploration and adventure. Explorations could not, however,
be carried forward without the concurrence and guidance
of the favages by whom he was immediately furrounded.
Friendly relations exifted between the French and the united
tribes of Montagnais, Hurons, and Algonquins, who occupied the northern fhores of the St. Lawrence and the great
lakes. A burning hatred exifted between thefe tribes and
the Iroquois, occupying the fouthern fhores of the fame river.
A deadly warfare was their chief employment, and every
fummer each party was engaged either in repelling an invafion

vafion or in making one in the territory of the other. Thofe friendly to Champlain were quite ready to act as pioneers in his explorations and difcoveries, but they expected and demanded in return that he fhould give them active perfonal affiftance in their wars.  Influenced, doubtlefs, by policy, the fpirit of the age, and his early education in the civil conflicts of France, Champlain did not hefitate to enter into an alliance and an exchange of fervices on thefe terms.

In the preceding year, two journeys into diftant regions had been planned for exploration and difcovery.  One beginning at Three Rivers, was to furvey, under the guidance of the Montagnais, the river St. Maurice to its fource, and thence, by different channels and portages, reach Lake St. John, returning by the Saguenay, making in the circuit a diftance of not lefs than eight hundred miles.  The other plan was to explore, under the direction of the Hurons and Algonquins, the vaft country over which they were accuftomed to roam, paffing up the Ottawa, and reaching in the end the region of the copper mines on Lake Superior, a journey not lefs than twice the extent of the former.

Neither of thefe explorations could be undertaken the prefent year.  Their importance, however, to the future progrefs of colonization in New France is fufficiently obvious. The purpofe of making thefe furveys fhows the breadth and wifdom of Champlain's views, and that hardfhips or dangers were not permitted to interfere with his patriotic fenfe of duty.

Soon after his arrival at Quebec, the favages began to affemble to engage in their ufual fummer's entertainment of making war upon the Iroquois.  Sixty Montagnais, equipped
in

in their rude armor, were haftening to the rendezvous which,
by agreement made the year before, was to be at the mouth
of the Richelieu.[69]  Hither were to come the three allied
tribes, and pafs together up this river into Lake Champlain,
the "gate" or war-path through which thefe hoftile clans
were accuftomed to make their yearly pilgrimage to meet
each other in deadly conflict.  Sending forward four barques
for trading purpofes, Champlain repaired to the mouth of
the Richelieu, and landed, in company with the Montagnais,
on the Ifland St. Ignace, on the 19th of June.  While preparations were making to receive their Algonquin allies from
the region of the Ottawa, news came that they had already
arrived, and that they had difcovered a hundred Iroquois
ftrongly barricaded in a log fort, which they had haftily
thrown together on the brink of the river not far diftant, and
to capture them the affiftance of all parties was needed without
delay.  Champlain, with four Frenchmen and the fixty Montagnais, left the ifland in hafte, paffed over to the mainland,
where they left their canoes, and eagerly rufhed through the
marfhy foreft a diftance of two miles.  Burdened with their
heavy armor, half confumed by mofquitoes which were fo thick
that they were fcarcely able to breathe, covered with mud
and water, they at length ftood before the Iroquois fort.[70]  It
was a ftructure of logs laid one upon another, braced and
held together by pofts coupled by withes, and of the ufual
circular form.  It offered a good protection in favage warfare.

[69] The mouth of the Richelieu was
the ufual place of meeting.  In 1603, the
allied tribes were there when Champlain
afcended the St. Lawrence.  They had
a fort, which he defcribes. — *Vide poftea,*
p. 243.

[70] Champlain's defcription does not
enable us to identify the place of this
battle with exactnefs.  It will be obferved, if we refer to his text, that, leaving the ifland of St. Ignace, and going
*half*

fare. Even the French arquebus difcharged through the crevices did flow execution.

It was obvious to Champlain that, to enfure victory, the fort muft be demolifhed. Huge trees, fevered at the bafe, falling upon it, did not break it down. At length, directed by Champlain, the favages approached under their fhields, tore away the fupporting pofts, and thus made a breach, into which rufhed the infuriated befiegers, and in hot hafte finifhed their deadly work. Fifteen of the Iroquois were taken prifoners; a few plunged into the river and were drowned; the reft perifhed by mufket-fhots, arrow-wounds, the toma-hawk, and the war-club. Of the allied favages three were killed and fifty wounded. Champlain himfelf did not efcape altogether

*half a league,* croffing the river, they landed, when they were plainly on the mainland near the mouth of the Riche-lieu. They then went *half a league,* and finding themfelves outrun by their Indian guides and loft, they called to two favages, whom they faw going through the woods, to guide them. Go-ing a *fhort diftance,* they were met by a meffenger from the fcene of conflict, to urge them to haften forwards. Then, after going *lefs than an eighth of a league,* they were within the found of the voices of the combatants at the fort. Thefe diftances are eftimated without meafurement, and, of courfe, are inex-act: but, putting the diftances men-tioned altogether, the journey through the woods to the fort was apparently a little more than two miles. Had they followed the courfe of the river, the dif-tance would probably have been fome-what more: perhaps nearly three miles. Champlain does not pofitively fay that the fort was on the Richelieu, but the whole narrative leaves no doubt that fuch was the fact. This river was the

avenue through which the Iroquois were accuftomed to come, and they would naturally encamp here where they could choofe their own ground, and where their enemies were fure to approach them. If we refer to Champlain's illuftration of *Fort des Iroquois,* Vol. II. p. 241, we fhall ob-ferve that the river is pictured as com-paratively narrow, which could hardly be a true reprefentation if it were in-tended for the St. Lawrence. The ef-caping Iroquois are reprefented as fwimming towards the right, which was probably in the direction of their homes on the fouth, the natural courfe of their retreat. The fhallop of Des Prairies, who arrived late, is on the left of the fort, at the exact point where he would naturally difembark if he came up the Richelieu from the St. Lawrence. From a ftudy of the whole narrative, together with the map, we infer that the fort was on the weftern bank of the Richelieu, between two and three miles from its mouth. We are confident that its lo-cation cannot be more definitely fixed.

altogether unharmed. An arrow, armed with a sharp point of stone, pierced his ear and neck, which he drew out with his own hand. One of his companions received a similar wound in the arm. The victors scalped the dead as usual, ornamenting the prows of their canoes with the bleeding heads of their enemies, while they severed one of the bodies into quarters, to eat, as they alleged, in revenge.

The canoes of the savages and a French shallop having come to the scene of this battle, all soon embarked and returned to the Island of St. Ignace. Here the allies, joined by eighty Huron warriors who had arrived too late to participate in the conflict, remained three days, celebrating their victory by dancing, singing, and the administration of the usual punishment upon their prisoners of war. This consisted in a variety of exquisite tortures, similar to those inflicted the year before, after the victory on Lake Champlain, horrible and sickening in all their features, and which need not be spread upon these pages. From these tortures Champlain would gladly have snatched the poor wretches, had it been in his power, but in this matter the savages would brook no interference. There was a solitary exception, however, in a fortunate young Iroquois who fell to him in the division of prisoners. He was treated with great kindness, but it did not overcome his excessive fear and distrust, and he soon sought an opportunity and escaped to his home."[71]

When the celebration of the victory had been completed, the Indians departed to their distant abodes. Champlain, however,

[71] For a full account of the Indian treatment of prisoners, *vide antea*, pp. 94, 95. Also Vol. II. pp. 224–227, 244–246.

however, before their departure, very wifely entered into an agreement that they fhould receive for the winter a young Frenchman who was anxious to learn their language, and, in return, he was himfelf to take a young Huron, at their fpecial requeft, to pafs the winter in France. This judicious arrangement, in which Champlain was deeply interefted and which he found fome difficulty in accomplifhing, promifed an important future advantage in extending the knowledge of both parties, and in ftrengthening on the foundation of perfonal experience their mutual confidence and friendfhip.

After the departure of the Indians, Champlain returned to Quebec, and proceeded to put the buildings in repair and to fee that all neceffary arrangements were made for the fafety and comfort of the colony during the next winter.

On the 4th of July, Des Marais, in charge of the veffel belonging to De Monts and his company, which had been left behind and had been expected foon to follow, arrived at Quebec, bringing the intelligence that a fmall revolution had taken place in Brouage, the home of Champlain, that the Proteftants had been expelled, and an additional guard of fol-diers had been placed in the garrifon. Des Marais alfo brought the ftartling news that Henry IV. had been affaffinated on the 14th of May. Champlain was penetrated by this an-nouncement with the deepeft forrow. He fully faw how great a public calamity had fallen upon his country. France had loft, by an ignominious blow, one of her ableft and wifeft fovereigns, who had, by his marvellous power, gradually united and compacted the great interefts of the nation, which had been fhattered and torn by half a century of civil con-flicts and domeftic feuds. It was alfo to him a perfonal lofs.

The

The king had taken a fpecial intereft in his undertakings, had been his patron from the time of his firft voyage to New France in 1603, had fuftained him by an annual penfion, and on many occafions had fhown by word and deed that he fully appreciated the great value of his explorations in his American domains. It was difficult to fee how a lofs fo great both to his country and himfelf could be repaired. A cloud of doubt and uncertainty hung over the future. The condition of the company, likewife, under whofe aufpices he was acting, prefented at this time no very encouraging features. The returns from the fur-trade had been fmall, owing to the lofs of the monopoly which the company had formerly enjoyed, and the exceffive competition which free-trade had ftimulated. Only a limited attention had as yet been given to the cultivation of the foil. Garden vegetables had been placed in cultivation, together with fmall fields of Indian corn, wheat, rye, and barley. Thefe attempts at agriculture were doubtlefs experiments, while at the fame time they were ufeful in fupplementing the ftores needed for the colony's confumption.

Champlain's perfonal prefence was not required at Quebec during the winter, as no active enterprife could be carried forward in that inclement feafon, and he decided, therefore, to return to France. The little colony now confifted of fixteen men, which he placed in charge, during his abfence, of Sieur Du Parc. He accordingly left Tadouffac on the 13th of Auguft, and arrived at Honfleur in France on the 27th of September, 1610.

During the autumn of this year, while refiding in Paris, Champlain became attached to Hélène Boullé, the daughter
of

of Nicholas Boullé, fecretary of the king's chamber. She was at that time a mere child, and of too tender years to act for herfelf, particularly in matters of fo great importance as thofe which relate to marital relations. However, agreeably to a cuftom not infrequent at that period, a marriage contract [71] was entered into on the 27th of December with her parents, in which, neverthelefs, it was ftipulated that the nuptials fhould not take place within at leaft two years from that date. The dowry of the future bride was fixed at fix thoufand livres *tournois*, three fourths of which were paid and receipted for by Champlain two days after the figning of the contract. The marriage was afterward confummated, and Helen Boullé, as his wife, accompanied Champlain to Quebec, in 1620, as we fhall fee in the fequel.

Notwithftanding the difcouragements of the preceding year and the fmall profpect of future fuccefs, De Monts and the merchants affociated with him ftill perfevered in fending another expedition, and Champlain left Honfleur for New France on the firft day of March, 1611. Unfortunately, the voyage had been undertaken too early in the feafon for thefe northern waters, and long before they reached the Grand Banks, they encountered ice-floes of the moft dangerous character. Huge blocks of cryftal, towering two hundred feet above the furface of the water, floated at times near them,

---

[71] *Vide Contrat de mariage de Samuel de Champlain, Œuvres de Champlain,* Quebec ed. Vol. VI., *Pièces Juftificatives,* p. 33.

Among the early marriages not uncommon at that period, the following are examples. Céfar, the fon of Henry IV., was efpoufed by public ceremonies to the daughter of the Duke de Mercœur in 1598. The bridegroom was four years old and the bride-elect had juft entered her fixth year. The great Condé, by the urgency of his avaricious father, was unwillingly married at the age of twenty, to Claire Clemence de Maillé Brézé, the niece of Cardinal Richelieu, when fhe was but thirteen years of age.

them, and at others they were furrounded and hemmed in
by vaft fields of ice extending as far as the eye could reach.
Amid thefe ceafelefs perils, momentarily expecting to be
crufhed between the floating iflands wheeling to and fro
about them, they ftruggled with the elements for nearly two
months, when finally they reached Tadouffac on the 13th of
May.

## CHAPTER VII.

THE FUR-TRADE AT MONTREAL. — COMPETITION AT THE RENDEZVOUS. —
NO EXPLORATIONS. — CHAMPLAIN RETURNS TO FRANCE. — REORGANIZA-
TION OF THE COMPANY. — COUNT DE SOISSONS, HIS DEATH. — PRINCE
DE CONDÉ. — CHAMPLAIN'S RETURN TO NEW FRANCE AND TRADE WITH
THE INDIANS. — EXPLORATION AND DE VIGNAN, THE FALSE GUIDE. —
INDIAN CEREMONY AT CHAUDIÈRE FALLS.

HAMPLAIN loft no time in haftening to Quebec, where he found Du Parc, whom he had left
in charge, and the colony in excellent health.
The paramount and immediate object which
now engaged his attention was to fecure for the
prefent feafon the fur-trade of the Indians. This furnifhed
the chief pecuniary fupport of De Monts's company, and
was abfolutely neceffary to its exiftence. He foon, therefore,
took his departure for the Falls of St. Louis, fituated a fhort
diftance above Montreal, and now better known as La Chine
Rapids. In the preceding year, this place had been agreed
upon as a rendezvous by the friendly tribes. But, as they
had not arrived, Champlain proceeded to make a thorough
exploration on both fides of the St. Lawrence, extending his
journeys more than twenty miles through the forefts and
along

along the ſhores of the river, for the purpoſe of ſelecting a
proper ſite for a trading-houſe, with doubtleſs an ultimate
purpoſe of making it a permanent ſettlement.   After a full
ſurvey, he finally fixed upon a point of land which he named
*La Place Royale*, ſituated within the preſent city of Montreal,
on the eaſtern ſide of the little brook Pierre, where it flows
into the St. Lawrence, at Point à Callière.   On the banks
of this ſmall ſtream there were found evidences that the land
to the extent of ſixty acres had at ſome former period been
cleared up and cultivated by the ſavages, but more recently
had been entirely abandoned on account of the wars, as he
learned from his Indian guides, in which they were inceſ-
ſantly engaged.

Near the ſpot which had thus been ſelected for a future
ſettlement, Champlain diſcovered a depoſit of excellent clay,
and, by way of experiment, had a quantity of it manufactured into bricks, of which he made a wall on the brink of
the river, to teſt their power of reſiſting the froſts and the
floods.   Gardens were alſo made and ſeeds ſown, to prove the
quality of the ſoil.   A weary month paſſed ſlowly away, with
ſcarcely an incident to break the monotony, except the
drowning of two Indians, who had unwiſely attempted to
paſs the rapids in a bark canoe overloaded with heron, which
they had taken on an iſland above.   In the mean time, Champlain had been followed to his rendezvous by a herd of adventurers from the maritime towns of France, who, ſtimulated by the freedom of trade, had flocked after him in
numbers out of all proportion to the amount of furs which
they could hope to obtain from the wandering bands of ſavages that might chance to viſit the St. Lawrence.   The river
was

was lined with thefe voracious cormorants, anxioufly watching the coming of the favages, all impatient and eager to fecure as large a fhare as poffible of the uncertain and meagre booty for which they had croffed the Atlantic. Fifteen or twenty barques were moored along the fhore, all feeking the beft opportunity for the difplay of the worthlefs trinkets for which they had avaricioufly hoped to obtain a valuable cargo of furs.

A long line of canoes was at length feen far in the diftance. It was a fleet of two hundred Hurons, who had fwept down the rapids, and were now approaching flowly and in a dignified and impreffive order. On coming near, they fet up a fimultaneous fhout, the token of favage greeting, which made the welkin ring. This falute was anfwered by a hundred French arquebufes from barque and boat and fhore. The unexpected multitude of the French, the newnefs of the firearms to moft of them, filled the favages with difmay. They concealed their fear as well and as long as poffible. They deliberately built their cabins on the fhore, but foon threw up a barricade, then called a council at midnight, and finally, under pretence of a beaver-hunt, fuddenly removed above the rapids, where they knew ·the French barques could not come. When they were thus in a place of fafety, they confeffed to Champlain that they had faith in him, which they confirmed by valuable gifts of furs, but none whatever in the grafping herd that had followed him to the rendezvous. The trade, meagre in the aggregate, divided among fo many, had proved a lofs to all. It was foon completed, and the favages departed to their homes. Subfequently, thirty-eight canoes, with eighty or a hundred Algonquin

gonquin warriors, came to the rendezvous. They brought, however, but a fmall quantity of furs, which added little to the lucrative charaĉter of the fummer's trade.

The reader will bear in mind that Champlain was not here merely as the fuperintendent and refponfible agent of a trading expedition. This was a fubordinate purpofe, and the refult of circumftances which his principal did not choofe, but into which he had been unwillingly forced. It was neceffary not to overlook this intereft in the prefent exigency, neverthelefs De Monts was fuftained by an ulterior purpofe of a far higher and nobler charaĉter. He ftill entertained the hope that he fhould yet fecure a royal charter under which his afpirations for colonial enterprife fhould have full fcope, and that his ambition would be finally crowned with the fuccefs which he had fo long coveted, and for which he had fo affiduoufly labored. Champlain, who had been for many years the geographer of the king, who had carefully reported, as he advanced into unexplored regions, his furveys of the rivers, harbors, and lakes, and had given faithful defcriptions of the native inhabitants, knowledge abfolutely neceffary as a preliminary ftep in laying the foundation of a French empire in America, did not for a moment lofe fight of this ulterior purpofe. Amid the commercial operations to which for the time being he was obliged to devote his chief attention, he tried in vain to induce the Indians to conduĉt an exploring party up the St. Maurice, and thus reach the headwaters of the Saguenay, a journey which had been planned two years before. They had excellent excufes to offer, and the undertaking was neceffarily deferred for the prefent. He, however, obtained much valuable information from

from them in converfations, in regard to the fource of the
St. Lawrence, the topography of the country which they
inhabited, and even drawings were executed by them to
illuftrate to him other regions which they had perfonally
vifited.

On the 18th of July, Champlain left the rendezvous,
and arrived at Quebec on the evening of the next day.
Having ordered all neceffary repairs at the fettlement, and,
not unmindful of its adornment, planted rofe-bufhes about
it, and taking fpecimens of oak timber to exhibit in France,
he left for Tadouffac, and finally for France on the 11th of
Auguft, and arrived at Rochelle on the 16th of September, 1611.

Immediately on his arrival, Champlain repaired to the city
of Pons, in Saintonge, of which De Monts was governor,
and laid before him the fituation of his affairs at Quebec.
De Monts ftill clung to the hope of obtaining a royal commiffion for the exclufive right of trade, but his affociates
were wholly difheartened by the competition and confequent
loffes of the laft year, and had the fagacity to fee that there
was no hope of a remedy in the future. They accordingly
declined to continue further expenditures. De Monts purchafed their intereft in the eftablifhment at Quebec, and,
notwithftanding the obftacles which had been and were ftill
to be encountered, was brave enough to believe that he could
ftem the tide unaided and alone. He haftened to Paris to
fecure the much coveted commiffion from the king. Important bufinefs, however, foon called him in another direction,
and the whole matter was placed in the hands of Champlain,
with the underftanding that important modifications were to
be

be introduced into the conftitution and management of the company.

The burden thus unexpectedly laid upon Champlain was not a light one. His experience and perfonal knowledge led him to appreciate more fully than any one elfe the difficulties that environed the enterprife of planting a colony in New France. He faw very clearly that a royal commiffion merely, with whatever exclufive rights it conferred, would in itfelf be ineffectual and powerlefs in the prefent complications. It was obvious to him that the adminiftration muft be adapted to the ftate of affairs that had gradually grown up at Quebec, and that it muft be fuftained by powerful perfonal influence.

Champlain proceeded, therefore, to draw up certain rules and regulations which he deemed neceffary for the management of the colony and the protection of its interefts. The leading characteriftics of the plan were, firft, an affociation of which all who defired to carry on trade in New France might become members, fharing equally in its advantages and its burdens, its profits and its loffes : and, fecondly, that it fhould be prefided over by a viceroy of high pofition and commanding influence. De Monts, who had thus far been at the head of the undertaking, was a gentleman of great refpectability, zeal, and honefty, but his name did not, as fociety was conftituted at that time in France, carry with it any controlling weight with the merchants or others whofe views were adverfe to his own. He was unable to carry out any plans which involved expenfe, either for the exploration of the country or for the enlargement and growth of the colony. It was neceffary, in the opinion of Champlain, to
place

place at the head of the company a man of fuch exalted
official and focial pofition that his opinions would be liftened
to with refpect and his wifhes obeyed with alacrity.

He fubmitted his plan to De Monts and likewife to Prefident Jeannin,[73] a man venerable with age, diftinguifhed for
his wifdom and probity, and at this time having under his
control the finances of the kingdom. They both pronounced
it excellent and urged its execution.

Having thus obtained the cordial and intelligent affent of
the higheft authority to his fcheme, his next ftep was to fecure a viceroy whofe exalted name and ftanding fhould con-
form to the requirements of his plan. This was an object
fomewhat difficult to attain. It was not eafy to find a nobleman who poffeffed all the qualities defired. After careful
confideration, however, the Count de Soiffons[74] was thought

to

---

[73] Pierre Jeannin was born at Autun, in 1540, and died about 1622. He be-gan the practice of law at Dijon, in 1569. Though a Catholic, he always counfelled tolerant meafures in the treatment of the Proteftants. By his in-fluence he prevented the maffacre of the Proteftants at Dijon in 1572. He was a Councillor, and afterward Prefident, of the Parliament of Dijon. He was the private advifer of the Duke of May-enne. He united himfelf with the party of the League in 1589. He negotiated the peace between Mayenne and Henry IV. The king became greatly attached to him, and appointed him a Councillor of State and Superintendent of Finan-ces. He held many offices and did great fervice to the State. After the death of the king, Marie de Médicis, the regent, continued him as Superintendent of Finances.

[74] Count de Soiffons, Charles de Bour-bon, was born at Nogent-le-Rotrou, in 1556, and died Nov. 1, 1612. He was educated in the Catholic religion. He acted for a time with the party of the League, but, falling in love with Cather-ine, the fifter of Henry IV., better to fecure his object he abandoned the League and took a military command under Henry III., and diftinguifhed himfelf for bravery when the king was befieged in Tours. After the death of the king, he efpoufed the caufe of Henry IV., was made Grand Mafter of France, and took part in the fiege of Paris. He attempted a fecret marriage with Catherine, but was thwarted; and the unhappy lovers were compelled, by the Duke of Sully, to renounce their matrimonial intentions. He had been Governor of Dauphiny, and, at the time of his death, was Governor of Normandy, with a penfion of 50,000 crowns.

to unite better than any other the characteristics which the office required. Champlain, therefore, laid before the Count, through a member of the king's council, a detailed exhibition of his plan and a map of New France executed by himself. He soon after received an intimation from this nobleman of his willingness to accept the office, if he should be appointed. A petition was sent by Champlain to the king and his council, and the appointment was made on the 8th of October, 1612, and on the 15th of the same month the Count issued a commission appointing Champlain his lieutenant.

Before this commission had been published in the ports and the maritime towns of France, as required by law, and before a month had elapsed, unhappily the death of the Count de Soissons suddenly occurred at his Château de Blandy. Henry de Bourbon, the Prince de Condé,[75] was hastily appointed his successor, and a new commission was issued to Champlain on the 22d of November of the same year.

The appointment of this prince carried with it the weight of high position and influence, though hardly the character which

[75] Prince de Condé, Henry de Bourbon II., the posthumous son of the first Henry de Bourbon, was born at Saint Jean d'Angely, in 1588. He married, in 1609, Charlotte Marguerite de Montmorency, the sister of Henry, the Duke de Montmorency, who succeeded him as the Viceroy of New France. To avoid the impertinent gallantries of Henry IV., who had fallen in love with this beautiful Princess, Condé and his wife left France, and did not return till the death of the king. He headed a conspiracy against the Regent, Marie de Médicis, and was thrown into prison on the first of September, 1616, where he remained three years. Influenced by ambition, and more particularly by his avarice, he forced his son Louis, Le Grand Condé, to marry the niece of Cardinal Richelieu, Claire Clémence de Maillé-Brézé. He did much to confer power and influence upon his family, largely through his avarice, which was his chief characteristic. The wit of Voltaire attributes his crowning glory to his having been the father of the great Condé. During the detention of the Prince de Condé in prison, the Maréchal de Thémins was Acting Viceroy of New France, having been appointed by Marie de Médicis, the Queen Regent. — *Vide Voyages du Sieur de Champlain*, Paris, 1632, p. 211.

15

which would have been moft defirable under the circumftances. He was, however, a potent fafeguard againft the
final fuccefs, though not indeed of the attempt on the part
of enemies, to break up the company, or to interfere with its
plans. No fooner had the publication of the commiffion
been undertaken, than the merchants, who had fchemes of
trade in New France, put forth a powerful oppofition. The
Parliamentary Court at Rouen even forbade its publication
in that city, and the merchants of St. Malo renewed their
oppofition, which had before been fet forth, on the flimfy
ground that Jacques Cartier, the difcoverer of New France,
was a native of their municipality, and therefore they had
rights prior and fuperior to all others.

After much delay and feveral journeys by Champlain to
Rouen, thefe difficulties were overcome. There was, indeed,
no folid ground of oppofition, as none were debarred from
engaging in the enterprife who were willing to fhare in the
burdens as well as the profits.

Thefe delays prevented the complete organization of the
company contemplated by Champlain's new plan, but it was
neverthelefs neceffary for him to make the voyage to Quebec the prefent feafon, in order to keep up the continuity of
his operations there, and to renew his friendly relations with
the Indians, who had been greatly difappointed at not feeing
him the preceding year. Four veffels, therefore, were authorized to fail under the commiffion of the viceroy, each of
which was to furnifh four men for the fervice of Champlain
in explorations and in aid of the Indians in their wars, if it
fhould be neceffary.

He accordingly left Honfleur in a veffel belonging to his
old

old friend Pont Gravé, on the 6th of March, 1613, and arrived at Tadouffac on the 29th of April. On the 7th of May he reached Quebec, where he found the little colony in excellent condition, the winter having been exceedingly mild and agreeable, the river not having been frozen in the fevereft weather. He repaired at once to the trading rendezvous at Montreal, then commonly known as the Falls of St. Louis. He learned from a trading barque that had preceded him, that a fmall band of Algonquins had already been there on their return from a raid upon the Iroquois. They had, however, departed to their homes to celebrate a feaft, at which the torture of two captives whom they had taken from the Iroquois was to form the chief element in the entertainment. A few days later, three Algonquin canoes arrived from the interior with furs, which were purchafed by the French. From them they learned that the ill treatment of the previous year, and their difappointment at not having feen Champlain there as they had expected, had led the Indians to abandon the idea of again coming to the rendezvous, and that large numbers of them had gone on their ufual fummer's expedition againft the Iroquois.

Under thefe circumftances, Champlain refolved, in making his explorations, to vifit perfonally the Indians who had been accuftomed to come to the Falls of St. Louis, to affure them of kind treatment in the future, to renew his alliance with them againft their enemies, and, if poffible, to induce them to come to the rendezvous, where there was a large quantity of French goods awaiting them.

It will be remembered that an ulterior purpofe of the French, in making a fettlement in North America, was to
enable

enable them better to explore the interior and difcover an avenue by water to the Pacific Ocean. This fhorter paffage to Cathay, or the land of fpicery, had been the day-dream of all the great navigators in this direction for more than a hundred years. Whoever fhould difcover it would confer a boon of untold commercial value upon his country, and crown himfelf with imperifhable honor. Champlain had been infpired by this dream from the firft day that he fet his foot upon the foil of New France. Every indication that pointed in this direction he watched with care and feized upon with avidity. In 1611, a young man in the colony, Nicholas de Vignan, had been allowed, after the trading feafon had clofed, to accompany the Algonquins to their diftant homes, and pafs the winter with them. This was one of the methods which had before been fuccefsfully reforted to for obtaining important information. De Vignan returned to Quebec in the fpring of 1612, and the fame year to France. Having heard apparently fomething of Hudfon's difcovery and its accompanying difafter, he made it the bafis of a ftory drawn wholly from his own imagination, but which he well knew muft make a ftrong impreffion upon Champlain and all others interefted in new difcoveries. He ftated that, during his abode with the Indians, he had made an excurfion into the forefts of the north, and that he had actually difcovered a fea of falt water; that the river Ottawa had its fource in a lake from which another river flowed into the fea in queftion ; that he had feen on its fhores the wreck of an Englifh fhip, from which eighty men had been taken and flain by the favages ; and that they had among them an Englifh boy, whom they were keeping to prefent to him.

As

As was expected, this ftory made a ftrong impreffion upon the mind of Champlain. The pricelefs object for which he had been in fearch fo many years feemed now within his grafp. The fimplicity and directnefs of the narrative, and the want of any apparent motive for deception, were a ftrong guaranty of its truth. But, to make affurance doubly fure, Vignan was crofs-examined and tefted in various ways, and finally, before leaving France, was made to certify to the truth of his ftatement in the prefence of two notaries at Rochelle. Champlain laid the ftory before the Chancellor de Sillery, the Prefident Jeannin, the old Marfhal de Briffac, and others, who affured him that it was a queftion of fo great importance, that he ought at once to teft the truth of the narrative by a perfonal exploration. He refolved, therefore, to make this one of the objects of his fummer's excurfion.

With two bark canoes, laden with provifions, arms, and a few trifles as prefents for the favages, an Indian guide, four Frenchmen, one of whom was the mendacious Vignan, Champlain left the rendezvous at Montreal on the 27th of May. After getting over the Lachine Rapids, they croffed Lake St. Louis and the Two Mountains, and, paffing up the Ottawa, now expanding into a broad lake and again contracting into narrows, whence its pent-up waters fwept over precipices and boulders in furious, foaming currents, they at length, after incredible labor, reached the ifland Allumette, a diftance of not lefs than two hundred and twenty-five miles. In no expedition which Champlain had thus far undertaken had he encountered obftacles fo formidable. The falls and rapids in the river were numerous and difficult to pafs. Sometimes a portage was impoffible on account
of

of the denfenefs of the forefts, in which cafe they were compelled to drag their canoes by ropes, wading along the edge
of the water, or clinging to the precipitous banks of the river
as beft they could.   When a portage could not be avoided,
it was neceffary to carry their armor, provifions, clothing,
and canoes through the forefts, over precipices, and fometimes over ftretches of territory where fome tornado had
proftrated the huge pines in tangled confufion, through
which a pathway was almoft impoffible.⁷⁸   To lighten their
burdens, nearly every thing was abandoned but their canoes.
Fifh and wild-fowl were an uncertain reliance for food, and
fometimes they toiled on for twenty-four hours with fcarcely
any thing to appeafe their craving appetites.

Overcome with fatigue and oppreffed by hunger, they at
length arrived at Allumette Ifland, the abode of the chief
Teffoüat, by whom they were cordially entertained.   Nothing
but the hope of reaching the north fea could have fuftained
them amid the perils and fufferings through which they had
paffed in reaching this inhofpitable region.   The Indians had
chofen this retreat not from choice, but chiefly on account of
its great inacceffibility to their enemies.   They were aftonifhed to fee Champlain and his company, and facetioufly
fuggefted that it muft be a dream, or that thefe new-comers
had

⁷⁸ In making the portage from what
is now known as Portage du Fort to
Mufkrat Lake, a diftance of about nine
miles, Champlain, though lefs heavily
loaded than his companions, carried
three French arquebuffes, three oars,
his cloak, and fome fmall articles, and
was at the fame time bitterly oppreffed
by fwarms of hungry and infatiable
mofquitoes.   On the old portage road,
traverfed by Champlain and his party
at this time, in 1613, an aftrolabe, infcribed 1603, was found in 1867.   The
prefumptive evidence that this inftrument was loft by Champlain is ftated in
a *brochure* by Mr. O. H. Marfhall.
—*Vide Magazine of American Hiftory*
for March, 1879.

had fallen from the clouds.  After the ufual ceremonies of
feafting and fmoking, Champlain was permitted to lay before
Teffoüat and his chiefs the objeét of his journey.  When he
informed them that he was in fearch of a falt fea far to the
north of them, which had been aétually feen two years before by one of his companions, he learned to his difappointment and mortification that the whole ftory of Vignan was
a fheer fabrication.  The mifcreant had indeed paffed a
winter on the very fpot where they then were, but had never
been a league further north.  The Indians themfelves had
no knowledge of the north fea, and were highly enraged at
the bafenefs of Vignan's falfehood, and craved the opportunity of defpatching him at once.  They jeered at him, calling
him a " liar," and even the children took up the refrain, vo-
ciferating vigoroufly and heaping maledictions upon his
head.

Indignant as he was, Champlain had too much philofophy
in his compofition to commit an indifcretion at fuch a moment as this.  He accordingly reftrained the favages and his
own anger, bore his infult and difappointment with exemplary patience, giving up all hope of feeing the falt fea in
this direétion, as he humoroufly added, "except in imagination."

Before leaving Allumette Ifland on his return, Champlain
invited Teffoüat to fend a trading expedition to the Falls of
St. Louis, where he would find an ample opportunity for an
exchange of commodities.  The invitation was readily accepted, and information was at once fent out to the neighboring chiefs, requefting them to join in the enterprife.
The favages foon began to affemble, and when Champlain
left,

left, he was accompanied by forty canoes well laden with furs; others joined them at different points on the way, and on reaching Montreal the number had fwollen to eighty.

An incident occurred on their journey down the river worthy of record. When the fleet of favage fur-traders had arrived at the foot of the Chaudière Falls, not a hundred rods diftant from the fite of the prefent city of Ottawa, having completed the portage, they all affembled on the fhore, before relaunching their canoes, to engage in a cere-mony which they never omitted when paffing this fpot. A wooden plate of fuitable dimenfions was paffed round, into which each of the favages caft a fmall piece of tobacco. The plate was then placed on the ground, in the midft of the company, and all danced around it, finging at the fame time. An addrefs was then made by one of the chiefs, fetting forth the great importance of this time-honored cuftom, particu-larly as a fafeguard and protection againft their enemies. Then, taking the plate, the fpeaker caft its contents into the boiling cauldron at the bafe of the falls, the act being accompanied by a loud fhout from the affembled multitude. This fall, named the *Chaudière*, or cauldron, by Champlain, formed in fact the limit above which the Iroquois rarely if ever went in hoftile purfuit of the Algonquins. The region above was exceedingly difficult of approach, and from which it was ftill more difficult, in cafe of an attack, to retreat. But the Iroquois often lingered here in ambufh, and fell upon the unfufpecting inhabitants of the upper Ottawa as they came down the river. It was, therefore, a place of great danger; and the Indians, enflaved by their fears and fuper-ftitions, did not believe it poffible to make a profperous jour-

ney,

ney, without obferving, as they paffed, the ceremonies above
defcribed.

On reaching Montreal, three additional fhips had arrived
from France with a licenfe to carry on trade from the Prince
de Condé, the viceroy, making feven in all in port. The trade
with the Indians for the furs brought in the eighty canoes,
which had come with Champlain to Montreal, was foon
defpatched. Vignan was pardoned on the folemn promife,
a condition offered by himfelf, that he would make a journey
to the north fea and bring back a true report, having made
a moft humble confeffion of his offence in the prefence of
the whole colony and the Indians, who were purpofely affembled to receive it. This public and formal adminiftration of
reproof was well adapted to produce a powerful effect upon
the mind of the culprit, and clearly indicates the moderation
and wifdom, fo uniformly characteriftic of Champlain's adminiftration.

The bufinefs of the feafon having been completed, Champlain returned to France, arriving at St. Malo on the 26th of
Auguft, 1613. Before leaving, however, he arranged to fend
back with the Algonquins who had come from Ifle Allumette two of his young men to pafs the winter, for the purpofe, as on former occafions, of learning the language and
obtaining the information which comes only from an intimate
and prolonged affociation.

CHAPTER VIII.

## CHAPTER VIII.

CHAMPLAIN OBTAINS MISSIONARIES FOR NEW FRANCE.—MEETS THE INDI-
ANS AT MONTREAL AND ENGAGES IN A WAR AGAINST THE IROQUOIS.
—HIS JOURNEY TO THE HURONS, AND WINTER IN THEIR COUNTRY.

URING the whole of the year 1614, Champlain remained in France, occupied for the moſt part in adding new members to his company of aſſociates, and in forming and perfecting ſuch plans as were clearly neceſſary for the proſperity and ſucceſs of the colony. His mind was particularly abſorbed in deviſing means for the eſtabliſhment of the Chriſtian faith in the wilds of America. Hitherto nothing whatever had been done in this direction, if we except the efforts of Poutrincourt on the Atlantic coaſt, which had already terminated in diſaſter.[77] No miſſionary of any ſort had

[77] De Poutrincourt obtained a confirmation from Henry IV. of the gift to him of Port Royal by De Monts, and proceeded to eſtabliſh a colony there in 1608. In 1611, a Jeſuit miſſion was planted by the Fathers Pierre Biard and Enemond Maſſé. It was chiefly patronized by a bevy of ladies, under the leaderſhip of the Marchioneſs de Guerchville, in cloſe aſſociation with Marie de Médicis, the queen-regent, Madame de Verneuil, and Madame de Soudis. Although De Poutrincourt was a devout member of the Roman Church, the miſſionaries were received with reluctance, and between them and the patentee and his lieutenant there was a conſtant and irrepreſſible diſcord. The lady patroneſs, the Marchioneſs de Guerchville, determined to abandon Port Royal and plant a new colony at Kadeſquit, on the ſite of the preſent city of Bangor, in the State of Maine. A colony was accordingly organized, which included the fathers, Quentin and Lalemant with the lay brother, Gilbert du Thet, and arrived at La Hève in La Cadie, on the 6th of May, 1613, under the conduct of Sieur de la Sauſſaye. From there they proceeded to Port Royal, took the two miſſionaries, Biard and Maſſé, on board, and coaſted along the borders of Maine till they came to Mount Deſert, and finally determined to plant their colony on that iſland. A ſhort time after the arrival of the colony, before they were in any condition for defence, Captain Samuel Argall, from the Engliſh colony in Virginia, ſuddenly appeared, and captured and

had hitherto fet his foot upon that part of the foil of New
France lying within the Gulf of St. Lawrence.[78]   A frefh
intereft had been awakened in the mind of Champlain.   He
faw its importance in a new light.   He fought counfel and
advice from various perfons whofe wifdom commended them to
his attention.   Among the reft was Louis Houêl, an intimate
friend, who held fome office about the perfon of the king,
and who was the chief manager of the falt works at Brouage.   This gentleman took a hearty intereft in the projeƈt,
and affured Champlain that it would not be difficult to raife
the means of fending out three or four Fathers, and, moreover, that he knew fome of the order of the Recolleƈts, belonging to a convent at Brouage, whofe zeal he was fure
would be equal to the undertaking.   On communicating
with them, he found them quite ready to engage in the work.
Two of them were fent to Paris to obtain authority and encouragement from the proper fources.   It happened that
about this time the chief dignitaries of the church were in
Paris, attending a feffion of the Eftates.   The bifhops and
cardinals were waited upon by Champlain, and their zeal
awakened and their co-operation fecured in raifing the neceffary means for fuftaining the miffion.   After the ufual negotiations and delays, the objeƈt was fully accomplifhed; fifteen
hundred

and tranfported the whole colony, and
fubfequently that at Port Royal, on the
alleged ground that they were intruders on Englifh foil.   Thus difaftroufly
ended Poutrincourt's colony at Port
Royal, and the Marchionefs de Guerchville's miffion at Mount Defert. — *Vide
Voyages par le Sr. de Champlain*,
Paris ed. 1632, pp. 98–114.   *Shea's
Charlevoix*, Vol. I. pp. 260–286.

[78] Champlain had tried to induce
Madame de Guerchville to fend her
miffionaries to Quebec, to avoid the obftacles which they had encountered at
Port Royal; but, for the fimple reafon
that De Monts was a Calvinift, fhe would
not liften to it. — *Vide Shea's Charlevoix*,
Vol. I. p. 274; *Voyages dv Sievr de
Champlain*, Paris ed. 1632, pp. 112,
113.

hundred *livres* were placed in the hands of Champlain for outfit and expenfes, and four Recollect friars embarked with him at Honfleur, on the fhip "St. Étienne," on the 24th of April, 1615, viz., Denis Jamay, Jean d'Olbeau, Jofeph le Caron, and the lay-brother Pacifique du Pleffis.[70]

On their arrival at Quebec, Champlain addreffed himfelf immediately to the preparation of lodgings for the miffionaries and the erection of a chapel for the celebration of divine fervice. The Fathers were impatient to enter the fields of labor feverally affigned to them. Jofeph le Caron was appointed to vifit the Hurons in their diftant foreft home, concerning which he had little or no information; but he neverthelefs entered upon the duty with manly courage and Chriftian zeal. Jean D'Olbeau affumed the miffion to the Montagnais, embracing the region about Tadouffac and the river Saguenay, while Denis Jamay and Pacifique du Pleffis took charge of the chapel at Quebec.

At the earlieft moment poffible Champlain haftened to the rendezvous at Montreal, to meet the Indians who had already reached there on their annual vifit for trade. The chiefs were in raptures of delight on feeing their old friend again, and had a grand fcheme to propofe. They had not forgotten that Champlain had often promifed to aid them in their wars. They approached the fubject, however, with moderation and diplomatic wifdom. They knew perfectly well that the trade in peltry was greatly defired, in fact that it was indifpenfable to the French. The fubftance of what they had to fay was this. It had become now, if not impoffible, exceedingly hazardous, to bring their furs to market.

Their

[70] *Vide Hiftoire du Canada, par Gabriel Sagard*, Paris, 1636, pp. 11-12.

Their enemies, the Iroquois, like fo many prowling wolves, were fure to be on their trail as they came down the Ottawa, and, incumbered with their loaded canoes, the ftruggle muft be unequal, and it was nearly impoffible for them ever to be winners. The only folution of the difficulty known to them, or which they cared to confider, as in all Indian warfare, was to annihilate their enemies utterly and wipe out their name for ever. Let this be done, and the fruits of peace would return, their commerce would be fafe, profperous, and greatly augmented.

Such were the reafons prefented by the allies. But there were other confiderations, likewife, which influenced the mind of Champlain. It was neceffary to maintain a clofe and firm alliance with the Indians in order to extend the French difcoveries and domain into new and more diftant regions, and on this extenfion of French influence depended their hope of converting the favages to the Chriftian faith. The force of thefe confiderations could not be refifted. Champlain decided that, under the circumftances, it was neceffary to give them the defired affiftance.

A general affembly was called, and the nature and extent of the campaign fully confidered. It was to be of vaftly greater proportions than any that had hitherto been propofed. The Indians offered to furnifh two thoufand five hundred and fifty men, but they were to be gathered together from different and diftant points. The journey muft, therefore, be long and perilous. The objective point, viz., a celebrated Iroquois fort, could not be reached by the only feafible route in a lefs diftance than eight hundred or nine hundred miles, and it would require an abfence of three or four months.

Preparations

Preparations for the journey were entered upon at once. Champlain vifited Quebec to make arrangements for his long abfence. On his return to Montreal, the Indians, impatient of delay, had already departed, and Father Jofeph le Caron had gone with them to his diftant field of miffionary labor among the Hurons.

On the 9th of July, 1615, Champlain embarked, taking with him an interpreter, probably Étienne Brûlé, a French fervant, and ten favages, who, with their equipments, were to be accommodated in two canoes. They entered the Rivière des Prairies, which flows into the St. Lawrence fome leagues eaft of Montreal, croffing the Lake of the Two Mountains, paffed up the Ottawa, taking the fame route which he had traverfed fome years before, revifiting its long fucceffion of reaches, its placid lakes, impetuous rapids, and magnificent falls, and at length arrived at the point where the river, by an abrupt angle, begins to flow from the northweft. Here, leaving the Ottawa, they entered the Mattawan, paffing down this river into Lac du Talon, thence into Lac la Tortue, and by a fhort portage, into Lake Nipiffing. After remaining here two days, entertained generoufly by the Nipiffingian chiefs, they croffed the lake, and, following the channel of French River, entered Lake Huron, or rather the Georgian Bay. They coafted along until they reached the northern limits of the county of Simcoe. Here they difembarked and entered the territory of their old friends and allies, the Hurons.

The domain of this tribe confifted of a peninfula formed by the Georgian Bay, the river Severn, and Lake Simcoe, at the fartheft, not more than forty by twenty-five miles in
extent,

extent, but more generally cultivated by the native population, and of a richer foil than any region hitherto explored
north of the St. Lawrence and the lakes.   They vifited four
of their villages and were cordially received and feafted on
Indian corn, fquafhes, and fifh, with fome variety in the
methods of cooking.  They then proceeded to Carhagouha,[10]
a town fortified with a triple palifade of wood thirty-five
feet in height.   Here they found the Recolleét Father Jofeph
Le Caron, who, having preceded them but a few days,
and not anticipating the vifit, was filled with raptures of
aftonifhment and joy.   The good Father was intent upon
his pious work.   On the 12th of Auguft, furrounded by his
followers, he formally erected a crofs as a fymbol of the
faith, and on the fame day they celebrated the mafs and
chanted TE DEUM LAUDAMUS for the firft time.

Lingering but two days, Champlain and ten of the French,
eight of whom had belonged to the fuite of Le Caron, proceeded flowly towards Cahiagué,[11] the rendezvous where the
muftering hofts of the favage warriors were to fet forth together upon their hoftile excurfion into the country of the
Iroquois.  Of the Huron villages vifited by them, fix are
particularly mentioned as fortified by triple palifades of
wood.   Cahiagué, the capital, encircled two hundred large
cabins within its wooden walls.   It was fituated on the north
of

[10] *Carhagouha,* named by the French *Saint Gabriel.*  Dr. J. C. Taché, of Ottawa, Canada, who has given much attention to the fubject, fixes this village in the central part of the prefent townfhip of Tiny, in the county of Simcoe. — *MS. Letter,* Feb. 11, 1880.

[11] *Cahiagué.*  Dr. Taché places this village on the extreme eaftern limit of the townfhip of Orillia, in the fame county, in the bend of the river Severn, a fhort diftance after it leaves Lake Couchiching.  The Indian warriors do not appear to have launched their flotilla of bark canoes until they reached the fifhing ftation at the outlet of Lake Simcoe.   This village was fubfequently known as *Saint-Jean Baptifte.*

of Lake Simcoe, ten or twelve miles from this body of water, furrounded by a country rich in corn, fquafhes, and a great variety of fmall fruits, with plenty of game and fifh. When the warriors had moftly affembled, the motley crowd, bearing their bark canoes, meal, and equipments on their fhoulders, moved down in a fouthwefterly direction till they reached the narrow ftrait that unites Lake Chouchiching with Lake Simcoe, where the Hurons had a famous fifhing wear. Here they remained fome time for other more tardy bands to join them. At this point they defpatched twelve of the moft ftalwart favages, with the interpreter, Étienne Brûlé, on a dangerous journey to a diftant tribe dwelling on the weft of the Five Nations, to urge them to haften to the fort of the Iroquois, as they had already received word from them that they would join them in this campaign.

Champlain and his allies foon left the fifhing wear and coafted along the northeaftern fhore of Lake Simcoe until they reached its moft eaftern border, when they made a portage to Sturgeon Lake, thence fweeping down Pigeon and Stony Lakes, through the Otonabee into Rice Lake, the River Trent, the Bay of Quinté, and finally rounding the eaftern point of Amherft Ifland, they were fairly on the waters of Lake Ontario, juft as it merges into the great River St. Lawrence, and where the Thoufand Iflands begin to loom into fight. Here they croffed the extremity of the lake at its outflow into the river, paufing at this important geographical point to take the latitude, which, by his imperfect inftruments, Champlain found to be 43° north.[52]

Sailing

[52] The latitude of Champlain is here far from correct. It is not poffible to determine the exact place at which it was taken. It could not, however have been at a point much below 44°7′.

Sailing down to the fouthern fide of the lake, after a diftance, by their eftimate, of about fourteen leagues, they landed
and concealed their canoes in a thicket near the fhore.
Taking their arms, they proceeded along the lake fome ten
miles, through a country diverfified with meadows, brooks,
ponds, and beautiful forefts filled with plenty of wild game,
when they ftruck inland, apparently at the mouth of Little
Salmon River. Advancing in a foutherly direction, along
the courfe of this ftream, they croffed Oneida River, an outlet of the lake of the fame name. When within about ten
miles of the fort which they intended to capture, they met a
fmall party of favages, men, women, and children, bound on
a fifhing excurfion. Although unarmed, neverthelefs, according to their cuftom, they took them all prifoners of war, and
began to inflict the ufual tortures, but this was dropped on
Champlain's indignant interference. The next day, on the
10th of October, they reached the great fortrefs of the Iroquois, after a journey of four days from their landing, a diftance loofely eftimated at from twenty-five to thirty leagues.
Here they found the Iroquois in their fields, induftrioufly
gathering in their autumnal harveft of corn and fquafhes.
A fkirmifh enfued, in which feveral were wounded on both
fides.

The fort, a drawing of which has been left us by Champlain, was fituated a few miles fouth of the eaftern terminus
of Oneida Lake, on a fmall ftream that winds its way in a
northwefterly direction, and finally lofes itfelf in the fame
body of water. This rude military ftructure was hexagonal
in form, one of its fides bordering immediately upon a
fmall pond, while four of the other laterals, two on the

17                                                           right

right and two on the left, were wafhed by a channel of water flowing along their bafes.⁸³ The fide oppofite the pond alone had

⁸³ There has naturally been fome difficulty in fixing fatisfactorily the fite of the Iroquois fort attacked by Champlain and his allies.

The fources of information on which we are to rely in identifying the fite of this fort are in general the fame that we refort to in fixing any locality mentioned in his explorations, and are to be found in Champlain's journal of this expedition, the map contained in what is commonly called his edition of 1632, and the engraved picture of the fort executed by Champlain himfelf, which was publifhed in connection with his journal. The information thus obtained is to be confidered in connection with the natural features of the country through which the expedition paffed, with fuch allowance for inexactness as the hiftory, nature, and circumftances of the evidence render neceffary.

The map of 1632 is only at beft an outline, drafted on a very fmall fcale, and without any exact meafurements or actual furveys. It pictures general features, and in connection with the journal may be of great fervice.

Champlain's diftances, as given in his journal, are eftimates made under circumftances in which accuracy was fcarcely poffible. He was journeying along the border of lakes and over the face of the country, in company with fome hundreds of wild favages, hunting and fifhing by the way, marching in an irregular and defultory manner, and his ftatements of diftances are wifely accompanied by very wide margins, and are of little fervice, taken alone, in fixing the fite of an Indian town. But when natural features, not fubject to change, are defcribed, we can eafily comprehend the meaning of the text.

The engraving of the fort may or may not have been fketched by Champlain on the fpot: parts of it may have been and doubtlefs were fupplied by memory, and it is decifive authority, not in its minor, but in its general features.

With thefe obfervations, we are prepared to examine the evidence that points to the fite of the Iroquois fort.

When the expedition, emerging from Quinté Bay, arrived at the eaftern end of Lake Ontario, at the point where the lake ends and the River St. Lawrence begins, they croffed over the lake, paffing large and beautiful iflands. Some of thefe iflands will be found laid down on the map of 1632. They then proceeded, a diftance, according to their eftimation, of about fourteen leagues, to the fouthern fide of Lake Ontario, where they landed and concealed their canoes. The diftance to the fouthern fide of the lake is too indefinitely ftated, even if we knew at what precife point the meafurement began, to enable us to fix the exact place of the landing.

They marched along the fandy fhore about four leagues, and then ftruck inland. If we turn to the map of 1632, on which a line is drawn to rudely reprefent their courfe, we fhall fee that on ftriking inland they proceeded along the banks of a fmall river to which feveral fmall lakes or ponds are tributary. Little Salmon River being fed by numerous fmall ponds or lakes may well be the ftream figured by Champlain. The text fays they difcovered an excellent country along the lake before they ftruck inland, with fine foreft-trees, efpecially the chefnut, with abundance of vines. For feveral miles along Lake Ontario on the north-eaft of Little Salmon River the country anfwers to this defcription. —*Vide*

had an unobſtructed land approach. As an Indian military work, it was of great ſtrength. It was made of the trunks of trees,

—*Vide MS. Letters of the Rev. James Cross, D.D., LL.D, and of S. D. Smith, Eſq.*, of Mexico, N.Y.

The text ſays they continued their courſe about twenty-five or thirty leagues. This again is indefinite, allowing a margin of twelve or fifteen miles ; but the text alſo ſays they croſſed a river flowing from a lake in which were certain beautiful iſlands, and moreover that the river ſo croſſed diſcharged into Lake Ontario. The lake here referred to muſt be the Oneida, ſince that is the only one in the region which contains any iſlands whatever, and therefore the river they croſſed muſt be the Oneida River, flowing from the lake of the ſame name into Lake Ontario.

Soon after they croſſed Oneida River, they met a band of ſavages who were going fiſhing, whom they made priſoners. This occurred, the text informs us, when they were about four leagues from the fort. They were now ſomewhere ſouth of Oneida Lake. If we conſult the map of 1632, we ſhall find repreſented on it an expanſe of water from which a ſtream is repreſented as flowing into Lake Ontario, and which is clearly Oneida Lake, and ſouth of this lake a ſtream is repreſented as flowing from the eaſt in a northweſterly direction and entering this lake towards its weſtern extremity, which muſt be Chittenango Creek or one of its branches. A fort or encloſed village is alſo figured on the map, of ſuch huge dimenſions that it ſubtends the angle formed by the creek and the lake, and appears to reſt upon both. It is plain, however, from the text that the fort does not reſt upon Oneida Lake ; we may infer therefore that it reſted upon the creek figured on the map, which from its courſe, as we have

already ſeen, is clearly intended to repreſent Chittenango Creek or one of its branches. A note explanatory of the map informs us that this is the village where Champlain went to war againſt the "Antouhonorons," that is to ſay, the Iroquois. The text informs us that the fort was on a pond, which furniſhed a perpetual ſupply of water. We therefore look for the ſite of the ancient fort on ſome ſmall body of water connected with Chittenango Creek.

If we examine Champlain's engraved repreſentation of the fort, we ſhall ſee that it is ſituated on a peninſula, that one ſide reſts on a pond, and that two ſtreams paſs it, one on the right and one on the left, and that one ſide only has an unobſtructed land-approach. Theſe channels of water courſing along the ſides are ſuch marked characteriſtics of the fort as repreſented by Champlain, that they muſt be regarded as important features in the identification of its ancient ſite.

On Nichols's Pond, near the northeaſtern limit of the townſhip of Fenner in Madiſon County, N.Y., the ſite of an Indian fort was ſome years ſince diſcovered, identified as ſuch by broken bits of pottery and ſtone implements, ſuch as are uſually found in localities of this fort. It is ſituated on a peculiarly formed peninſula, its northern ſide reſting on Nichols's Pond, while a ſmall ſtream flowing into the pond forms its weſtern boundary, and an outlet of the pond about thirty-two rods eaſt of the inlet, running in a ſouth-eaſterly direction, forms the eaſtern limit of the fort. The outlet of this pond, deflecting to the eaſt and then ſweeping round to the north, at length finds its way in a winding courſe into Cowaſhalon Creek, thence

into

trees, as large as could be conveniently tranfported. Thefe
were fet in the ground, forming four concentric palifades, not
more than fix inches apart, thirty feet in height, interlaced and
bound together near the top, fupporting a gallery of double
paling extending around the whole enclofure, proof not only
againft the flint-headed arrows of the Indian, but againft the
leaden bullets of the French arquebus.   Port-holes were
opened along the gallery, through which effective fervice
could be done upon affailants by hurling ftones and other
miffiles with which they were well provided.   Gutters were
laid along between the palifades to conduct water to every
part

into the Chittenango, through which it
flows into Oneida Lake, at a point north-
weft of Nichols's Pond.

If we compare the geographical fituation of Champlain's fort as figured on
his map of 1632, particularly with reference to Oneida Lake, we fhall obferve
a remarkable correfpondence between
it and the fite of the Indian fort at
Nichols's Pond.  Both are on the fouth
of Oneida Lake, and both are on
ftreams which flow into that lake by
running in a north-wefterly direction.
Moreover, the fite of the old fort at
Nichols's Pond is fituated on a peninfula
like that of Champlain; and not only
fo, but it is on a peninfula formed by a
pond on one fide, and by two ftreams of
water on two other oppofite fides; thus
fulfilling in a remarkable degree the
conditions contained in Champlain's
drawing of the fort.

If the reader has carefully examined
and compared the evidences referred to
in this note, he will have feen that all
the diftinguifhing circumftances contained in the text of Champlain's journal, on the map of 1632, and in his
drawing of the fort, converge to and
point out this fpot on Nichols's Pond,

as the probable fite of the palifaded
Iroquois town attacked by Champlain
in 1615.

We are indebted to General John S.
Clark, of Auburn, N.Y., for pointing out
and identifying the peninfula at Nichols's Pond as the fite of the Iroquois
fort. — *Vide Shea's Notes on Champlain's Expedition into Weftern New
York in 1615, and the Recent Identification of the Fort*, by General John S.
Clark, *Pennfylvania Magazine of Hiftory*, Philadelphia, Vol. II. pp. 103-108;
alfo *A Loft Point in Hiftory*, by L. W.
Ledyard, *Cazenovia Republican*, Vol.
XXV. No. 47; *Champlain's Invafion
of Onondaga*, by the Rev. W. M. Beau-
champ, *Baldwinfville Gazette*, for June
27, 1879.

We are indebted to Orfamus H. Marfhall, Efq., of Buffalo, N.Y., for proving
the fite of the Iroquois fort to be in the
neighborhood of Oneida Lake, and not
at a point farther weft as claimed by
feveral authors. — *Vide Proceedings of
the New York Hiftorical Society* for
1849, p. 96; *Magazine of American
Hiftory*, New York, Vol. I. pp. 1-13,
Vol. II. pp. 470-483.

part of the fortification for extinguifhing fire, in cafe of
need.

It was obvious to Champlain that this fort was a complete
protection to the Iroquois, unlefs an opening could be made
in its walls. This could not be eafily done by any force
which he and his allies had at their command. His only
hope was in fetting fire to the palifades on the land fide.
This required the diflodgement of the enemy, who were pofted
in large numbers on the gallery, and the protection of the
men in kindling the fire, and fhielding it, when kindled,
againft the extinguifhing torrents which could be poured
from the water-fpouts and gutters of the fort. He confequently ordered two inftruments to be made with which
he hoped to overcome thefe obftacles. One was a wooden
tower or frame-work, dignified by Champlain as a *cavalier*,
fomewhat higher than the palifades, on the top of which
was an enclofed platform where three or four fharp-fhooters
could in fecurity clear the gallery, and thus deftroy the effective force of the enemy. The other was a large wooden
fhield, or *mantelet*, under the protection of which they could
in fafety approach and kindle a fire at the bafe of the fort,
and protect the fire thus kindled from being extinguifhed by
water coming from above.

When all was in readinefs, two hundred favages bore the
framed tower and planted it near the palifades. Three ar-
quebusiers mounted it and poured a deadly fire upon the
defenders on the gallery. The battle now began and raged
fiercely for three hours, but Champlain ftrove in vain to carry
out any plan of attack. The favages rufhed to and fro in a
frenzy of excitement, filling the air with their difcordant
yells,

yells, obferving no method and heeding no commands. The wooden fhields were not even brought forward, and the burning of the fort was undertaken with fo little judgment and fkill that the fire was inftantly extinguifhed by the fountains of water let loofe by the fkilful defenders through the gutters and water-fpouts of the fort.

The fharp-fhooters on the tower killed and wounded a large number, but neverthelefs no effective impreffion was made upon the fortrefs. Two chiefs and fifteen men of the allies were wounded, while one was killed, or died of wounds received in a fkirmifh before the formal attack upon the fort began. After a frantic and defultory fight of three hours, the attacking favages loft their courage and began to clamor for a retreat. No perfuafions could induce them to renew the attack.

After lingering four days in vain expectation of the arrival of the allies to whom Brûlé had been fent, the retreat began. Champlain had been wounded in the knee and leg, and was unable to walk. Litters in the form of bafkets were fabricated, into which the wounded were packed in a conftrained and uncomfortable attitude, and carried on the fhoulders of the men. As the tafk of the carriers was lightened by frequent relays, and, as there was little baggage to impede their progrefs, the march was rapid. In three days they had reached their canoes, which had remained in the place of their concealment near the fhore of the lake, an eftimated diftance of twenty-five or thirty leagues from the fort.

Such was the character of a great battle among the contending favages, an undifciplined hoft, without plan or well-defined

defined purpofe, rufhing in upon each other in the heat of a
fudden frenzy of paffion, ftriking an aimlefs blow, and following it by a hafty and cowardly retreat.   They had, for the
time being at leaft, no ulterior defign.   They fought and expected no fubftantial reward of their conflict.   The fweet-
nefs of perfonal revenge and the blotting out a few human
lives were all they hoped for or cared at this time to attain.
The invading party had apparently deftroyed more than they
had themfelves loft, and this was doubtlefs a fuitable reward
for the hazards and hardfhips of the campaign.

The retreating warriors lingered ten days on the fhore of
Lake Ontario, at the point where they had left their canoes,
beguiling the time in preparing for hunting and fifhing excurfions, and for their journey to their diftant homes.   Champlain here took occafion to call the attention of the allies to
their promife to conduct him fafely to his home.   The
head of the St. Lawrence as it flows from the Ontario is lefs
than two hundred miles from Montreal, a journey by canoes
not difficult to make.   Champlain defired to return this way,
and demanded an efcort.   The chiefs were reluctant to grant
his requeft.   Mafters in the art of making excufes, they faw
many infuperable obftacles.   In reality, they did not defire
to part with him, but wifhed to avail themfelves of his
knowledge, counfel, and perfonal aid againft their enemies.
When one obftacle after another gave way, and when volun-
teers were found ready to accompany him, no canoes could
be fpared for the journey.   This clofed the debate.   Champlain was not prepared for the expofure and hardfhip of a
winter among the favages, but there was left to him no
choice.   He fubmitted as gracefully as he could, and with
                                                    fuch

fuch patience as neceffity made it poffible for him to command.

The bark flotilla was at length ready to leave the borders
of the prefent State of New York. According to their
ufual cuftom in canoe navigation, they crept along the fhore
of the Ontario, revifiting an ifland at the eaftern extremity
of the lake, not unlikely the fame place where Champlain
had ftopped to take the latitude a few weeks before. Croffing over from the ifland to the mainland on the north, they
appear to have continued up the Cataraqui Creek eaft of
Kingfton, and, after a fhort portage, entered Loughborough
Lake, a fheet of water then renowned as a refort of water-
fowl in vaft numbers and varieties. Having bagged all
they defired, they proceeded inland twenty or thirty miles,
to the objective point of their excurfion, which was a famous hunting-ground for wild game. Here they conftructed a deer-trap, an enclofure into which the unfufpecting
animals were beguiled and from which it was impoffible for
them to efcape. Deer-hunting was of all purfuits, if we
except war, the moft exciting to the Indians. It not only
yielded the richeft returns to their larder, and fupplied more
fully other domeftic wants, but it poffeffed the element of
fafcination, which has always given zeft and infpiration to
the fportfman.

They lingered here thirty-eight days, during which time they
captured one hundred and twenty deer. They purpofely
prolonged their ftay that the froft might feal up the marfhes,
ponds, and rivers over which they were to pafs. Early in
December they began to arrange into convenient packages
their peltry and venifon, the fat of which was to ferve as
butter

butter in their rude huts during the icy months of winter. On the 4th of the month they broke camp and began their weary march, each favage bearing a burden of not lefs than a hundred pounds, while Champlain himfelf carried a package of about twenty. Some of them conftructed rude fledges, on which they eafily dragged their luggage over the ice and fnow. During the progrefs of the journey, a warm current came fweeping up from the fouth, melted the ice, flooded the marfhes, and for four days the overburdened and weary travellers ftruggled on, knee-deep in mud and water and flufh. Without experience, a lively imagination alone can picture the toil, fuffering, and expofure of a journey through the tangled forefts and half-fubmerged bogs and marfhes of Canada, in the moft inclement feafon of the year.

At length, on the 23d of December, after nineteen days of exceffive toil, they arrived at Cahiagué, the chief town of the Hurons, the rendezvous of the allied tribes, whence they had fet forth on the firft of September, nearly four months before, on what may feem to us a bootlefs raid. To the favage warriors, however, it doubtlefs feemed a different thing. They had been enabled to bring home valuable provifions, which were likely to be important to them when an unfuccefsful hunt might, as it often did, leave them nearly deftitute of food. They had loft but a fingle man, and this was lefs than they had anticipated, and, moreover, was the common fortune of war. They had invaded the territory and made their prefence felt in the very home of their enemies, and could rejoice in having inflicted upon them more injury than they had themfelves received. Though they had not captured

tured or annihilated them, they had done enough to infpire and fully fuftain their own grovelling pride.

To Champlain even, although the expedition had been accompanied by hardfhip and fuffering and fome difappointments, it was by no means a failure. He had explored an interefting and important region; he had gone where European feet had never trod, and had feen what European eyes had never feen; he had, moreover, planted the lilies of France in the chief Indian towns, and at all fuitable and important points, and thefe were to be witneffes of poffeffion and ownerfhip in what his exuberant imagination faw as a vaft French empire rifing into power and opulence in the weftern world.

It was now the laft week in December, and the deep fnows and piercing cold rendered it impoffible for Champlain or even the allied warriors to continue their journey further. The Algonquins and Nipiffings became guefts of the Hurons for the winter, encamping within their principal walled town, or perhaps in fome neighboring village not far removed.

After the reft of a few days at Cahiagué, where he had been hofpitably entertained, Champlain took his departure for Carhagouha, a fmaller village, where his friend the Recollect Father, Jofeph le Caron, had taken up his abode as the pioneer miffionary to the Hurons. It was important for Le Caron to obtain all the information poffible, not only of the Hurons, but of all the furrounding tribes, as he contemplated returning to France the next fummer to report to his patrons upon the character, extent, and hopefulnefs of the miffionary field which he had been fent out to explore.

Champlain

Champlain was happy to avail himfelf of his company in executing the explorations which he defired to make.

They accordingly fet out together on the 15th of January, and penetrated the tracklefs and fnow-bound forefts, and, proceeding in a weftern direction, after a journey of two days, reached a tribe called *Petuns,* an agricultural people, fimilar in habits and mode of life to the Hurons. By them they were hofpitably received, and a great feftival, in which all their neighbors participated, was celebrated in honor of their new guefts. Having vifited feven or eight of their villages, the explorers pufhed forward ftill further weft, when they came to the fettlement of an interefting tribe, which they named *Cheveux-Relevés,* or the "lofty haired," an appellation fuggefted by the mode of dreffing their hair.

On their return from this expedition, they found, on reaching the encampment of the Nipiffings, who were wintering in the Huron territory, that a difagreement had arifen between the Hurons and their Algonquin guefts, which had already affumed a dangerous character. An Iroquois captive taken in the late war had been awarded to the Algonquins, according to the cuftom of dividing the prifoners among the feveral bands of allies, and, finding him a fkilful hunter, they refolved to fpare his life, and had actually adopted him as one of their tribe. This had offended the Hurons, who expected he would be put to the ufual torture, and they had commiffioned one of their number, who had inftantly killed the unfortunate prifoner by plunging a knife into his heart. The affaffin, in turn, had been fet upon by the Algonquins and put to death on the fpot. The perpetrators of this laft act had regretted the occurrence, and had
done

done what they could to heal the breach by prefents : but there was, neverthelefs, a fmouldering feeling of hoftility ftill lingering in both parties, which might at any moment break out into open conflict.

It was obvious to Champlain that a permanent difagree- ment between thefe two important allies would be a great calamity to themfelves as well as difaftrous to his own plans. It was his purpofe, therefore, to bring them, if poffible, to a cordial pacification. Proceeding cautioufly and with great deliberation, he made himfelf acquainted with all the facts of the quarrel, and then called an affembly of both parties and clearly fet before them in all its lights the utter foolifh- nefs of allowing a circumftance of really fmall importance to interfere with an alliance between two great tribes ; an alliance neceffary to their profperity, and particularly in the war they were carrying on againft their common enemy, the Iroquois. This appeal of Champlain was fo convincing that when the affembly broke up all profeffed themfelves entirely fatisfied, although the Algonquins were heard to mutter their determination never again to winter in the territory of the Hurons, a wife and not unnatural conclufion.

Champlain's conftant intercourfe with thefe tribes for many months in their own homes, his explorations, obfervations, and inquiries, enabled him to obtain a comprehenfive, defi- nite, and minute knowledge of their character, religion, government, and mode of life. As the fruit of thefe invef- tigations, he prepared in the leifure of the winter an elabo- rate memoir, replete with difcriminating details, which is and muft always be an unqueftionable authority on the fubject of which it treats.

CHAPTER IX.

## CHAPTER IX.

CHAMPLAIN'S RETURN FROM THE HURON COUNTRY AND VOYAGE TO FRANCE.
— THE CONTRACTED VIEWS OF THE COMPANY OF MERCHANTS. — THE
PRINCE DE CONDÉ SELLS THE VICEROYALTY TO THE DUKE DE MONT-
MORENCY. — CHAMPLAIN WITH HIS WIFE RETURNS TO QUEBEC, WHERE
HE REMAINS FOUR YEARS. — HAVING REPAIRED THE BUILDINGS AND
ERECTED THE FORTRESS OF ST. LOUIS, CHAMPLAIN RETURNS TO FRANCE.
— THE VICEROYALTY TRANSFERRED TO HENRY DE LEVI, AND THE COM-
PANY OF THE HUNDRED ASSOCIATES ORGANIZED.

BOUT the 20th of May, Champlain, accompanied by the miffionary, Le Caron, efcorted by a
delegation of favages, fet out from the Huron
capital, in the prefent county of Simcoe, on
their return to Quebec.  Purfuing the fame
circuitous route by which they had come, they were forty
days in reaching the Falls of St. Louis, near Montreal,
where they found Pont Gravé, juft arrived from France, who,
with the reft, was much rejoiced at feeing Champlain, fince a
rumor had gone abroad that he had perifhed among the
favages.

The party arrived at Quebec on the 11th of July.  A public fervice of thankfgiving was celebrated by the Recollect
Fathers for their fafe return.  The Huron chief, D'Arontal,
with whom Champlain had paffed the winter and who had
accompanied him to Quebec, was greatly entertained and
delighted with the eftablifhment of the French, the buildings
and other acceffories of European life, fo different from his
own, and earneftly requefted Champlain to make a fettlement at Montreal, that his whole tribe might come and
refide

reside near them, safe under their protection against their Iroquois enemies.

Champlain did not remain at Quebec more than ten days, during which he planned and put in execution the enlargement of their houses and fort, increasing their capacity by at least one third. This he found neceffary to do for the greater convenience of the little colony, as well as for the occasional entertainment of strangers. He left for France on the 20th day of July, in company with the Recollect Fathers, Joseph le Caron and Denis Jamay, the commiffary of the miffion, taking with them specimens of French grain which had been produced near Quebec, to testify to the excellent quality of the soil. They arrived at Honfleur in France on the 10th of September, 1616.

The exploration in the distant Indian territories which we have just described in the preceding pages was the last made by Champlain. He had plans for the survey of other regions yet unexplored, but the favorable opportunity did not occur. Henceforth he directed his attention more exclusively than he had hitherto done to the enlargement and strengthening of his colonial plantation, without such succefs, we regret to say, as his zeal, devotion, and labors fitly deferved. The obstacles that lay in his way were infurmountable. The establishment or factory, we can hardly call it a plantation, at Quebec, was the creature of a company of merchants. They had invested confiderable fums in shipping, buildings, and in the employment of men, in order to carry on a trade in furs and peltry with the Indians, and they naturally defired remunerative returns. This was the limit of their purpofe in making the inveftment. The corporators

tors faw nothing in their organization but a commercial enterprife yielding immediate refults. They were infpired by
no generofity, no loyalty, or patriotifm that could draw from
them a farthing to increafe the wealth, power, or aggrandizement of France.  Under thefe circumftances, Champlain
ftruggled on for years againft a current which he could
barely direct, but by no means control.

Champlain made voyages to New France both in 1617 and
in 1618.  In the latter year, among the Indians who came
to Quebec for the purpofe of trade, appeared Étienne Brulé,
the interpreter, who it will be remembered had been defpatched in 1615, when Champlain was among the Hurons,
to the Entouhonorons at Carantouan, to induce them to join
in the attack of the Iroquois in central New York.  During
the three years that had intervened, nothing had been heard
from him.  Brulé related the ftory of his extraordinary adventures, which Champlain has preferved, and which may be
found in the report of the voyage of 1618, in Volume III.
of this work.[84]

At Quebec, he met numerous bands of Indians from remote
regions,

[84] The character of Étienne Brulé,
either for honor or veracity, is not improved by his fubfequent conduct.  He
appears in 1629 to have turned traitor,
to have fold himfelf to the Englifh, and
to have piloted them up the river in
their expedition againft Quebec.
Whether this conduct, bafe certainly
it was, ought to affect the credibility
of his ftory, the reader muft judge.
Champlain undoubtedly believed it
when he firft related it to him.  He
probably had no means then or afterwards of tefting its truth.  In the edition of 1632, Brulé's ftory is omitted.
It does not neceffarily follow that it
was omitted becaufe Champlain came
to difcredit the ftory, fince many paffages contained in his preceding publications are omitted in the edition of
1632, but they are not generally paffages
of fo much geographical importance as
this, if it be true.  The map of 1632
indicates the country of the Carantou-
anais; but this information might have
been obtained by Champlain from the
Hurons, or the more weftern tribes
which he vifited during the winter of
1615-16. — *Vide* ed. 1632, p. 220.

regions, whom he had vifited in former years, and who, in fulfilment of their promifes, had come to barter their peltry for
fuch commodities as fuited their need or fancy, and to renew
and ftrengthen their friendfhip with the French. By thefe re-
peated interviews, and the cordial reception and generous
entertainment which he always gave them, the Indians
dwelling on the upper waters of the Ottawa, along the borders of Lake Huron, or on the Georgian Bay, formed a
ftrong perfonal attachment to Champlain, and yearly brought
down their fleets of canoes heavily freighted with the valuable furs which they had diligently fecured during the preceding winter. His perfonal influence with them, a power
which he exercifed with great delicacy, wifdom, and fidelity,
contributed largely to the revenues annually obtained by the
affociated merchants.

But Champlain defired more than this. He was not fatisfied to be the agent and chief manager of a company organized merely for the purpofe of trade. He was anxious
to elevate the meagre factory at Quebec into the dignity and
national importance of a colonial plantation. For this purpofe he had tefted the foil by numerous experiments, and
had, from time to time, forwarded to France fpecimens of
ripened grain to bear teftimony to its productive quality.
He even laid the fubject before the Council of State, and
they gave it their cordial approbation. By thefe means giving emphafis to his perfonal appeals, he fucceeded at length
in extorting from the company a promife to enlarge the eftablifhment to eighty perfons, with fuitable equipments, farm-
ing implements, all kinds of feeds and domeftic animals,
including cattle and fheep. But when the time came, this
promife

promife was not fulfilled.  Differences, bickerings, and feuds fprang up in the company.  Some wanted one thing, and fome wanted another.  Even religion caft in an apple of dif- cord.  The Catholics wifhed to extend the faith of their church into the wilds of Canada, while the Huguenots de- fired to prevent it, or at leaft not to promote it by their own contributions.  The company, infpired by avarice and a de- fire to reftrict the eftablifhment to a mere trading poft, raifed an iffue to difcredit Champlain.  It was gravely propofed that he fhould devote himfelf exclufively to exploration, and that the government and trade fhould henceforth be under the direction and control of Pont Gravé.  But Champlain was not a man to be ejected from an official pofition by thofe who had neither the authority to give it to him or the power to take it away.  Pont Gravé was his intimate, long-tried, and trufted friend; and, while he regarded him with filial refpect and affection, he could not yield, even to him, the rights and honors which had been accorded to him as a rec- ognition, if not a reward, for many years of faithful fervice, which he had rendered under circumftances of perfonal hardfhip and danger.  The king addreffed a letter to the company, in which he directed them to aid Champlain as much as poffible in making explorations, in fettling the country, and cultivating the foil, while with their agents in the traffic of peltry there fhould be no interference.  But the fpirit of avarice could not be fubdued by the mandate of the king.  The affociated merchants were ftill obftinate. Champlain had intended to take his family to Canada that year, but he declined to make the voyage under any impli- cation of a divided authority.  The veffel in which he was

to

to fail departed without him, and Pont Gravé fpent the winter in charge of the company's affairs at Quebec.

Champlain, in the mean time, took fuch active meafures as fcemed neceffary to eftablifh his authority as lieutenant of the viceroy, or governor of New France. He appeared before the Council of State at Tours, and after an elaborate argument and thorough difcuffion of the whole fubject, obtained a decree ordering that he fhould have the command at Quebec and at all other fettlements in New France, and that the company fhould abftain from any interference with him in the difcharge of the duties of his office.

The Prince de Condé having recently been liberated from an imprifonment of three years, governed by his natural avarice, was not unwilling to part with his viceroyalty, and early in 1620 transferred it, for the confideration of eleven thoufand crowns, or about five hundred and fifty pounds fterling, to his brother-in-law, the Duke de Montmorency,[85] at that time high-admiral of France. The new viceroy appointed Champlain his lieutenant, who immediately prepared to leave for Quebec. But when he arrived at Honfleur, the company, difpleafed at the recent change, again brought forward the old queftion of the authority which the lieutenant was to exercife in New France. The time for difcuffion had, however, paffed. No further words were now to be wafted.

The

[85] Henry de Montmorency II. was born at Chantilly in 1595, and was beheaded at Touloufe Oct. 30, 1632. He was created admiral at the age of feventeen. He commanded the Dutch fleet at the fiege of Rochelle. He made the campaigns of 1629 and 1630 in Piedmont, and was created a marfhal of France after the victory of Veillane. He adopted the party of Gafton, the Duke of Orleans, and having excited the province of Languedoc of which he was governor to rebellion, he was defeated, and executed as guilty of high treafon. He was the laft fcion of the elder branch of Montmorency. and his death was a fatal blow to the reign of feudalifm.

The viceroy fent them a peremptory order to defift from further interferences, or otherwife their fhips, already equipped
for their yearly trade, would not be permitted to leave port.
This meffage from the high-admiral of France came with
authority and had the defired effect.

Early in May, 1620, Champlain failed from Honfleur, accompanied by his wife and feveral Recollect friars, and, after
a voyage of two months, arrived at Tadouffac, where he was
cordially greeted by his brother-in-law, Euftache Boullé, who
was very much aftonifhed at the arrival of his fifter, and particularly that fhe was brave enough to encounter the dangers
of the ocean and take up her abode in a wildernefs at once
barren of both the comforts and refinements of European
life.

On the 11th of July, Champlain left Tadouffac for Quebec, where he found the whole eftablifhment, after an abfence
of two years, in a condition of painful neglect and diforder.
He was cordially received, and becoming ceremonies were
obferved to celebrate his arrival. A fermon compofed for
the occafion was delivered by one of the Recollect Fathers,
the commiffion of the king and that of the viceroy appointing him to the fole command of the colony were publicly
read, cannon were difcharged, and the little populace, from
loyal hearts, loudly vociferated *Vive le Roy !*

The attention of the lieutenant was at firft directed to reftoration and repairs. The roof of the buildings no longer
kept out the rain, nor the walls the piercing fury of the
winds. The gardens were in a ftate of ruinous neglect, and
the fields poorly and fcantily cultivated. But the zeal, energy, and induftry of Champlain foon put every thing in
repair,

repair, and gave to the little fettlement the afpeƐt of neat-
nefs and thrift. When this was accomplifhed, he laid the
foundations of a fortrefs, which he called the *Fort Saint
Louis*, fituated on the creft of the rocky elevation in the
rear of the fettlement, about a hundred and feventy-two feet
above the furface of the river, a pofition which commanded
the whole breadth of the St. Lawrence at that narrow point.

This work, fo neceffary for the proteƐtion and fafety of
the colony, involving as it did fome expenfe, was by no
means fatisfaƐtory to the Company of Affociates.[86] Their
general fault-finding and chronic difcontent led the Duke
de Montmorency to adopt heroic meafures to filence their
complaints. In the fpring of 1621, he fummarily diffolved the affociation of merchants, which he denominated
the " Company of Rouen and St. Malo," and eftablifhed
another in its place. He continued Champlain in the office
of lieutenant, but committed all matters relating to trade to
William de Caen, a merchant of high ftanding, and to Émeric de Caen the nephew of the former, a good naval captain.
This new and hafty reorganization, arbitrary if not illegal,
however important it might feem to the profperity and fuccefs of the colony, laid upon Champlain new refponfibilities
and duties at once delicate and difficult to difcharge. Though
in form fuppreffed, the company did not yield either its exiftence or its rights. Both the old and the new company
were, by their agents, early in New France, clamoring for
their

[86] Among other annoyances which Champlain had to contend againft was the contraband trade carried on by the unlicenfed Rochellers, who not only carried off quantities of peltry, but even fupplied the Indians with fire-arms and ammunition. This was illegal, and en-dangered the fafety of the colony. — *Vide Voyages par De Champlain*, Paris, 1632, Sec. Partie, p. 3.

their refpective interefts.   De Caen, in behalf of the new, infifted that the lieutenant ought to prohibit all trade with the Indians by the old company, and, moreover, that he ought to feize their property and hold it as fecurity for their unpaid obligations.   Champlain, having no written authority for fuch a proceeding, and De Caen declining to produce any, did not approve the meafure and declined to act.   The threats of De Caen that he would take the matter into his own hands, and feize the veffel of the old company commanded by Pont Gravé and then in port, were fo violent that Champlain thought it prudent to place a body of armed men in his little fort ftill unfinifhed, until the fury of the altercation fhould fubfide.[87]   This decifive meafure, and time, the natural emollient of irritated tempers, foon reftored peace to the contending parties, and each was allowed to carry on its trade unmolefted by the other.   The prudence of Champlain's conduct was fully juftified, and the two companies, by mutual confent, were, the next year, confolidated into one.

Champlain remained at Quebec four years before again returning to France.   His time was divided between many local enterprifes of great importance.   His fpecial attention was given to advancing the work on the unfinifhed fort, in order to provide againft incurfions of the hoftile Iroquois,[88] who at one time approached the very walls of Quebec, and attacked unfuccefsfully the guarded houfe of the Recollects on the St. Charles.[89]   He undertook the reconftruction of
the

[87] *Vide* ed. 1632. Sec. Partie, Chap. III.
[88] *Vide Hift. New France,* by Charlevoix, Shea's Trans., Vol. II. p. 32.

[89] The houfe of the Recollects on the St. Charles was erected in 1620, and was called the *Couuent de Noftre Dame*

the buildings of the fettlement from their foundations. The main ftructure was enlarged to a hundred and eight feet<sup>90</sup> in length, with two wings of fixty feet each, having fmall towers at the four corners. In front and on the borders of the river a platform was erected, on which were placed cannon, while the whole was furrounded by a ditch fpanned by drawbridges.

Having placed every thing at Quebec in as good order as his limited means would permit, and given orders for the completion of the works which he had commenced, leaving Émeric de Caen in command, Champlain determined to return to France with his wife, who, though devoted to a religious life, we may well fuppofe was not unwilling to exchange the rough, monotonous, and dreary mode of living at Quebec for the more congenial refinements to which fhe had always been accuftomed in her father's family near the court of Louis XIII. He accordingly failed on the 15th of Auguft, and arrived at Dieppe on the 1ft of October, 1624. He haftened to St. Germain, and reported to the king and the viceroy what had occurred and what had been done during the four years of his abfence.

The interefts of the two companies had not been adjufted and they were ftill in conflict. The Duke de Montmorency about this time negotiated a fale of his viceroyalty to his nephew, Henry de Levi, Duke de Ventadour. This nobleman,

*Dame des Anges.* The Father Jean d'Olbeau laid the firft ftone on the 3d of June of that year. — *Vide Hiftoire du Canada* par Gabriel Sagard, Paris, 1636, Trois ed., 1866, p. 67; *Découvertes et Établiffements des Français, dans l'oueft et dans le fud de L'Ame-* *rique Septentrionale* 1637, par Pierre Margry, Paris, 1876, Vol. I. p. 7.
<sup>90</sup> *Hundred and eight feet,* dix-huict toyfes. The *toife* is here eftimated at fix feet. Compare *Voyages de Champlain,* Laverdière's ed., Vol. I. p. lii, and ed. 1632, Paris, Partie Seconde, p. 63.

bleman, of a deeply religious caſt of mind, had taken holy orders, and his chief purpoſe in obtaining the viceroyalty was to encourage the planting of Catholic miſſions in New France. As his ſpiritual directors were Jeſuits, he naturally committed the work to them. Three fathers and two lay brothers of this order were ſent to Canada in 1625, and others ſubſequently joined them. Whatever were the fruits of their labors, many of them periſhed in their heroic undertaking, manfully ſuffering the exquiſite pains of mutilation and torture.

Champlain was reappointed lieutenant, but remained in France two years, fully occupied with public and private duties, and in frequent conſultations with the viceroy as to the beſt method of advancing the future intereſts of the colony. On the 15th of April, 1626, with Euſtache Boullé, his brother-in-law, who had been named his aſſiſtant or lieutenant, he again ſailed for Quebec, where he arrived on the 5th of July. He found the coloniſts in excellent health, but nevertheleſs approaching the borders of ſtarvation, having nearly exhauſted their proviſions. The work that he had laid out to be done on the buildings had been entirely neglected. One important reaſon for this neglect, was the neceſſary employment of a large number of the moſt efficient laborers, for the chief part of the ſummer in obtaining forage for their cattle in winter, collecting it at a diſtance of twenty-five or thirty miles from the ſettlement. To obviate this inconvenience, Champlain took an early opportunity to erect a farm-houſe near the natural meadows at Cape Tourmente, where the cattle could be kept with little attendance, appointing at the ſame time an overſeer for the men, and making a weekly
viſit

vifit to this eftablifhment for perfonal infpection and over-fight.

The fort, which had been erected on the creft of the rocky height in the rear of the dwelling, was obvioufly too fmall for the protection of the whole colony in cafe of an attack by hoftile favages. He confequently took it down and erected another on the fame fpot, with earthworks on the land fide, where alone, with difficulty, it could be approached. He alfo made extenfive repairs upon the ftore-houfe and dwelling.

During the winter of 1626–27, the friendly Indians, the Montagnais, Algonquins, and others gave Champlain much anxiety by unadvifedly entering into an alliance, into which they were enticed by bribes, with a tribe dwelling near the Dutch, in the prefent State of New York, to affift them againft their old enemies, the Iroquois, with whom, however, they had for fome time been at peace. Champlain juftly looked upon this foolifh undertaking as hazardous not only to the profperity of thefe friendly tribes, but to their very exiftence. He accordingly fent his brother-in-law to Three Rivers, the rendezvous of the favage warriors, to convince them of their error and avert their purpofe. Boullé fucceeded in obtaining a delay until all the tribes fhould be affembled and until the trading veffels fhould arrive from France. When Émeric de Caen was ready to go to Three Rivers, Champlain urged upon him the great importance of fuppreffing this impending conflict with the Iroquois. The efforts of De Caen were, however, ineffectual. He forthwith wrote to Champlain that his prefence was neceffary to arreft thefe hoftile proceedings. On his arrival, a grand council

was

was affembled, and Champlain fucceeded, after a full ftatement of all the evils that muft evidently follow, in reverfing
their decifion, and meffengers were fent to heal the breach.
Some weeks afterward news came that the embaffadors were
inhumanly maffacred.

Crimes of a ferious nature were not unfrequently committed againft the French by Indians belonging to tribes,
with which they were at profound peace. On one occafion
two men, who were conducting cattle by land from Cape
Tourmente to Quebec, were affaffinated in a cowardly manner. Champlain demanded of the chiefs that they fhould
deliver to him the perpetrators of the crime. They expreffed genuine forrow for what had taken place, but were
unable to obtain the criminals. At length, after confulting
with the miffionary, Le Caron, they offered to prefent to
Champlain three young girls as pledges of their good faith,
that he might educate them in the religion and manners of
the French. The gift was accepted by Champlain, and
thefe favage maidens became exceedingly attached to their
fofter-father, as we fhall fee in the fequel.

The end of the year 1627 found the colony, as ufual, in a
depreffed ftate. As a colony, it had never profpered. The
average number compofing it had not exceeded about fifty
perfons. At this time it may have been fomewhat more,
but did not reach a hundred. A fingle family only appears
to have fubfifted by the cultivation of the foil.[91] The reft
were

---

[91] There was but one private houfe
at Quebec in 1623, and that belonged
to Madame Hébert, whofe hufband was
the firft to attempt to obtain a living by
the cultivation of the foil. — *Vide Sa-*
*gard, Hift. du Canada,* 1636, Trois ed.
Vol. I. p. 163. There were fifty-one
inhabitants at Quebec in 1624, including men, women, and children. — *Vide*
*Champlain,* ed. 1632, p. 76.

were fuftained by fupplies fent from France. From the beginning difputes and contentions had prevailed in the corporation. Endlefs bickerings fprung up between the Huguenots and Catholics, each fenfitive and jealous of their rights.[91] All expenditures were the fubject of cenforious criticifm. The neceffary repairs of the fort, the enlargement and improvement of the buildings from time to time, were too often refifted as unneceffary and extravagant. The company, as a mere trading affociation, was doubtlefs fuccefsful. Large quantities of peltry were annually brought by the Indians for traffic to the Falls of St. Louis, Three Rivers, Quebec, and Tadouffac. The average number of beaver-fkins annually purchafed and tranfported to France was probably not far from fifteen thoufand to twenty thoufand, and in a moft favorable year it mounted up to twenty-two thoufand.[93] The large dividends that they were able to make, intimated by Champlain to be not far from forty per centum yearly, were, of courfe, highly fatisfactory to the company. They defired not to impair this characteriftic of their enterprife. They had, therefore, a prime motive for not wifhing to lay out a fingle unneceffary franc on the eftablifhment.

Their

[91] *Vide Champlain*, ed. 1632, pp. 107, 108, for an account of the attempt on the part of the Huguenot, Émeric de Caen, to require his failors to chaunt pfalms and fay prayers on board his fhip after entering the River St. Lawrence, contrary to the direction of the Viceroy, the Duke de Ventadour. As two thirds of them were Huguenots, it was finally agreed that they fhould continue to fay their prayers, but muft omit their pfalm-finging.

[92] Father Lalemant enumerates the kind of peltry obtained by the French from the Indians, and the amount, as follows : "En efchange ils emportent des peaux d'Orignac, de Loup Ceruier, de Renard, de Loutre, et quelquefois il f'en rencontre de noires, de Martre, de Blaireau et de Rat Musqué, mais principalement de Caftor qui eft le plus grand de leur gain. On m'a dit que pour vne année ils en auoyent emporté jufques à 22000. L'ordinaire de chaque année eft de 15000, ou 20000, à vne piftole la piece, ce n'eft pas mal allé." — *Vide Rélation de la Nouvelle France en l'Annea* 1626, Quebec ed. p. 5.

Their policy was to keep the expenfes at the minimum and the net income at the maximum. Under thefe circumftances, nearly twenty years had elapfed fince the founding of Quebec, and it ftill poffeffed only the character of a trading poft, and not that of a colonial plantation. This progrefs was fatisfactory neither to Champlain, to the viceroy, nor the council of ftate. In the view of thefe feveral interefted parties, the time had come for a radical change in the organization of the company. Cardinal de Richelieu had rifen by his extraordinary ability as a ftatefman, a fhort time anterior to this, into fupreme authority, and had affumed the office of grand mafter and chief of the navigation and commerce of France. His fagacious and comprehenfive mind faw clearly the intimate and interdependent relations between thefe two great national interefts and the enlargement and profperity of the French colonies in America. He loft no time in organizing meafures which fhould bring them into the clofeft harmony. The company of merchants whofe finances had been fo fkilfully managed by the Caens was by him at once diffolved. A new one was formed, denominated *La Compagnie de la Nouvelle-France*, confifting of a hundred or more members, and commonly known as the Company of the Hundred Affociates. It was under the control and management of Richelieu himfelf. Its members were largely gentlemen in official pofitions about the court, in Paris, Rouen, and other cities of France. Among them were the Marquis Deffiat, fuperintendent of finances, Claude de Roquemont, the Commander de Razilly, Captain Charles Daniel, Sébaftien Cramoify, the diftinguifhed Paris printer, Louis Houêl, the controller of the falt works in

Brouage,

Brouage, Champlain, and others well known in public circles.

The new company had many charaĉteriftics which feemed
to affure the folid growth and enlargement of the colony.   Its
authority extended over the whole domain of New France
and Florida.   It provided in its organization for an aĉtual
capital of three hundred thoufand livres.   It entered into an
obligation to fend to Canada in 1628 from two to three
hundred artifans of all trades, and within the fpace of fifteen years to tranfport four thoufand colonifts to New
France.   The colonifts were to be wholly fupported by the
company for three years, and at the expiration of that period were to be affigned as much land as they needed for
cultivation.   The fettlers were to be native-born Frenchmen,
exclufively of the Catholic faith, and no foreigner or Huguenot was to be permitted to enter the country.[94]   The charter accorded to the company the exclufive control of trade,
and

[94] This exclufivenefs was charaĉter-
iftic of the age.   Cardinal Richelieu
and his affociates were not qualified by
education or by any tendency of their
natures to inaugurate a reformation in
this direĉtion.   The experiment of
amalgamating Catholic and Huguenot
in the enterprifes of the colony had been
tried but with ill fuccefs.   Contentions
and bickerings had been inceffant, and
subverfive of peace and good neighborhood.   Neither party had the fpirit of
praĉtical toleration as we underftand it,
and which we regard at the prefent day
as a pricelefs boon.   Nor was it underftood anywhere for a long time afterward.   Even the Puritans of Maffachufetts Bay did not comprehend it, and
took heroic meafures to exclude from
their commonwealth thofe who differed
from them in their religious faith.   We
certainly cannot cenfure them for not
being in advance of their times.   It
would doubtlefs have been more manly
in them had they excluded all differing
from them by plain legal enaĉtment, as
did the Society of the Hundred Affociates, rather than to imprifon or banifh
any on charges which all fubfequent generations muft pronounce unfuftained.  —
*Vide Memoir of the Rev. John Wheel-
wright*, by Charles H. Bell, Prince Society, ed.  1876, pp.  9-31 *et paffim;
Hutchinfon Papers*, Prince Society ed.,
1865, Vol. I. pp. 79-113.   *American
Criminal Trials*, by Peleg W. Chandler,
Bofton, 1841, Vol. 1. p. 29.

and all goods manufactured in New France were to be free of imposts on exportation. Besides these, it secured to the corporators other and various exclusive privileges of a semifeudal character, suppofed, however, to contribute to the prosperity and growth of the colony.

The organization of the company, having received the formal approbation of Richelieu on the 29th of April, 1627, was ratified by the Council of State on the 6th of May, 1628.

## CHAPTER X.

THE FAVORABLE PROSPECTS OF THE COMPANY OF NEW FRANCE. — THE ENGLISH INVASION OF CANADA AND THE SURRENDER OF QUEBEC. — CAPTAIN DANIEL PLANTS A FRENCH COLONY NEAR THE GRAND CIBOU. — CHAMPLAIN IN FRANCE, AND THE TERRITORIAL CLAIMS OF THE FRENCH AND ENGLISH STILL UNSETTLED.

THE Company of New France, or of the Hundred Affociates, loft no time in carrying out the purpofe of its organization. Even before the ratification of its charter by the council, four armed veffels had been fitted out and had already failed under the command of Claude de Roquemont, a member of the company, to convoy a fleet of eighteen tranfports laden with emigrants and ftores, together with one hundred and thirty-five pieces of ordnance to fortify their fettlements in New France.

The company, thus compofed of noblemen, wealthy merchants, and officials of great perfonal influence, with a large capital, and Cardinal Richelieu, who really controlled and
                                              fhaped

fhaped the policy of France at that period, at its head, poffeffed fo many elements of ftrength that, in the reafonable
judgment of men, fuccefs was affured, failure impoffible.[95]

To Champlain, the vifion of a great colonial eftablifhment
in New France, that had fo long floated before him in the
diftance, might well feem to be now almoft within his grafp.

But difappointment was near at hand. Events were already tranfpiring which were deftined to caft a cloud over
thefe brilliant hopes. A fleet of armed veffels was already
croffing the Atlantic, bearing the Englifh flag, with hoftile
intentions to the fettlements in New France. Here we muft
paufe in our narrative to explain the origin, charaćter, and
purpofe of this armament, as unexpećted to Champlain as it
was unwelcome.

The reader muft be reminded that no boundaries between
the French and Englifh territorial poffeffions in North
America at this time exifted. Each of thefe great nations
was putting forth claims fo broad and extenfive as to utterly
exclude the other. By their refpećtive charters, grants, and
conceffions, they recognized no fovereignty or ownerfhip but
their own.

Henry IV. of France, made, in 1603, a grant to a favorite
nobleman, De Monts, of the territory lying between the fortieth and the forty-fixth degrees of north latitude. James I.
of England, three years later, in 1606, granted to the Virginia

[95] The affociation was a joint-ftock
company. Each corporator was bound
to pay in three thoufand livres ; and as
there were over a hundred, the quick
capital amounted to over 300,000 livres.
— *Vide Mercure François*, Paris, 1628,
Tome XIV. p. 250.

For a full ftatement of the organiza-
tion and conftitution of the Company of
New France, *Vide Mercure François*,
Tome XIV. pp. 232–267. *Vide* alfo
*Charlevoix's Hift. New France*, Shea's
Trans. Vol. II. pp. 39–44.

ginia Companies the territory lying between the thirty-fourth
and the forty-eighth degrees of north latitude, covering the
whole grant made by the French three years before. Creuxius, a French hiftorian of Canada, writing fome years later
than this, informs us that New France, that is, the French
poffeffions in North America, then embraced the immenfe
territory extending from Florida, or from the thirty-fecond
degree of latitude, to the polar circle, and in longitude from
Newfoundland to Lake Huron. It will, therefore, be feen
that each nation, the Englifh and the French, claimed at
that time fovereignty over the fame territory, and over nearly
the whole of the continent of North America.    Under
thefe circumftances, either of thefe nations was prepared to
avail itfelf of any favorable opportunity to difpoffefs the
other.

The Englifh, however, had, at this period, particular and
fpecial reafons for defiring to accomplifh this important object.  Sir William Alexander,[96] Secretary of State for Scotland at the court of England, had received, in 1621, from
James I., a grant, under the name of New Scotland, of a
large territory, covering the prefent province of Nova Scotia,
New Brunfwick, and that part of the province of Quebec
lying eaft of a line drawn from the head-waters of the River
St. Croix in a northerly direction to the River St. Lawrence.
He had affociated with him a large number of Scottifh noblemen and merchants, and was taking active meafures to
eftablifh Scottifh colonies on this territory.   The French
had made a fettlement within its limits, which had been
                                                      broken

[96] *Vide Sir William Alexander and American Colonization*, Prince Society,
Bofton, 1873.

broken up and the colony difperfed in 1613, by Captain
Samuel Argall, under the authority of Sir Thomas Dale,
governor of the colony at Jameftown, Virginia. A defultory
and ftraggling French population was ftill in occupation, under the nominal governorfhip of Claude La Tour. Sir William Alexander and his affociates naturally looked for more
or lefs inconvenience and annoyance from the claims of the
French. It was, therefore, an objeét of great perfonal importance and particularly defired by him, to extinguifh all
French claims, not only to his own grant, but to the neighboring fettlement at Quebec. If this were done, he might
be fure of being unmolefted in carrying forward his colonial
enterprife.

A war had broken out between France and England the
year before, for the oftenfible purpofe, on the part of the
Englifh, of relieving the Huguenots who were fhut up in
the city of Rochelle, which was beleaguered by the armies
of Louis XIII., under the direétion of his prime minifter,
Richelieu, who was refolved to reduce this laft ftronghold to
obedience. The exiftence of this war offered an opportunity and pretext for difpoffeffing the French and extinguifhing their claims under the rules of war. This objeét could
not be attained in any other way. The French were too
deeply rooted to be removed by any lefs violent or decifive
means. No time was, therefore, loft in taking advantage of
this opportunity.

Sir William Alexander applied himfelf to the formation of
a company of London merchants who fhould bear the expenfe of fitting out an armament that fhould not only overcome and take poffeffion of the French fettlements and forts

wherever

wherever they fhould be found, but plant colonies and erect fuitable defences to hold them in the future. The company was fpeedily organized, confifting of Sir William Alexander, junior, Gervafe Kirke, Robert Charlton, William Berkeley, and perhaps others, diftinguifhed merchants of London.[77] Six fhips were equipped with a fuitable armament and letters of marque, and defpatched on their hoftile errand. Capt. David Kirke, afterwards Sir David, was appointed admiral of the fleet, who likewife commanded one of the fhips.[98] His brothers, Lewis Kirke and Thomas Kirke, were in command of two others. They failed under a royal patent executed in favor of Sir William Alexander, junior, fon of the fecretary, and others, granting exclufive authority to trade, feize, and confifcate French or Spanifh fhips and deftroy the French fettlements on the river and Gulf of St. Lawence and parts adjacent.

Kirke

[77] *Vide Colonial Papers*, Vol. V. 87, III. We do not find the mention of any others as belonging to the Company of Merchant Adventurers to Canada.

[98] Sir David Kirke was one of five brothers, the fons of Gervafe or Gervais Kirke, a merchant of London, and his wife, Elizabeth Goudon of Dieppe in France. The grandfather of Sir David was Thurfton Kirke of Norton, a fmall town in the northern part of the county of Derby, known as the birthplace of the fculptor Chantrey. This little hamlet had been the home of the Kirkes for feveral generations. Gervafe Kirke had, in 1629, refided in Dieppe for the moft of the forty years preceding, and his children were probably born there. Sir David Kirke was married to Sarah, daughter of Sir Jofeph Andrews. In early life he was a wine-merchant at Bordeaux and Cognac. He was knighted by Charles I. in 1633, in recognition of his fervices in taking Quebec. On the 13th of November, 1637, he received a grant of "the whole continent, ifland, or region called Newfoundland." In 1638, he took up his refidence at Ferryland, Newfoundland, in the houfe built by Lord Baltimore. He was a friend and correfpondent of Archbifhop Laud, to whom he wrote, in 1639, "That the ayre of Newfoundland agrees perfectly well with all God's creatures, except Jefuits and fchifmatics." He remained in Newfoundland nearly twenty years, where he died in 1655–56, having experienced many difappointments occafioned by his loyalty to Charles I. — *Vide Colonial Papers*, Vol. IX. No. 76; *The Firft Englifh Conqueft of Canada*, by Henry Kirke, London, 1871, *paffim ; Les Voyages dv Sievr de Champlain*, Paris ed. 1632, p. 257.

21

Kirke failed, with a part if not the whole of his fleet, to Annapolis Bafin in the Bay of Fundy, and took poffeffion of the defultory French fettlement to which we have already referred. He left a Scotch colony there, under the command of Sir William Alexander, junior, as governor. The fleet finally rendezvoufed at Tadouffac, capturing all the French fifhing barques, boats, and pinnaces which fell in its way on the coaft of Nova Scotia, including the Ifland of Cape Breton.

From Tadouffac, Kirke defpatched a fhallop to Quebec, in charge of fix Bafque fifhermen whom he had recently captured. They were bearers of an official communication from the admiral of the Englifh fleet to Champlain. About the fame time he fent up the river, likewife, an armed barque, well manned, which anchored off Cape Tourmente, thirty miles below Quebec, near an outpoft which had been eftablifhed by Champlain for the convenience of forage and pafturage for cattle. Here a fquad of men landed, took four men, a woman, and little girl prifoners, killed fuch of the cattle as they defired for ufe and burned the reft in the ftables, as likewife two fmall houfes, pillaging and laying wafte every thing they could find. Having done this, the barque haftily returned to Tadouffac.

We muft now afk the reader to return with us to the little fettlement at Quebec. The proceedings which we have juft narrated were as yet unknown to Champlain. The fummer of 1628 was wearing on, and no fupplies had arrived from France. It was obvious that fome accident had detained the tranfports, and they might not arrive at all. His provifions were nearly exhaufted. To fubfift without a refupply
was

was impoffible. Each weary day added a new keennefs to his anxiety. A winter of deftitution, of ftarvation and death for his little colony of well on towards a hundred perfons was the painful picture that now conftantly haunted his mind. To avoid this cataftrophe, if poffible, he ordered a boat to be conftructed, to enable him to communicate with the lower waters of the gulf, where he hoped he might obtain provifions from the fifhermen on the coaft, or tranfportation for a part or the whole of his colony to France.

On the 9th of July, two men came up from Cape Tourmente to announce that an Indian had brought in the news that fix large fhips had entered and were lying at anchor in the harbor of Tadouffac. The fame day, not long after, two canoes arrived, in one of which was Foucher, the chief herdfman at Cape Tourmente, who had efcaped from his captors, from whom Champlain firft learned what had taken place at that outpoft.

Sufficiently affured of the character of the enemy, Champlain haftened to put the unfinifhed fort in as good condition as poffible, appointing to every man in the little garrifon his poft, fo that all might be ready for duty at a moment's warning. On the afternoon of the next day a fmall fail came into the bay, evidently a ftranger, directing its courfe not through the ufual channel, but towards the little River St. Charles. It was too infignificant to caufe any alarm. Champlain, however, fent a detachment of arquebufiers to receive it. It proved to be Englifh, and contained the fix Bafque fifhermen already referred to, charged by Kirke with defpatches for Champlain. They had met the armed barque returning to Tadouffac, and had taken off and brought up with them
the

the woman and little girl who had been captured the day before at Cape Tourmente.

The defpatch, written two days before, and bearing date July 8th, 1628, was a courteous invitation to furrender Quebec into the hands of the Englifh, affigning feveral natural and cogent reafons why it would be for the intereft of all parties for them to do fo. Under different circumftances, the reafoning might have had weight; but this Englifh admiral had clearly conceived a very inadequate idea of the character of Champlain, if he fuppofed he would furrender his poft, or even take it into confideration, while the enemy demanding it and his means of enforcing it were at a diftance of at leaft a hundred miles. Champlain fubmitted the letter to Pont Gravé and the other gentlemen of the colony, and we concluded, he adds, that if the Englifh had a defire to fee us nearer, they muft come to us, and not threaten us from fo great a diftance.

Champlain returned an anfwer declining the demand, couched in language of refpectful and dignified politenefs. It is eafy, however, to detect a tinge of farcafm running through it, fo delicate as not to be offenfive, and yet fufficiently obvious to convey a ferene indifference on the part of the French commander as to what the Englifh might think it beft to do in the fequel. The tone of the reply, the air of confidence pervading it, led Kirke to believe that the French were in a far better condition to refift than they really were. The Englifh admiral thought it prudent to withdraw. He deftroyed all the French fifhing veffels and boats at Tadouffac, and proceeded down the gulf, to do the fame along the coaft.

We

We have already alluded, in the preceding pages, to De
Roquemont, the French admiral, who had been charged by
the Company of the Hundred Affociates to convoy a fleet
of tranfports to Canada. Wholly ignorant of the importance of an earlier arrival at Quebec, he appears to have
moved leifurely, and was now, with his whole fleet, lying at
anchor in the Bay of Gafpé. Hearing that Kirke was in
the gulf, he very unwifely prepared to give him battle, and
moved out of the bay for that purpofe. On the 18th of
July the two armaments met. Kirke had fix armed veffels
under his command, while De Roquemont had but four.
The conflict was unequal. The Englifh veffels were unen-
cumbered and much heavier than thofe of the French. De
Roquemont [90] was foon overpowered and compelled to furrender. His whole fleet of twenty-two veffels, with a hundred and thirty-five pieces of ordnance, together with fupplies
and colonifts for Quebec, were all taken. Kirke returned to
England laden with the rich fpoils of his conqueft, having
practically accomplifhed, if not what he had intended, nevertheleſs that which fatisfied the avarice of the London merchants under whofe aufpices the expedition had failed. The
capture of Quebec had from the beginning been the objective
purpofe of Sir William Alexander. The taking of this fleet
and the cutting off their fupplies was an important ftep in
this undertaking. The conqueft was thereby affured, though
not completed.

Champlain,

[90] Champlain criticifes with merited
feverity the conduct of De Roquemont,
and clofes in the following words : " Le
merite d'un bon Capitaine n'eft pas
feulemēt au courage, mais il doit eftre
accōpagné de prudēce, qui eft ce qui
les fait eftimer, cōme eftāt fuiuy de
rufes, ftratagefmes. & d'inventiōs : plufieurs auec peu ont beaucoup fait, & fe
font rēdus glorieux & redoubtables." —
*Vide Les Voyages dv Sievr de Cham-
plain,* ed. 1632, part II p. 166.

Champlain, having defpatched his reply to Kirke, naturally
fuppofed he would foon appear before Quebec to carry out his
threat.  He awaited this event with great anxiety.  About ten
days after the meffengers had departed, a young Frenchman,
named Defdames, arrived in a fmall boat, having been
fent by De Roquemont, the admiral of the new company,
to inform Champlain that he was then at Gafpé with a large
fleet, bringing colonifts, arms, ftores, and provifions for the
fettlement.  Defdames alfo ftated that De Roquemont intended to attack the Englifh, and that on his way he had
heard the report of cannon, which led him to believe that
a conflict had already taken place.  Champlain heard nothing
more from the lower St. Lawrence until the next May, when
an Indian from Tadouffac brought the ftory of De Roquemont's defeat.

In the mean time, Champlain reforted to every expedient
to provide fubfiftence for his famifhing colony.  Even at the
time when the furrender was demanded by the Englifh, they
were on daily rations of feven ounces each.  The means of
obtaining food were exceedingly flender.  Fifhing could not
be profecuted to any extent, for the want of nets, lines, and
hooks.  Of gunpowder they had lefs than fifty pounds, and
a poffible attack by treacherous favages rendered it inexpedient to expend it in hunting game.  Moreover, they had no
falt for curing or preferving the flefh of fuch wild animals as
they chanced to take.  The few acres cultivated by the miffionaries and the Hébert family, and the fmall gardens
about the fettlement, could yield but little towards fuftaining
nearly a hundred perfons for the full term of ten months,
the fhorteft period in which they could reafonably expect
                                                         fupplies

fupplies from France. A fyftem of the utmoft economy was
inftituted. A few eels were purchafed by exchange of beaver-fkins from the Indians. Peafe were reduced to flour firft
by mortars and later by hand-mills conftructed for the purpofe, and made into a foup to add flavor to other lefs palatable
food. Thus economifing their refources, the winter finally
wore away, but when the fpring came, their fcanty means
were entirely exhaufted. Henceforth their fole reliance was
upon the few fifh that could be taken from the river, and the
edible roots gathered day by day from the fields and forefts.
An attempt was made to quarter fome of the men upon the
friendly Indians, but with little fuccefs. Near the laft of
June, thirty of the colony, men, women, and children, unwilling to remain longer at Quebec, were defpatched to Gafpé,
twenty of them to refide there with the Indians, the others
to feek a paffage to France by fome of the foreign fifhing-
veffels on the coaft. This detachment was conducted by
Euftache Boullé, the brother-in-law of Champlain. The remnant of the little colony, difheartened by the gloomy profpect before them and exhaufted by hunger, continued to
drag out a miferable exiftence, gathering fuftenance for the
wants of each day, without knowing what was to fupply the
demands of the next.

On the 19th of July, 1629, three Englifh veffels were feen
from the fort at Quebec, diftant not more than three miles,
approaching under full fail.[100]   Their purpofe could not be
miftaken.   Champlain called a council, in which it was decided

[100] On the 13th of March, 1629, letters of marque were iffued to Capt.
David Kirke, Thomas Kirke, and others, in favor of the "Abigail," 300
tons, the "William," 200 tons, the
"George" of London, and the "Jarvis."

cided at once to furrender, but only on good terms; otherwife, to refift to their utmoft with fuch flender means as they
had. The little garrifon of fixteen men, all his available
force, haftened to their pofts. A flag of truce foon brought
a fummons from the brothers, Lewis and Thomas Kirke,
couched in courteous language, afking the furrender of the
fort and fettlement, and promifing fuch honorable and reafonable terms as Champlain himfelf might dictate.

To this letter Champlain [101] replied that he had not, in his
prefent circumftances, the power of refifting their demand,
and that on the morrow he would communicate the conditions on which he would deliver up the fettlement; but, in
the mean time, he muft requeft them to retire beyond can-
non-fhot, and not attempt to land. On the evening of the
fame day the articles of capitulation were delivered, which
were finally, with very little variation, agreed to by both
parties.

The whole eftablifhment at Quebec, with all the mov-
able property belonging to it, was to be furrendered into the
hands of the Englifh. The colonifts were to be tranfported
to France, neverthelefs, by the way of England. The officers were permitted to leave with their arms, clothes, and the
peltries belonging to them as perfonal property. The fol-
diers were allowed their clothes and a beaver-robe each; the
miffionaries, their robes and books. This agreement was
fubfequently ratified at Tadouffac by David Kirke, the admiral of the fleet, on the 19th of Auguft, 1629.

On the 20th of July, Lewis Kirke, vice-admiral, at the
head

---

[101] This correfpondence is preferved *le Sievr de Champlain*, Paris, 1632, pp.
by Champlain. — *Vide Les Voyages par* 215-219.

head of two hundred armed men,[102] took formal poffeffion of Quebec, in the name of Charles I., the king of England. The Englifh flag was hoifted over the Fort of St. Louis. Drums beat and cannon were difcharged in token of the accomplifhed victory.

The Englifh demeaned themfelves with exemplary courtefy and kindnefs towards their prifoners of war. Champlain was requefted to continue to occupy his accuftomed quarters until he fhould leave Quebec; the holy mafs was celebrated at his requeft; and an inventory of what was found in the habitation and fort was prepared and placed in his hand, a document which proved to be of fervice in the fequel. The colonifts were naturally anxious as to the difpofition of their lands and effects; but their fears were quieted when they were all cordially invited to remain in the fettlement, affured, moreover, that they fhould have the fame privileges and fecurity of perfon and property which they had enjoyed from their own government. This generous offer of the Englifh, and their kind and confiderate treatment of them, induced the larger part of the colonifts to remain.

On the 24th of July, Champlain, exhaufted by a year of diftreffing anxiety and care, and depreffed by the adverfe proceedings going on about him, embarked on the veffel of Thomas Kirke for Tadouffac, to await the departure of the fleet for England. Before reaching their deftination, they encountered a French fhip laden with merchandife and fupplies, commanded by Émeric de Caen, who was endeavoring to

[102] *Vide Abftract of the Depofition of* endar of State Papers, Colonial, 1574– *Capt. David Kirke and Others.* Cal-   1660, p. 103.

22

to reach Quebec for the purpofe of trade and obtaining certain peltry and other property ftored at that place, belonging to his uncle, William de Caen. A conflict was inevitable. The two veffels met. The ftruggle was fevere, and, for a time, of doubtful refult. At length the French cried for quarter. The combat ceafed. De Caen afked permiffion to fpeak with Champlain. This was accorded by Kirke, who informed him, if another fhot were fired, it would be at the peril of his life. Champlain was too old a foldier and too brave a man to be influenced by an appeal to his perfonal fears. He coolly replied, It will be an eafy matter for you to take my life, as I am in your power, but it would be a difgraceful act, as you would violate your facred promife. I cannot command the men in the fhip, or prevent their doing their duty as brave men fhould ; and you ought to commend and not blame them.

De Caen's fhip was borne as a prize into the harbor of Tadouffac, and paffed for the prefent into the vortex of general confifcation.

Champlain remained at Tadouffac until the fleet was ready to return to England. In the mean time, he was courteoufly entertained by Sir David Kirke. He was, however, greatly pained and difappointed that the admiral was unwilling that he fhould take with him to France two Indian girls who had been prefented to him a year or two before, and whom he had been carefully inftructing in religion and manners, and whom he loved as his own daughters. Kirke, however, was inexorable. Neither reafon, entreaty, nor the tears of the unhappy maidens could move him. As he could not take them with him, Champlain adminiftered to them fuch
consolation

confolation as he could, counfelling them to be brave and virtuous, and to continue to fay the prayers that he had taught them. It was a relief to his anxiety at laft to be able to obtain from Mr. Couillard,[103] one of the earlieft fettlers at Quebec, the promife that they fhould remain in the care of his wife, while the girls, on their part, affured him that they would be as daughters to their new fofter-parents until his return to New France.

Quebec having been provifioned and garrifoned, the fleet failed for England about the middle of September, and arrived at Plymouth on the 20th of November. On the 27th, the miffionaries and others who wifhed to return to France, difembarked at Dover, while Champlain was taken to London, where he arrived on the 29th.

At Plymouth, Kirke learned that a peace between France and England had been concluded on the 24th of the preceding April, nearly three months before Quebec had been taken ; confequently, every thing that had been done by this expedition muft, fooner or later, be reverfed. The articles of peace had provided that all conquefts fubfequent to the date of that inftrument fhould be reftored. It was evident that Quebec, the peltry, and other property taken there, together with the fifhing-veffels and others captured in the gulf, muft be reftored to the French. To Kirke and the Company of London Merchants this was a bitter difappointment. Their expenditures had been large in the firft inftance ; the prizes of the year before, the fleet of the Hundred Affociates which

they

---

[108] *Couillard.* Champlain writes *Couillart.* This appears to have been William Couillard, the fon-in-law of Madame Hébert and one of the five families which remained at Quebec after it was taken by the Englifh. — *Vide Laverdière's note, Œuvres de Champlain,* Quebec ed. Vol. VI. p. 249.

they had captured, had probably all been abforbed in the
outfit of the prefent expedition, comprifing the fix veffels
and two pinnaces with which Kirke had failed for the conqueft of Quebec.   Sir William Alexander had obtained, in
the February preceding, from Charles I., a royal charter of
THE COUNTRY AND LORDSHIP OF CANADA IN AMERICA,[104]
embracing a belt of territory one hundred leagues in width,
covering both fides of the St. Lawrence from its mouth to
the Pacific Ocean.   This charter with the moft ample provifions had been obtained in anticipation of the taking of
Quebec, and in order to pave the way for an immediate occupation and fettlement of the country.   Thus a plan for
the eftablifhment of an Englifh colonial empire on the banks
of the St. Lawrence had been deliberately formed, and down
to the prefent moment offered every profpect of a brilliant
fuccefs.   But a cloud had now fwept along the horizon and
fuddenly obfcured the last ray of hope.   The proceeds of their
two years of inceffant labor, and the large fums which they
had rifked in the enterprife, had vanifhed like a mift in the
morning fun.   But, as the caufe of the Englifh became more
defperate, the hopes of the French revived.   The loffes of
the latter were great and difheartening; but they faw, neverthelefs, in the diftance, the long-cherifhed New France of the
paft rifing once more into renewed ftrength and beauty.

On his arrival at London, Champlain immediately put
himfelf in communication with Monfieur de Châteauneuf,
the French ambaffador, laid before him the original of the
capitulation,

[104] An Englifh tranflation of this
charter from the Latin original was
publifhed by the Prince Society in 1873.   *Vide Sir William Alexander and American Colonization*, Prince Society, Bof-
ton, pp. 239-249.

capitulation, a map of the country, and fuch other memoirs as were needed to fhow the fuperior claims of the French to Quebec on the ground both of difcovery and occupation.[105] Many queftions arofe concerning the poffeffion and owner-fhip of the peltry and other property taken by the Englifh, and, during his ftay, Champlain contributed as far as poffible to the fettlement of thefe complications. It is fomewhat remarkable that during this time the Englifh pretended to hold him as a prifoner of war, and even attempted to extort a ranfom from him,[106] preffing the matter fo far that Champlain felt compelled to remonftrate againft a demand fo extraordinary and fo obvioufly unjuft, as he was in no fenfe a prifoner of war, and likewife to ftate his inability to pay a ranfom, as his whole eftate in France did not exceed feven hundred pounds fterling.

After having remained a month in London, Champlain was permitted to depart for France, arriving on the laft day of December.

At Dieppe he met Captain Daniel, from whom he learned that

[105] Champlain publifhed, in 1632, a brief argument fetting forth the claims of the French, which he entitles, *Abregé des Defcouvertures de la Nouuelle France, tant de ce que nous auons defcouuert comme auffi les Anglois, depuis les Virgines iufqu'au Freton Dauis, & de cequ'eux & nous pouuons pretendre fuiuant le rapport des Hiftoriens qui en ont defcrit, que ie rapporte cy deffous, qui feront inger à vn chacun du tout fans paffion.* — *Vide* ed. 1632, p. 290. In this paper he narrates fuccinctly the early difcoveries made both by the French and Englifh navigators, and enforces the doctrine of the fuperior claims of the French with clearnefs and

ftrength. It contains, probably, the fubftance of what Champlain placed at this time in the hands of the French embaffador in London.

[106] It is difficult to conceive on what ground this ranfom was demanded, fince the whole proceedings of the Englifh againft Quebec were illegal, and contrary to the articles of peace which had juft been concluded. That fuch a demand was made would be regarded as incredible, did not the fact reft upon documentary evidence of undoubted authority. — *Vide Laverdière's* citation from State Papers Office, Vol. V. No. 33, Œuvres de Champlain, Quebec ed., Vol. VI. p. 1413.

that Richelieu and the Hundred Affociates had not been unmindful of the preffing wants of their colony at Quebec. Arrangements had been made early in the year 1629 to fend to Champlain fuccor and fupplies, and a fleet had been organized to be conducted thither by the Commander Ifaac de Razilly. While preparations were in progrefs, peace was concluded between France and England on the 24th of April. It was, confequently, deemed unneceffary to accompany the tranf-ports by an armed force, and thereupon Razilly's orders were countermanded, while Captain Daniel of Dieppe,[197] whofe fervices had been engaged, was fent forward with four veffels and a barque belonging to the company, to carry fupplies to Quebec. A ftorm fcattered his fleet, but the veffel under his immediate command arrived on the coaft of the Ifland of Cape Breton, and anchored on the 18th of September, *novo ftylo*, in the little harbor of Baleine, fituated about fix miles eafterly from the prefent fite of Louifburgh, now famous in the annals of that ifland. Here he was furprifed to find a Britifh fettlement. Lord Ochiltrie, better known as Sir James Stuart, a Scottifh nobleman, had obtained a grant, through Sir William Alexander, of the Ifland of Cape Breton, and had, on the 10th of July preceding, *novo ftylo*, planted there a colony of fixty perfons, men, women, and children, and had thrown up for their protection a temporary fort. Daniel confidered this an intrufion upon French foil. He accordingly made a bloodlefs capture of the fortrefs at Baleine,

[197] *Vide Relation dv Voyage fait par le Capitaine Daniel de Dieppe, année 1629, Les Voyages du Sieur de Champlain*, Paris, 1632, p. 271. Captain Daniel was enrolled by Creuxius in the Society of New France or the Hundred Affociates, as *Carolvs Daniel, nauticus Capitaneus. Vide Hiftoria Canadenfit* for the names of the Society of the Hundred Affociates.

Baleine, demolifhed it, and, failing to the north and fweeping round to the weft, entered an eftuary which he fays the
favages called *Grand Cibou*,[108] where he erected a fort and
left a garrifon of forty men, with provifions and all neceffary means of defence.  Having fet up the arms of the
King of France and thofe of Cardinal Richelieu, erected a
houfe, chapel, and magazine, and leaving two Jefuit miffionaries, the fathers Barthélemy Vimond and Alexander de
Vieuxpont, he departed, taking with him the Britifh colonifts,
forty-two of whom he landed near Falmouth in England,
and eighteen, including Lord Ochiltrie, he carried into
France.  This fettlement at the Bay of St. Anne, or Port
Dauphin, accidentally eftablifhed and inadequately fuftained,
lingered a few years and finally difappeared.

Having received the above narrative from Captain Daniel,
Champlain foon after proceeded to Paris, and laid the whole
fubject of the unwarrantable proceedings of the Englifh in
detail

[108] *Cibou.*  Sometimes written Chibou.  "Cibou means," fays Mr. J.
Hammond Trumball, "fimply river in
all eaftern Algonkin languages." — *MS.
letter.*  Nicholas Denys, in his very full
itinerary of the coaft of the ifland of
Cape Breton fpeaks alfo of the *entree
du petit Chibou ou de Labrador.*  This
*petit Chibou,* according to his defcription, is identical with what is now known
as the Little Bras d'Or, or fmaller paffage to Bras d'Or Lake.  It feems probable that the great Cibou of the Indians
was applied originally by them to what
we now call the Great Bras d'Or, or
larger paffage to Bras d'Or Lake.  It is
plain, however, that Captain Daniel
and other early writers applied it to an
eftuary or bay a little further weft than
the Great Bras d'Or, feparated from it
by Cape Dauphin, and now known as
St. Anne's Bay.  It took the name of
St. Anne's immediately on the planting
of Captain Daniel's colony, as Champlain calls it, *l'habitation fainéte Anne
en l'ifle du Cap Breton* in his relation
of what took place in 1631. — *Voyages,*
ed. 1632, p. 298.  A very good defcription of it by Père Perrault may be
found in *Jefuit Relations,* 1635, Quebec
ed. p. 42. — *Vide,* alfo, *Defcription de
l'Amerique Septentrionale par Monfieur Denys,* Paris, 1672, p. 155, where
is given an elaborate defcription of St.
Anne's Harbor.  *Granfibou* may be
feen on Champlain's map of 1632, but
the map is too indefinite to aid us in
fixing its exact location.

detail before the king, Cardinal Richelieu, and the Company of New France, and urged the importance of regaining poffeffion as early as poffible of the plantation from which they had been unjuftly ejected. The Englifh king did not hefitate at an early day to promife the reftoration of Quebec, and, in fact, after fome delay, all places which were occupied by the French at the outbreak of the war. The policy of the Englifh minifters appears, however, to have been to poftpone the execution of this promife as long as poffible, probably with the hope that fomething might finally occur to render its fulfilment unneceffary. Sir William Alexander, the Earl of Stirling, who had very great influence with Charles I., was particularly oppofed to the reftoration of the fettlement on the fhores of Annapolis Bafin. This fell within the limits of the grant made to him in 1621, under the name of New Scotland, and a Scotch colony was now in occupation. He contended that no proper French plantation exifted there at the opening of the war, and this was probably true; a few French people were, indeed, living there, but under no recognized, certainly no actual, authority or control of the crown of France, and confequently they were under no obligation to reftore it. But Charles I. had given his word that all places taken by the Englifh fhould be reftored as they were before the war, and no argument or perfuafions could change his refolution to fulfil his promife. It was not, however, till after the lapfe of more than two years, owing, chiefly, to the oppofition of Sir William Alexander, that the reftoration of Quebec and the plantation on Annapolis Bafin was fully affured by the treaty of St. Germain en Laye, bearing date March 29, 1632.

The

The reader muſt be reminded that the text of the treaty juſt mentioned and numerous contemporary documents ſhow that the reſtorations demanded by the French and granted by the Engliſh only related to the places occupied by the French before the outbreak of the war, and not to Canada or New France or to any large extent of provincial territory whatever.[109] When the reſtorations were completed, the boundary lines diſtinguiſhing the Engliſh and French poſſeſſions in America were ſtill unſettled, the territorial rights of both nations were ſtill undefined, and each continued, as they had done before the war, to claim the ſame territory as a part of their reſpective poſſeſſions. Hiſtorians, giving to this treaty a ſuperficial examination, and not conſidering it in connection with contemporary documents, have, from that time to the preſent, fallen into the looſe and unauthorized ſtatement that, by the treaty of St. Germain en Laye, the whole domain of Canada or New France was reſtored to the French.

Had the treaty of St. Germain en Laye, by which Quebec was reſtored to the French, fixed accurately the boundary lines between the two countries, it would probably have ſaved the expenditure of money and blood, which continued to be demanded from time to time until, after a century and a quarter, the whole of the French poſſeſſions were tranſferred, under the arbitration of war, to the Engliſh crown.

CHAPTER XI.

[109] *Vide Sir William Alexander and American Colonization*, Prince Society, 1873, pp. 66-72. — *Royal Letters, Charters, and Tracts relating to the Colonization of New Scotland*, Bannatyne Club, Edinburgh, 1867, p. 77 *et paſſim.*

## CHAPTER XI.

ÉMERIC DE CAEN TAKES POSSESSION OF QUEBEC. — CHAMPLAIN PUBLISHES HIS VOYAGES. — RETURNS TO NEW FRANCE, REPAIRS THE HABITATION, AND ERECTS A CHAPEL. — HIS LETTER TO CARDINAL DE RICHELIEU. — CHAMPLAIN'S DEATH.

N breaking up the fettlement at Quebec, the loffes of the De Caens were confiderable, and it was deemed an act of juftice to allow them an opportunity to retrieve them, at leaft in part; and, to enable them to do this, the monopoly of the fur-trade in the Gulf of St. Lawrence was granted to them for one year, and, on the retirement of the Englifh, Émeric de Caen, as provifional governor for that period, took formal poffeffion of Quebec on the 13th of July, 1632.

In the mean time, Champlain remained in France, devoting himfelf with characteriftic energy to the interefts of New France. Befide the valuable counfel and aid which he gave regarding the expedition then fitting out and to be fent to Quebec by the Company of New France, he prepared and carried through the prefs an edition of his Voyages, comprifing extended extracts from what he had already publifhed, and a continuation of the narrative to 1631. He alfo publifhed in the fame volume a Treatife on Navigation, and a Catechifm tranflated from the French by one of the Fathers into the language of the Montagnais.[110]

On

[110] This catechifm, bearing the following title, is contained on fifteen pages in the ed. of 1632 : *Doctrine Chreftienne, du R. P. Ledefme de la Compagnie de Iefus. Traduicte en Langage Cana-* *dois, autre que celuy des Montagnars, pour la Conuerfion des habitans dudit pays. Par le R. P. Brebœuf de la mefme Compagnie.* It is in double columns, one fide Indian and the other French.

On the 23d of March, 1633, having again been commiſ-
ſioned as governor, Champlain ſailed from Dieppe with a
fleet of three veſſels, the " Saint Pierre," the " Saint Jean,"
and the " Don de Dieu," belonging to the Company of New
France, conveying to Quebec a large number of coloniſts,
together with the Jeſuit fathers, Encmond Maſſé and Jean
de Brébeuf. The three veſſels entered the harbor of Quebec on the 23d of May. On the announcement of Champlain's arrival, the little colony was all aſtir. The cannon
at the Fort St. Louis boomed forth their hoarſe welcome
of his coming. The hearts of all, particularly of thoſe
who had remained at Quebec during the occupation of the
Engliſh, were overflowing with joy. The three years' ab-
ſence of their now venerable and venerated governor, and
the trials, hardſhips, and diſcouragements through which
they had in the mean time paſſed, had not effaced from their
minds the virtues that endeared him to their hearts. The
memory of his tender ſolicitude in their behalf, his brave
example of endurance in the hour of want and peril, and
the ſweetneſs of his parting counſels, came back afreſh to
awaken in them new pulſations of gratitude. Champlain's
heart was touched by his warm reception and the viſible
proofs of their love and devotion. This was a bright and
happy day in the calendar of the little colony.

Champlain addreſſed himſelf with his old zeal and a renewed ſtrength to every intereſt that promiſed immediate or
future good reſults. He at once directed the renovation and
improvement of the habitation and fort, which, after an occupation of three years by aliens, could not be delayed. He
then inſtituted means, holding councils and creating a new
                                                    trading-poſt,

trading-poft, for winning back the traffic of the allied tribes, which had been of late drawn away by the Englifh, who continued to fteal into the waters of the St. Lawrence for that purpofe. At an early day after his re-eftablifhment of himfelf at Quebec, Champlain proceeded to build a memo-rial chapel in clofe proximity to the fort which he had erected fome years before on the creft of the rocky eminence that overlooks the harbor. He gave it the appropriate and fig-nificant name, Notre Dame de Recouvrance, in grateful memory of the recent return of the French to New France.[111] It had long been an ardent defire of Champlain to eftablifh a French fettlement among the Hurons, and to plant a mif-fion there for the converfion of this favorite tribe to the Chriftian faith. Two miffionaries, De Brébeuf and De Noüé, were now ready for the undertaking. The governor fpared no pains to fecure for them a favorable reception, and vig-oroufly urged the importance of their miffion upon the Hurons affembled at Quebec.[112] But at the laft, when on the eve of fecuring his purpofe, complications arofe and fo much hof-tility was difplayed by one of the chiefs, that he thought it prudent

[111] The following extracts will fhow that the chapel was erected in 1633, that it was built by Champlain, and that it was called Notre Dame de Recouv-rance.
Nous les menafmes en noftre petite chapelle, qui a commencé cefte année à f'embellir.—*Vide Relations des Jéfuites.* Quebec ed. 1633, p. 30.
La fage conduite et la prudence de Monfieur de Champlain Gouuerneur de Kebec et du fleuue fainct Laurens, qui nous honore de fa bien-veillance, rete-nant vn chacun dans fon deuoir, a fait que nos paroles et nos predications

ayent efté bien receuës, et la Chapelle qu'il a fait dreffer proche du fort à l'hon-neur de noftre Dame, &c.—*Idem,* 1634, p. 2.
La troifiéme, que nous allons habiter cette Autome, la Refidence de Noftre-dame de Recourrance, à Kebec proche du Fort.—*Idem,* 1635, p. 3.
[112] According to Père Le Jeune, from five to feven hundred Hurons had af-fembled at Quebec in July, 1633. bring-ing their canoes loaded with merchan-dife.—*Vide Relations des Jéfuites,* Quebec ed. 1633, p. 34.

prudent to advife its poftponement to a more aufpicious moment. With thefe and kindred occupations growing out of
the refponfibilities of his charge, two years foon paffed away.

During the fummer of 1635, Champlain addreffed an interefting and important letter to Cardinal de Richelieu,
whofe authority at that time fhaped both the domeftic and
foreign policy of France. In it the condition and impera-
tive wants of New France are clearly fet forth. This document was probably the laft that Champlain ever penned, and
is, perhaps, the only autograph letter of his now extant.
His views of the richnefs and poffible refources of the country, the vaft miffionary field which it offered, and the policy
to be purfued, are fo clearly ftated that we need offer no
apology for giving the following free tranflation of the letter in thefe pages."³

### LETTER OF CHAMPLAIN TO CARDINAL DE RICHELIEU.

MONSEIGNEUR, — The honor of the commands that I have
received from your Eminence has infpired me with greater
courage to render to you every poffible fervice with all the
fidelity and affeftion that can be defired from a faithful fervant. I fhall fpare neither my blood nor my life whenever
the occafion fhall demand them.

There are fubjefts enough in thefe regions, if your Eminence, after confidering the charafter of the country, fhall
defire to extend your authority over them. This territory
is more than fifteen hundred leagues in length, lying between the fame parallels of latitude as our own France. It
is

---

¹¹ᵃ This letter was printed in Œuvres  nal is at Paris, in the Archives of For-
de Champlain. Quebec ed. Vol. vi.  eign Affairs.
*Pièces Juftificatives*, p. 35. The origi-

is watered by one of the fineſt rivers in the world, into which empty many tributaries more than four hundred leagues in length, beautifying a country inhabited by a vaſt number of tribes. Some of them are ſedentary in their mode of life, poſſeſſing, like the Muſcovites, towns and villages built of wood; others are nomadic, hunters and fiſhermen, all longing to welcome the French and religious fathers, that they may be inſtruéted in our faith.

The excellence of this country cannot be too highly eſtimated or praiſed, both as to the richneſs of the ſoil, the diverſity of the timber ſuch as we have in France, the abundance of wild animals, game, and fiſh, which are of extraordinary magnitude. All this invites you, Monſeigneur, and makes it ſeem as if God had created you above all your predeceſſors to do a work here more pleaſing to Him than any that has yet been accompliſhed.

For thirty years I have frequented this country, and have acquired a thorough knowledge of it, obtained from my own obſervation and the information given me by the native inhabitants. Monſeigneur, I pray you to pardon my zeal, if I ſay that, after your renown has ſpread throughout the Eaſt, you ſhould end by compelling its recognition in the Weſt.

Expelling the Engliſh from Quebec has been a very important beginning, but, neverthelefs, ſince the treaty of peace between the two crowns, they have returned to carry on trade and annoy us in this river; declaring that it was enjoined upon them to withdraw, but not to remain away, and that they have their king's permiſſion to come for the period of thirty years. But, if your Eminence wills, you can make them feel the power of your authority. This can, furthermore,

more, be extended at your pleaſure to him who has come here to bring about a general peace among theſe peoples, who are at war with a nation holding more than four hundred leagues in ſubjection, and who prevent the free uſe of the rivers and highways.  If this peace were made, we ſhould be in complete and eaſy enjoyment of our poſſeſſions.  Once eſtabliſhed in the country, we could expel our enemies, both Engliſh and Flemings, forcing them to withdraw to the coaſt, and, by depriving them of trade with the Iroquois, oblige them to abandon the country entirely.  It requires but one hundred and twenty men, light-armed for avoiding arrows, by whoſe aid, together with two or three thouſand ſavage warriors, our allies, we ſhould be, within a year, abſolute maſters of all theſe peoples, and, by eſtabliſhing order among them, promote religious worſhip and ſecure an incredible amount of traffic.

The country is rich in mines of copper, iron, ſteel, braſs, ſilver, and other minerals which may be found here.

The coſt, Monſeigneur, of one hundred and twenty men is a trifling one to his Majeſty, the enterpriſe the moſt noble that can be imagined.

All for the glory of God, whom I pray with my whole heart to grant you ever-increaſing proſperity, and to make me, all my life,

       Monſeigneur,

           Your moſt humble,

               Moſt faithful, and

                   Moſt obedient ſervant,

                      CHAMPLAIN.

AT QUEBEC, IN NEW FRANCE, the 15th of Auguſt, 1635.

                                  In

In this letter will be found the key to Champlain's war-policy with the Iroquois, no where elfe fo fully unfolded. We fhall refer to this fubject in the fequel.

Early in October, when the harveft of the year had ri-pened and been gathered in, and the leaves had faded and fallen, and the earth was mantled in the fymbols of general decay, in fympathy with all that furrounded him, in his chamber in the little fort on the creft of the rocky promon-tory at Quebec, lay the manly form of Champlain, fmitten with difeafe, which was daily breaking down the vigor and ftrength of his iron conftitution. From loving friends he re-ceived the miniftrations of tender and affiduous care. But his earthly career was near its end. The bowl had been broken at the fountain. Life went on ebbing away from week to week. At the end of two months and a half, on Chriftmas day, the 25th of December, 1635, his fpirit paffed to its final reft.

This otherwife joyous feftival was thus clouded with a deep forrow. No heart in the little colony was untouched by this event. All had been drawn to Champlain, fo many years their chief magiftrate and wife counfellor, by a fponta-neous and irrefiftible refpect, veneration, and love. It was meet, as it was the univerfal defire, to crown him, in his burial, with every honor which, in their circumftances, they could beftow. The whole population joined in a mournful proceffion. His fpiritual advifer and friend, Father Charles Lalemant, performed in his behalf the laft folemn fervice of the church. Father Paul Le Jeune pronounced a funeral difcourfe, reciting his virtues, his fidelity to the king and the Company of New France, his extraordinary love and devotion

tion to the families of the colony, and his laft counfels for their continued happinefs and welfare."[114]

When thefe ceremonies were over, his body was pioufly and tenderly laid to reft, and foon after a tomb was con-ftructed for its reception exprefsly in his honor as the bene-factor of New France."[115]  The place of his burial [116] was within the little chapel fubfequently erected, and which was reverently called *La Chapelle de M. de Champlain*, in grate-ful memory of him whofe body repofed beneath its fhelter-ing walls.

CHAPTER XII.

[114] *Vide Relations des Jéfuites*, Que-bec ed. 1636, p. 56.  *Creuxius, Hiftoria Canadenfis*, pp. 183-4.

[115] Monfieur le Gouuerneur, qui efti-moit fa vertu, defira qu'il fuft enterré prés du corps de feu Monfieur de Cham-plain, qui eft dans vn fepulchre par-ticulier, erigé exprés pour honorer la memoire de ce fignalé perfonnage qui a tant obligé la Nouuelle France. — *Vide Relations des Jéfuites*, Quebec ed. 1643, p. 3.

[116] The exact fpot where Champlain was buried is at this time unknown. Hiftorians and antiquaries have been much interefted in its difcovery.  In 1866, the Abbés Laverdière and Cafgrain were encouraged to believe that their fearches had been crowned with fuc-cefs.  They publifhed a ftatement of their difcovery.  Their views were con-troverted in feveral critical pamphlets that followed.  In the mean time, addi-tional refearches have been made.  The theory then broached that his burial was in the Lower Town, and in the Re-collect chapel built in 1615, has been abandoned.  The Abbé Cafgrain, in an able difcuffion of this fubject, in which he cites documents hitherto unpub-lifhed, fhows that Champlain was buried in a tomb within the walls of a chapel erected by his fucceffor in the Upper Town, and that this chapel was fituated fomewhere within the court-yard of the prefent poft-office.  Père Le Jeune, who records the death of Champlain in his Relation of 1636, does not men-tion the place of his burial; but the Père Vimont, in his Relation of 1643, in fpeaking of the burial of Père Charles Raymbault, fays, the "Gov-ernor defired that he fhould be buried near the *body of the late Monfieur de Champlain*, which is in a particular tomb erected exprefsly to honor the memory of that diftinguifhed perfonage, who had placed New France under fuch great obligation."  In the Parifh Reg-ifter of Notre Dame de Quebec, is the following entry:  "The 22d of October (1642), was interred *in the Chapel of M. De Champlain* the Père Charles Rimbault."  It is plain, therefore, that Champlain was buried in what was then commonly known as *the Chapel of M. de Champlain*.  By reference to ancient documents or deeds (one bearing date Feb. 10, 1649, and another 22d April, 1652, and in one of which the Chapel of Champlain is mentioned as contiguous to a piece of land therein defcribed), the Abbé

24

## CHAPTER XII.

CHAMPLAIN'S RELIGION. — HIS WAR POLICY. — HIS DOMESTIC AND SOCIAL LIFE. — CHAMPLAIN AS AN EXPLORER. — HIS LITERARY LABORS. — THE RESULTS OF HIS CAREER.

S Champlain had lived, fo he died, a firm and confiftent member of the Roman church. In harmony with his general character, his religious views were always moderate, never betraying him into exceffes, or into any merely partifan zeal. Born during the profligate, cruel, and perfidious reign of Charles IX., he was, perhaps, too young to be greatly affected by the evils characteriftic of that period, the maffacre of St. Bartholomew's and the numberlefs vices that fwept along in its train. His youth and early manhood, covering the plaftic and formative period, ftretched through the reign of Henry III., in which the ftandards of virtue and religion were little if in any degree improved. Early in the reign of Henry IV., when he had fairly entered upon his manhood, we find him clofely

Abbé Cafgrain proves that the *Chapel of M. de Champlain* was within the fquare where is fituated the prefent poft-office at Quebec, and, as the tomb of Champlain was within the chapel, it follows that Champlain was buried fomewhere within the poft-office fquare above mentioned.

Excavations in this fquare have been made, but no traces of the walls or foundations of the chapel have been found. In the excavations for cellars of the houfes conftructed along the fquare, the foundations of the chapel may have been removed. It is poffible that when the chapel was deftroyed, which was at a very early period, as no reference to its exiftence is found fubfequent to 1649, the body of Champlain and the others buried there may have been removed, and no record made of the removal. The Abbé Cafgrain expreffes the hope that other difcoveries may hereafter be made that fhall place this interefting queftion beyond all doubt. — *Vide Documents Inédits Relatifs au Tombeau de Champlain*, par l'Abbé H. R. Cafgrain, *L'Opinion Publique*, Montreal, 4 Nov. 1875.

clofely affociated with the moderate party, which encouraged
and fuftained the broad, generous, and catholic principles of
that diftinguifhed fovereign.

When Champlain became lieutenant-governor of New
France, his attention was naturally turned to the religious
wants of his diftant domain.   Proceeding cautioufly, after
patient and prolonged inquiry, he felected miffionaries who
were earneft, zealous, and fully confecrated to their work.
And all whom he fubfequently invited into the field were
men of character and learning, whofe brave endurance of
hardfhip, and manly courage amid numberlefs perils, fhed
glory and luftre upon their holy calling.

Champlain's fympathies were always with his miffionaries
in their pious labors.   Whether the enterprife were the
eftablifhment of a miffion among the diftant Hurons, among
the Algonquins on the upper St. Lawrence, or for the
enlargement of their accommodations at Quebec, the printing of a catechifm in the language of the aborigines, or if
the foundations of a college were to be laid for the education of the favages, his heart and hand were ready for the
work.

On the eftablifhment of the Company of New France, or
the Hundred Affociates, Proteftants were entirely excluded.
By its conftitution no Huguenots were allowed to fettle
within the domain of the company.   If this rule was not
fuggefted by Champlain, it undoubtedly exifted by his decided
and hearty concurrence.   The mingling of Catholics and
Huguenots in the early hiftory of the colony had brought
with it numberlefs annoyances.   By fifting the wheat before
it was fown, it was hoped to get rid of an otherwife inevitable
                                                        caufe

caufe of irritation and trouble. The correctnefs of the principle of Chriftian toleration was not admitted by the Roman
church then any more than it is now. Nor did the Proteftants of that period believe in it, or practife it, whenever
they poffeffed the power to do otherwife. Even the Puritans of Maffachufetts Bay held that their charter conferred
upon them the right and power of exclufion. It was not
eafy, it is true, to carry out this view by fquare legal enact-
ment without coming into conflict with the laws of England;
but they were adroit and fkilful, endowed with a marvellous
talent for finding fome indirect method of laying a heavy
hand upon Friend or Churchman, or the more independent
thinkers among their own numbers, who defired to make their
abode within the precincts of the bay. In the earlier years
of the colony at Quebec, when Proteftant and Catholic were
there on equal terms, Champlain's religious affociations led
him to fwerve neither to the right hand nor to the left. His
adminiftration was characterized by juftice, firmnefs, and
gentlenefs, and was defervedly fatisfactory to all parties.

In his later years, the little colony upon whofe welfare and
Chriftian culture he had beftowed fo much cheerful labor
and anxious thought, became every day more and more dear
to his heart. Within the ample folds of his charity were
likewife encircled the numerous tribes of favages, fpread over
the vaft domains of New France. He earneftly defired that
all of them, far and near, friend and foe, might be inftructed
in the doctrines of the Chriftian faith, and brought into willing and loving obedience to the crofs.

In its perfonal application to his own heart, the religion
of Champlain was diftinguifhed by a natural and gradual
progrefs,

progrefs. His warmth, tendernefs, and zeal grew deeper and ftronger with advancing years. In his religious life there was a clearly marked feed-time, growth, and ripening for the harveft. After his return to Quebec, during the laft three years of his life, his time was efpecially fyftematized and appropriated for intellectual and fpiritual improvement. Some portion was given every morning by himfelf and thofe who conftituted his family to a courfe of hiftorical reading, and in the evening to the memoirs of the faintly dead whofe lives he regarded as fuitable for the imitation of the living, and each night for himfelf he devoted more or lefs time to private meditation and prayer.

Such were the devout habits of Champlain's life in his later years. We are not, therefore, furprifed that the hiftorian of Canada, twenty-five years after his death, fhould place upon record the following concife but comprehenfive eulogy : —

" His furpaffing love of juftice, piety, fidelity to God, his king, and the Society of New France, had always been confpicuous. But in his death he gave fuch illuftrious proofs of his goodnefs as to fill every one with admiration." [117]

The reader of thefe memoirs has doubtlefs obferved with furprife and perhaps with difappointment, the readinefs with which Champlain took part in the wars of the favages. On his firft vifit to the valley of the St. Lawrence, he found the Indians dwelling on the northern fhores of the river and the lakes engaged in a deadly warfare with thofe on the fouthern, the Iroquois tribes occupying the northern limits of the present

[117] *Vide Creuxius, Hiftoria Canadenfis,* pp. 183, 184.

prefent State of New York, generally known as the Five
Nations.   The hoftile relations between thefe favages were
not of recent date.   They reached back to a very early but
indefinite period.   They may have exifted for feveral centuries.   When Champlain planted his colony at Quebec, in
1608, he at once entered into friendly relations with all the
tribes which were his immediate neighbors.   This was eminently a fuitable thing to do, and was, moreover, neceffary
for his fafety and protection.

But a permanent and effective alliance with thefe tribes
carried with it of neceffity a folemn affurance of aid againft
their enemies.   This Champlain promptly promifed without
hefitation, and the next year he fulfilled his promife by leading them to battle on the fhores of Lake Champlain.   At
all fubfequent periods he regarded himfelf as committed to
aid his allies in their hoftile expeditions againft the Iroquois.
In his printed journal, he offers no apology for his conduct
in this refpect, nor does he intimate that his views could be
queftioned either in morals or found policy.   He rarely
affigns any reafon whatever for engaging in thefe wars.   In
one or two inftances he ftates that it feemed to him neceffary
to do fo in order to facilitate the difcoveries which he wifhed
to make, and that he hoped it might in the end be the means
of leading the favages to embrace Chriftianity.   But he no-
where enters upon a full difcuffion of this point.   It is enough
to fay, in explanation of this filence, that a private journal like
that publifhed by Champlain, was not the place in which to
forefhadow a policy, efpecially as it might in the future be
fubject to change, and its fuccefs might depend upon its
being known only to thofe who had the power to fhape and
                                                      direct

direct it. But neverthelefs the filence of Champlain has
doubtlefs led fome hiftorians to infer that he had no good
reafons to give, and unfavorable criticifms have been beftowed
upon his conduct by thofe, who did not underftand the circumftances which influenced him, or the motives which controlled his action.

The war-policy of Champlain was undoubtedly very plainly
fet forth in his correfpondence and interviews with the viceroys and feveral companies under whofe authority he acted.
But thefe difcuffions, whether oral or written, do not appear
in general to have been preferved. Fortunately a fingle document of this character is ftill extant, in which his views
are clearly unfolded. In Champlain's remarkable letter to
Cardinal de Richelieu, which we have introduced a few pages
back, his policy is fully ftated. It is undoubtedly the fame
that he had acted upon from the beginning, and explains the
franknefs and readinefs with which, firft and laft, as a faithful
ally, he had profeffed himfelf willing to aid the friendly tribes
in their wars againft the Iroquois. The object which he
wifhed to accomplifh by this tribal war was, as fully ftated
in the letter to which we have referred, firft, to conquer the
Iroquois or Five Nations; to introduce peaceful relations between them and the other furrounding tribes; and, fecondly,
to eftablifh a grand alliance of all the favage tribes, far and
near, with the French. This could only be done in the order
here ftated. No peace could be fecured from the Iroquois,
except by their conqueft, the utter breaking down of their
power. They were not fufceptible to the influence of reafon.
They were implacable, and had been brutalized by long-
inherited habits of cruelty. In the total annihilation of their
power

power was the only hope of peace. This being accomplifhed,
the furviving remnant would, according to the ufual cuftom
among the Indians, readily amalgamate with the victorious
tribes, and then a general alliance with the French could
be eafily fecured. This was what Champlain wifhed to
accomplifh. The pacification of all the tribes occupying
both fides of the St. Lawrence and the chain of northern lakes would place the whole domain of the American
continent, or as much of it as it would be defirable to
hold, under the eafy and abfolute control of the French
nation.

Such a pacification as this would fecure two objects;
objects eminently important, appealing ftrongly to all who
defired the aggrandizement of France and the progrefs and
fupremacy of the Catholic faith. It would fecure for ever
to the French the fur-trade of the Indians, a commerce then
important and capable of vaft expanfion. The chief ftrength
and refources of the favages allied with the French, the
Montagnais, Algonquins, and Hurons, were at that period
expended in their wars. On the ceffation of hoftilities, their
whole force would naturally and inevitably be given to the
chafe. A grand field lay open to them for this exciting
occupation. The fur-bearing country embraced not only
the region of the St. Lawrence and the lakes, but the vaft
and unlimited expanfe of territory ftretching out indefinitely
in every direction. The whole northern half of the continent
of North America, filled with the moft valuable fur-producing
mammalia, would be open to the enterprife of the French,
and could not fail to pour into their treafury an incredible
amount of wealth. This Champlain was far-fighted enough
to

to fee, and his patriotic zeal led him to defire that France fhould avail herfelf of this opportunity."[118]

But the conqueft of the Iroquois would not only open to France the profpect of exhauftlefs wealth, but it would render acceffible a broad, extenfive, and inviting field of miffionary labor. It would remove all external and phyfical obftacles to the fpeedy tranfmiffion and offer of the Chriftian faith to the numberlefs tribes that would thus be brought within their reach.

The defire to bring about thefe two great ulterior purpofes, the augmentation of the commerce of France in the full development of the fur-trade, and the gathering into the Catholic church the favage tribes of the wildernefs, explains the readinefs with which, from the beginning, Champlain encouraged his Indian allies and took part with them in their wars againft the Five Nations. In the very laft year of his life, he demanded of Richelieu the requifite military force to carry on this war, reminding him that the coft would be trifling to his Majefty, while the enterprife would be the moft noble that could be imagined.

In regard to the domeftic and focial life of Champlain, fcarcely any documents remain that can throw light upon the

---

[118] The juftnefs of Champlain's conception of the value of the fur-trade has been verified by its fubfequent hiftory. The Hudfon's Bay Company was organized for the purpofe of carrying on this trade, under a charter granted by Charles II., in 1670. A part of the trade has at times been conducted by other affociations. But this company is ftill in active and vigorous operation. Its capital is $10,000,000. At its reorganization in 1863, it was eftimated that it would yield a net annual income, to be divided among the corporators, of $400,000. It employs twelve hundred fervants befide its chief factors. It is eafy to fee what a vaft amount of wealth in the fhape of furs and peltry has been pouring into the European markets, for more than two hundred years, from this fur-bearing region, and the fources of this wealth are probably little, if in any degree, diminifhed.

the fubject.  Of his parents we have little information
beyond that of their refpectable calling and ftanding.  He
was probably an only child, as no others are on any occafion mentioned or referred to.  He married, as we have feen,
the daughter of the Secretary of the King's Chamber, and
his wife, Hélène Boullé, accompanied him to Canada in 1620,
where fhe remained four years.  They do not appear to have
had children, as the names of none are found in the records
at Quebec, and, at his death, the only claimant as an heir,
was a coufin, Marie Cameret, who, in 1639, refided at Rochelle, and whofe hufband was Jacques Herfant, controller
of duties and impofts.  After Champlain's deceafe, his wife,
Hélène Boullé, became a novice in an Urfuline convent in
the faubourg of St. Jacques in Paris.  Subfequently, in
1648, fhe founded a religious houfe of the fame order in the
city of Meaux, contributing for the purpofe the fum of
twenty thoufand livres and fome part of the furnifhing.  She
entered the houfe that fhe had founded, as a nun, under the
name of Sifter *Hélène de St. Auguftin,* where, as the
foundrefs, certain privileges were granted to her, fuch as a
fuperior quality of food for herfelf, exemption from attendance upon fome of the longer fervices, the reception into the
convent, on her recommendation, of a young maiden to be
a nun of the choir, with fuch pecuniary affiftance as fhe
might need, and the letters of her brother, the Father Euftache Boullé, were to be exempted from the ufual infpection.
She died at Meaux, on the 20th day of December, 1654, in
the convent which fhe had founded."[119]

As

[119] *Vide Documents inédits fur Sa-*    ravay,  archivifte-paléographe,  Paris,
*muel de Champlain,* par Étienne Cha-   1875.

As an explorer, Champlain was unfurpaffed by any who
vifited the northern coafts of America anterior to its permanent fettlement.  He was by nature endowed with a love of
ufeful adventure, and for the difcovery of new countries he
had an infatiable thirft.  It began with him as a child, and
was frefh and irrepreffible in his lateft years.  Among the
arts, he affigned to navigation the higheft importance.  His
broad appreciation of it and his ftrong attachment to it, are
finely ftated in his own compact and comprehenfive defcription.

"Of all the moft ufeful and excellent arts, that of navigation
has always feemed to me to occupy the firft place.  For the
more hazardous it is, and the more numerous the perils and
loffes by which it is attended, fo much the more is it efteemed
and exalted above all others, being wholly unfuited to the timid
and irrefolute.  By this art we obtain a knowledge of different countries, regions, and realms.  By it we attract and bring
to our own land all kinds of riches; by it the idolatry of
paganifm is overthrown and Chriftianity proclaimed throughout all the regions of the earth.  This is the art which won
my love in my early years, and induced me to expofe myfelf
almoft all my life to the impetuous waves of the ocean, and
led me to explore the coafts of a part of America, efpecially
thofe of New France, where I have always defired to fee the
Lily flourifh, together with the only religion, catholic, apo-
ftolic, and Roman."

In addition to his natural love for difcovery, Champlain
had a combination of other qualities which rendered his
explorations pre-eminently valuable.  His intereft did not
vanifh with feeing what was new.  It was by no means a

mere

mere fancy for fimple fight-feeing. Reftleffnefs and volatility
did not belong to his temperament. His inveftigations were
never made as an end, but always as a means. His undertakings in this direction were for the moft part fhaped and
colored by his Chriftian principle and his patriotic love of
France. Sometimes one and fometimes the other was more
prominent.

His voyage to the Weft Indies was undertaken under a
twofold impulfe. It gratified his love of exploration and
brought back rare and valuable information to France.
Spain at that time did not open her ifland-ports to the commerce of the world. She was drawing from them vaft revenues in pearls and the precious metals. It was her policy to
keep this whole domain, this rich archipelago, hermetically
fealed, and any foreign veffel approached at the rifk of capture and confifcation. Champlain could not, therefore,
explore this region under a commiffion from France. He
accordingly fought and obtained permiffion to vifit thefe
Spanifh poffeffions under the authority of Spain herfelf. He
entered and perfonally examined all the important ports that
furround and encircle the Caribbean Sea, from the pearl-
bearing Margarita on the fouth, Defeada on the eaft, to Cuba
on the weft, together with the city of Mexico, and the Ifthmus of Panama on the mainland. As the fruit of thefe jour-
neyings, he brought back a report minute in defcription, rich
in details, and luminous with illuftrations. This little brochure, from the circumftances attendant upon its origin, is
unfurpaffed in hiftorical importance by any fimilar or com-
peting document of that period. It muft always remain of
the higheft value as a truftworthy, original authority, without
                                                      which

which it is probable that the hiftory of thofe iflands, for that period, could not be accurately and truthfully written.

Champlain was a pioneer in the exploration of the Atlantic coaft of New England and the eaftern provinces of Canada. From the Strait of Canfeau, at the northeaftern extremity of Nova Scotia, to the Vineyard Sound, on the fouthern limits of Maffachufetts, he made a thorough furvey of the coaft in 1605 and 1606, perfonally examining its moft important harbors, bays, and rivers, mounting its headlands, penetrating its forefts, carefully obferving and elaborately defcribing its foil, its products, and its native inhabitants. Befides lucid and definite defcriptions of the coaft, he executed topographical drawings of numerous points of intereft along our fhores, as Plymouth harbor, Naufet Bay, Stage Harbor at Chatham, Gloucefter Bay, the Bay of Saco, with the long ftretch of Old Orchard Beach and its interfperfed iflands, the mouth of the Kennebec, and as many more on the coaft of New Brunfwick and Nova Scotia. To thefe he added defcriptions, more or lefs definite, of the harbors of Barnftable, Wellfleet, Bofton, of the headland of Cape Anne, Merrimac Bay, the Ifles of Shoals, Cape Porpoife, Richmond's Ifland, Mount Defert, Ifle Haute, Seguin, and the numberlefs other iflands that adorn the exquifite fea-coaft of Maine, as jewels that add a new luftre to the beauty of a peerlefs goddefs.

Other navigators had coafted along our fhores. Some of them had touched at fingle points, of which they made meagre and unfatisfactory furveys. Gofnold had, in 1602, difcovered Savage Rock, but it was fo indefinitely located and defcribed that it cannot even at this day be identified. Re-
folving

folving to make a fettlement on one of the barren iflands
forming the group named in honor of Queen Elizabeth and
ftill bearing her name, after fome weeks fpent in erecting a
ftorehoufe, and in collecting a cargo of "furrs, fkyns, faxa-
fras, and other commodities," the project of a fettlement was
abandoned and he returned to England, leaving, however,
two permanent memorials of his voyage, in the names which
he gave refpectively to Martha's Vineyard and to the headland of Cape Cod.

Captain Martin Pring came to our fhores in 1603, in fearch
of a cargo of faffafras. There are indications that he entered
the Penobfcot. He afterward paid his refpects to Savage
Rock, the undefined *bonanza* of his predeceffor. He foon
found his defired cargo on the Vineyard Iflands, and haftily
returned to England.

Captain George Weymouth, in 1605, was on the coaft of
Maine concurrently, or nearly fo, with Champlain, where he
paffed a month, explored a river, fet up a crofs, and took poffeffion of the country in the name of the king. But where
thefe tranfactions took place is ftill in difpute, fo indefinitely
does his journalift defcribe them.

Captain John Smith, eight years later than Champlain,
furveyed the coaft of New England while his men were collecting a cargo of furs and fifh. He wrote a defcription of
it from memory, part or all of it while a prifoner on board a
French fhip of war off Fayall, and executed a map, both
valuable, but neverthelefs exceedingly indefinite and general
in their character.

Thefe flying vifits to our fhores were not unimportant,
and muft not be undervalued. They were neceffary fteps in
the

the progrefs of the grand hiftorical events that followed. But they were meagre and hafty and fuperficial, when compared to the careful, deliberate, extenfive, and thorough, not to fay exhauftive, explorations made by Champlain.

In the Gulf of St. Lawrence, Cartier had preceded Champlain by a period of more than fixty years. During this long, dreary half-century the ftillnefs of the primeval foreft had not been difturbed by the woodman's axe. When Champlain's eyes fell upon it, it was ftill the fame wild, unfrequented, unredeemed region that it had been to its firft difcoverer. The rivers, bays, and iflands defcribed by Cartier were identified by Champlain, and the names they had already received were permanently fixed by his added authority. The whole gulf and river were re-examined and defcribed anew in his journal. The exploration of the Richelieu and of Lake Champlain was pufhed into the interior three hundred miles from his bafe at Quebec. It reached into a wildernefs and along gentle waters never before feen by any civilized race. It was at once fafcinating and hazardous, environed as it was by vigilant and ferocious favages, who guarded its gates with the fleeplefs watchfulnefs of the fabled Cerberus.

The courage, endurance, and heroifm of Champlain were tefted in the ftill greater exploration of 1615. It extended from Montreal, the whole length of the Ottawa, to Lake Nipiffing, the Georgian Bay, Simcoe, the fyftem of fmall lakes on the fouth, acrofs the Ontario, and finally ending in the interior of the State of New York, a journey through tangled forefts and broken water-courfes of more than a thoufand miles, occupying nearly a year, executed in the

face

face of phyfical fuffering and hardfhip before which a nature
lefs intrepid and determined, lefs loyal to his great purpofe,
lefs generous and unfelfifh, would have yielded at the outfet.
Thefe journeys into the interior, along the courfes of navigable rivers and lakes, and through the primitive forefts, laid
open to the knowledge of the French a domain vaft and indefinite in extent, on which an empire broader and far richer
in refources than the old Gallic France might have been
fuccefsfully reared.

The perfonal explorations of Champlain in the Weft Indies, on the Atlantic coaft, in the Gulf of St. Lawrence, in
the State of New York and of Vermont, and among the
lakes in Canada and thofe that divide the Dominion from
the United States, including the full, explicit, and detailed
journals which he wrote concerning them, place Champlain
undeniably not merely in the front rank, but at the head of
the long lift of explorers and navigators, who early vifited
this part of the continent of North America.

Champlain's literary labors are interefting and important.
They were not profeffional, but incidental, and the natural
outgrowth of the career to which he devoted his life. He
had the fagacity to fee that the fields which he entered as
an explorer were new and important, that the afpect of every
thing which he then faw would, under the influence and
progrefs of civilization, foon be changed, and that it was
hiftorically important that a portrait fketched by an eye-
witnefs fhould be handed down to other generations. It
was likewife neceffary for the immediate and fuccefsful
planting of colonies, that thofe who engaged in the undertaking fhould have before them full information of all the
conditions

conditions on which they were to build their hopes of final fuccefs.

Infpired by fuch motives as thefe, Champlain wrote out an accurate journal of the events that tranfpired about him, of what he perfonally faw, and of the obfervations of others, authenticated by the beft tefts which, under the circumftances, he was able to apply. His natural endowments for this work were of the higheft order. As an obferver he was fagacious, difcriminating, and careful. His judgment was cool, comprehenfive, and judicious. His ftyle is in general clear, logical, and compact. His acquired ability was not, however, extraordinary. He was a fcholar neither by education nor by profeffion. His life was too full of active duties, or too remote from the centres of knowledge for acquifitions in the departments of elegant and refined learning. The period in which he lived was little diftinguifhed for literary culture. A more brilliant day was approaching, but it had not yet appeared. The French language was ftill crude and unpolifhed. It had not been difciplined and moulded into the excellence to which it foon after arofe in the reign of Louis XIV. We cannot in reafon look for a grace, refinement, and flexibility which the French language had not at that time generally attained. But it is eafy to fee under the rude, antique, and now obfolete forms which characterize Champlain's narratives, the elements of a ftyle which, under early difcipline, nicer culture, and a richer vocabulary, might have made it a model for all times. There are, here and there, fome involved, unfinifhed, and obfcure paffages, which feem, indeed, to be the offspring of hafte, or perhaps of carelefs and inadequate proof-reading. But in general his ftyle is with-

26                                                                    out

out ornament, fimple, dignified, concife, and clear. While
he was not a diffufive writer, his works are by no means limited in extent, as they occupy in the late erudite Laverdière's
edition, fix quarto volumes, containing fourteen hundred
pages. In them are three large maps, delineating the whole
northeaftern part of the continent, executed with great care
and labor by his own hand, together with numerous local
drawings, picturing not only bays and harbors, Indian canoes,
wigwams, and fortreffes, but feveral battle fcenes, conveying
a clear idea, not poffible by a mere verbal defcription, of the
favage implements and mode of warfare.[120] His works in-
clude, likewife, a treatife on navigation, full of excellent fuggeftions to the practical feaman of that day, drawn from
his own experience, ftretching over a period of more than
forty years.

The Voyages of Champlain, as an authority, muft always
ftand in the front rank. In truftworthinefs, in richnefs and
fullnefs of detail, they have no competitor in the field of
which they treat. His obfervations upon the character,
manners, cuftoms, habits, and utenfils of the aborigines, were
made before they were modified or influenced in their mode
of life by European civilization. The intercourfe of the
ftrolling fur-trader and fifhermen with them was fo infrequent and brief at that early period, that it made upon them
little or no impreffion. Champlain confequently pictures
the Indian in his original, primeval fimplicity. This will
always

[120] The later fketches made by Champlain are greatly fuperior to thofe which
he executed to illuftrate his voyage in
the Weft Indies. They are not only
accurate, but fome of them are fkilfully
done, and not only do no difcredit to an
amateur, but difcover marks of artiftic
tafte and fkill.

always give to his narratives, in the eye of the hiftorian, the ethnologift, and the antiquary, a peculiar and pre-eminent importance. The refult of perfonal obfervation, eminently truthful and accurate, their teftimony muft in all future time be incomparably the beft that can be obtained relating to the aborigines on this part of the American continent.

In completing this memoir, the reader can hardly fail to be impreffed, not to fay difappointed, by the fact that refults apparently infignificant fhould thus far have followed a life of able, honeft, unfelfifh, heroic labor. The colony was ftill fmall in numbers, the acres fubdued and brought into cultivation were few, and the aggregate yearly products were meagre. But it is to be obferved that the productivenefs of capital and labor and talent, two hundred and feventy years ago, cannot well be compared with the ftandards of to-day. Moreover, the refults of Champlain's career are infignificant rather in appearance than in reality. The work which he did was in laying foundations, while the fuperftructure was to be reared in other years and by other hands. The palace or temple, by its lofty and majeftic proportions, attracts the eye and gratifies the tafte; but its unfeen foundations, with their nicely adjufted arches, without which the fuperftructure would crumble to atoms, are not lefs the refult of the profound knowledge and practical wifdom of the architect. The explorations made by Champlain early and late, the organization and planting of his colonies, the refiftance of avaricious corporations, the holding of numerous favage tribes in friendly alliance, the daily adminiftration of the affairs of the colony, of the favages, and of the corporation in France, to
the

the eminent fatisfaction of all generous and noble-minded patrons, and this for a period of more than thirty years, are proofs of an extraordinary combination of mental and moral qualities. Without impulfivenefs, his warm and tender fympathies imparted to him an unufual power and influence over other men. He was wife, modeft, and judicious in council, prompt, vigorous, and practical in adminiftration, fimple and frugal in his mode of life, perfiftent and unyielding in the execution of his plans, brave and valiant in danger, unfelfifh, honeft, and confcientious in the difcharge of duty. Thefe qualities, rare in combination, were always confpicuous in Champlain, and juftly entitle him to the refpect and admiration of mankind.

## ANNOTATIONES POSTSCRIPTÆ.

USTACHE BOULLÉ. A brother-in-law of Champlain, who made his firſt viſit to Canada in 1618. He was an active aſſiſtant of Champlain, and in 1625 was named his lieutenant. He continued there until the taking of Quebec by the Engliſh in 1629. He ſubſequently took holy orders. —*Vide Doc. inédits ſur Samuel de Champlain*, par Étienne Charavay. Paris, 1875, p. 8.

PONT GRAVÉ. The whole career of this diſtinguiſhed merchant was cloſely aſſociated with Canadian trade. He was in the Gulf of St. Lawrence, in the intereſt of Chauvin, in 1599. He commanded the expedition ſent out by De ·Chaſte in 1603, when Champlain made his firſt exploration of the River St. Lawrence. He was intruſted with the chief management of the trade carried on with the Indians by the various companies and viceroys under Champlain's lieutenancy until the removal of the colony by the Engliſh, when his active life was cloſed by the infirmities of age. He was always a warm and truſted friend of Champlain, who ſought his counſel on all occaſions of importance.

THE

## 206 *Annotationes Postscriptæ.*

THE BIRTH OF CHAMPLAIN. All efforts to fix the exact date of his birth have been unfuccefsful. M. De Richemond, author of a *Biographie de la Charente Inférieure*, inftituted moft careful fearches, particularly with the hope of finding a record of his baptifm. The records of the parifh of Brouage extend back only to Auguft 11, 1615. The duplicates, depofited at the office of the civil tribunal of Marennes anterior to this date, were deftroyed by fire. — *MS. letter of M. De Richemond, Archivift of the Dep. of Charente Inférieure*, La Rochelle, July 17, 1875.

MARC LESCARBOT. We have cited the authority of this writer in this work on many occafions. He was born at Vervins, perhaps about 1585. He became an advocate, and a refident of Paris, and, according to Larouffe, died in 1630. He came to America in 1606, and paffed the winter of that year at the French fettlement near the prefent fite of Lower Granville, on the weftern bank of Annapolis Bafin in Nova Scotia. In the fpring of 1607 he croffed the Bay of Fundy, entered the harbor of St. John, N. B., and extended his voyage as far as De Monts's Ifland in the River St. Croix. He returned to France that fame year, on the breaking up of De Monts's colony. He was the author of the following works: *Hiftoire de la Nouvelle France*, 1609; *Les Mufes de la Nouvelle France ; Tableau de la Suiffe, auquel font décrites les Singularites des Alpes*, Paris, 1618 ; *La Chaffe aux Anglais dans l'ifle de Rhé et au Siège de la Rochelle, et la Réduction de cette Ville en* 1628. Paris, 1629.

PLYMOUTH HARBOR. This note will modify our remarks on p. 78, Vol. II. Champlain entered this harbor on the
18th

18th of July, 1605, and, lingering but a fingle day, failed out of it on the 19th. He named it *Port St. Louis*, or *Port du Cap St. Louis.* — *Vide antea*, pp. 53, 54; Vol. II., pp. 76–78. As the fruit of his brief ftay in the harbor of Plymouth, he made an outline fketch of the bay which preferves moft of its important features. He delineates what is now called on our Coaft Survey maps *Long Beach* and *Duxbury Beach.* At the fouthern extremity of the latter is the headland known as the *Gurnet.* Within the bay he figures two iflands, of which he fpeaks alfo in the text. Thefe two iflands are mentioned in Mourt's Relation, printed in 1622. — *Vide Dexter's ed.* p. 60. They are alfo figured on an old map of the date of 1616, found by J. R. Brodhead in the Royal Archives at the Hague ; likewife on a map by Lucini, without date, but, as it has Bofton on it, it muft have been executed after 1630. Thefe maps may be found in *Doc. His. of the State of New York*, Vol. I.; *Documents relating to the Colonial His. of the State of New York*, Vol. I., p. 13. The reader will find thefe iflands likewife indicated on the map of William Wood, entitled *The South part of New-England, as it is Planted this yeare*, 1634. — *Vide New England Profpect*, Prince Society ed. They appear alfo on Blafkowitz's "Plan of Plimouth," 1774. — *Vide Changes in the Harbor of Plymouth*, by Prof. Henry Mitchell, Chief of Phyfical Hydrography, U. S. Coaft Survey, Report of 1876, Appendix No. 9. In the collections of the Mafs. Hiftorical Society for 1793, Vol. II., in an article entitled *A Topographical Defcription of Duxborough*, but without the author's name, the writer fpeaks of two pleafant iflands within the harbor, and adds that Saquifh was joined to the
Gurnet

Gurnet by a narrow piece of land, but for feveral years the water had made its way acrofs and *infulated* it.

From the early maps to which we have referred, and the foregoing citations, it appears that there were two iflands in the harbor of Plymouth from the time of Champlain till about the beginning of the prefent century. A careful collation of Champlain's map of the harbor with the recent Coaft Survey Charts will render it evident that one of thefe iflands thus figured by Champlain, and by others later, is Saquifh Head; that fince his time a fand-bank has been thrown up and now become permanent, connecting it with the Gurnet by what is now called Saquifh Neck. Prof. Mitchell, in the work already cited, reports that there are now four fathoms lefs of water in the deeper portion of the roadftead than when Champlain explored the harbor in 1605. There muft, therefore, have been an enormous depofit of fand to produce this refult, and this accounts for the neck of fand which has been thrown up and become fixed or permanent, now connecting Saquifh Head with the Gurnet.

MOUNT DESERT. This ifland was difcovered on the fifth day of September, 1604. Champlain having been comiffioned by Sieur De Monts, the Patentee of La Cadie, to make difcoveries on the coaft fouthweft of the Saint Croix, left the mouth of that river in a fmall barque of feventeen or eighteen tons, with twelve failors and two favages as guides, and anchored the fame evening, apparently near Bar Harbor. While here, they explored Frenchman's Bay as far on the north as the Narrows, where Champlain fays the diftance acrofs to the mainland is not more than a hundred paces. The

The next day, on the fixth of the month, they failed two leagues, and came to Otter Creek Cove, which extends up into the ifland a mile or more, neftling between the fpurs of Newport Mountain on the eaft and Green Mountain on the weft. Champlain fays this cove is " at the foot of the mountains," which clearly identifies it, as it is the only one in the neighborhood anfwering to this defcription. In this cove they difcovered feveral favages, who had come there to hunt beavers and to fifh. On a vifit to Otter Cove Cliffs in June, 1880, we were told by an old fifherman ninety years of age, living on the borders of this cove, and the ftatement was confirmed by feveral others, that on the creek at the head of the cove, there was, within his memory, a well-known beaver dam.

The Indians whofe acquaintance Champlain made at this place conducted him among the iflands, to the mouth of the Penobfcot, and finally up the river, to the fite of the prefent city of Bangor. It was on this vifit, on the fifth of September, 1604, that Champlain gave the ifland the name of *Montsdéferts*. The French generally gave to places names that were fignificant. In this inftance they did not depart from their ufual cuftom. The fummits of most of the mountains on this ifland, then as now, were only rocks, being deftitute of trees, and this led Champlain to give its fignificant name, which, in plain Englifh, means the ifland of the defert, wafte, or uncultivatable mountains. If we follow the analogy of the language, either French or Englifh, it fhould be pronounced with the accent on the penult, Mount Défert, and not on the laft fyllable, as we fometimes hear it. This principle cannot be violated without giving to the word a

meaning

meaning which, in this connection, would be obviously inappropriate and abfurd.

CARTE DE LA NOVVELLE FRANCE, 1632. As the map of 1632 has often been referred to in this work, we have introduced into this volume a heliotype copy. The original was publifhed in the year of its date, but it had been completed before Champlain left Quebec in 1629. The reader will bear in mind that it was made from Champlain's perfonal explorations, and from fuch other information as could be obtained from the meagre fources which exifted at that early period, and not from any accurate or fcientific furveys. The information which he obtained from others was derived from more or lefs doubtful fources, coming as it did from fifhermen, fur-traders, and the native inhabitants. The two former undoubtedly conftructed, from time to time, rude maps of the coaft for their own ufe. From thefe Champlain probably obtained valuable hints, and he was thus able to fupplement his own knowledge of the regions with which he was leaft familiar on the Atlantic coaft and in the Gulf of St. Lawrence. Beyond the limits of his perfonal explorations on the weft, his information was wholly derived from the favages. No European had penetrated into thofe regions, if we except his fervant, Étienne Brûlé, whofe defcriptions could have been of very little fervice. The deficiencies of Champlain's map are here accordingly moft apparent. Rivers and lakes farther weft than the Georgian Bay, and fouth of it, are fometimes laid down where none exift, and, again, where they do exift, none are portrayed. The outline of Lake Huron, for illuftration, was entirely mifconceived. A river-like river-like line only of water reprefents Lake Erie, while Lake Michigan does not appear at all.

The delineation of Hudfon's Bay was evidently taken from the TABULA NAUTICA of Henry Hudfon, as we have fhown in Note 297, Vol. II., to which the reader is referred.

It will be obferved that there is no recognition on the map of any Englifh fettlement within the limits of New England. In 1629, when the *Carte de la Nouvelle France* was completed, an Englifh colony had been planted at Plymouth, Mafs., nine years, and another at Pifcataqua, or Portfmouth, N. H., fix years. The Rev. William Blaxton had been for feveral years in occupation of the peninfula of Shawmut, or Bofton. Salem had alfo been fettled one or two years. These laft two may not, it is true, have come to Champlain's knowledge. But none of thefe fettlements are laid down on the map. The reafon of thefe omiffions is obvious. The whole territory from at leaft the 40th degree of north latitude, ftretching indefinitely to the north, was claimed by the French. As poffeffion was, at that day, the moft potent argument for the juftice of a territorial claim, the recognition, on a French map, of thefe Englifh fettlements, would have been an indifcretion which the wife and prudent Champlain would not be likely to commit.

There is, however, a diftinct recognition of an Englifh fettlement farther fouth. Cape Charles and Cape Henry appear at the entrance of Chefapeake Bay. Virginia is infcribed in its proper place, while Jameftown and Point Comfort are referred to by numbers.

On the borders of the map numerous fifh belonging to thefe waters are figured, together with feveral veffels of different

ferent fizes and in different attitudes, thus preferving their
form and ftructure at that period. The degrees of latitude
and longitude are numerically indicated, which are convenient
for the references found in Champlain's journals, but are
neceffarily too inaccurate to be otherwife ufeful. But notwithftanding its defects, when we take into account the limited means at his command, the difficulties which he had to
encounter, the vaft region which it covers, this map muft be
regarded as an extraordinary achievement. It is by far the
moft accurate in outline, and the moft finifhed in detail, of
any that had been attempted of this region anterior to this
date.

THE PORTRAITS OF CHAMPLAIN. — Three engraved portraits of Champlain have come to our knowledge. All of
them appear to have been after an original engraved portrait
by Balthazar Moncornet. This artift was born in Rouen
about 1615, and died not earlier than 1670. He practifed
his art in Paris, where he kept a fhop for the fale of prints.
Though not eminently diftinguifhed as a fkilful artift, he
neverthelefs left many works, particularly a great number of
portraits. As he had not arrived at the age of manhood
when Champlain died, his engraving of him was probably
executed about fifteen or twenty years after that event. At
that time Madame Champlain, his widow, was ftill living, as
likewife many of Champlain's intimate friends. From fome
of them it is probable Moncornet obtained a fketch or portrait, from which his engraving was made.

Of the portraits of Champlain which we have feen, we
may mention firft that in Laverdière's edition of his works.
This

This is a half-length, with long, curling hair, mouftache and imperial. The fleeves of the clofe-fitting coat are flafhed, and around the neck is the broad linen collar of the period, faftened in front with cord and taffels. On the left, in the background, is the promontory of Quebec, with the reprefentation of feveral turreted buildings both in the upper and lower town. On the border of the oval, which inclofes the fubject, is the legend, *Moncornet Ex c. p.* The engraving is coarfely executed, apparently on copper. It is alleged to have been taken from an original Moncornet in France. Our inquiries as to where the original then was, or in whofe poffeffion it then was or is now, have been unfuccefsful. No original, when inquiries were made by Dr. Otis, a fhort time fince, was found to exift in the department of prints in the Bibliothèque Nationale in Paris.

Another portrait of Champlain is found in Shea's tranflation of Charlevoix's Hiftory of New France. This was taken from the portrait of Champlain, which, with that of Cartier, Montcalm, Wolfe, and others, adorns the walls of the reception room of the Speaker of the Houfe of Commons, in the Parliament Houfe at Ottawa, in Canada, which was painted by Thomas Hamel, from a copy of Moncornet's engraving obtained in France by the late M. Faribault. From the coftume and general features, it appears to be after the fame as that contained in Laverdière's edition of Champlain's works, to which we have already referred. The artift has given it a youthful appearance, which fuggefts that the original fketch was made many years before Champlain's death. We are indebted to the politenefs of Dr. Shea for the copies which accompany this work.

A

A third portrait of Champlain may be found in L'Hiſtoire de France, par M. Guizot, Paris, 1876, Vol. v. p. 149. The inſcription reads: " Champlain [Samuel de], d'après un portrait gravé par Moncornet." It is engraved on wood by E. Ronjat, and repreſents the ſubjeĉt in the advanced years of his life. In poſition, coſtume, and accefſories it is widely different from the others, and Moncornet muſt have left more than one engraving of Champlain, or we muſt conclude that the modern artiſts have taken extraordinary liberties with their ſubjeĉt. The features are ſtrong, ſpirited, and charaĉteriſtic. A heliotype copy accompanies this volume.

## PREFACE TO THE TRANSLATION.

THE journals of Champlain, commonly called his Voyages, were written and publifhed by him at intervals from 1603 to 1632. The firft volume was printed in 1603, and entitled, —

1. *Des Savvages, ov, Voyage de Samvel Champlain, de Brovage, faiĉt en la France Nouuelle, l'an mil fix cens trois. A Paris, chez Clavde de Monftr'oeil, tenant fa boutique en la Cour du Palais, au nom de Jefus.* 1604. *Auec priuilège du Roy.* 12mo. 4 preliminary leaves. Text 36 leaves. The title-page contains alfo a fub-title, enumerating in detail the fubjeĉts treated of in the work. Another copy with flight verbal changes has no date on the title-page, but in both the " privilège " is dated November 15, 1603. The copies which we have ufed are in the Library of Harvard College, and in that of Mrs. John Carter Brown, of Providence, R. I.

An Englifh tranflation of this iffue is contained in *Pvr-chas his Pilgrimes.* London, 1625, vol. iv., pp. 1605-1619.

The next publication appeared in 1613, with the following title : —

2. *Les Voyages dv Sievr de Champlain Xaintongeois, Capitaine ordinaire pour le Roy, en la marine. Divifez en devx livres. ou, jovrnal tref-fidele des obfervations faites és*
                                                                                    *defcouuertures*

*defcouuertures de la Nouuelle France: tant en la defcriptiõ
des terres, coftes, riuieres, ports, haures, leurs hauteurs, &
plufieurs delinaifons de la guide-aymant; qu'en la creãce des
peuples, leur fuperftition, façon de viure & de guerroyer:
enrichi de quantité de figures. A Paris, chez Jean Berjon,
rue S. Jean de Beauuais, au Cheual volant, & en fa boutique
au Palais, à la gallerie des prifonniers. M.DC.XIII. Avec
privilege dv Roy.* 4to. 10 preliminary leaves. Text, 325
pages; table 5 pp. One large folding map. One fmall
map. 22 plates. The title-page contains, in addition, a
fub-title in regard to the two maps.

The above-mentioned volume contains, alfo, the Fourth
Voyage, bound in at the end, with the following title: —

*Qvatriefme Voyage dv Sr de Champlain Capitaine ordin-
aire povr le Roy en la marine, & Lieutenant de Monfeigneur
le Prince de Condé en la Nouuelle France, fait en l'annee
1613.* 52 pages. Whether this was alfo iffued as a feparate work, we are not informed.

The copy of this publication of 1613 which we have ufed
is in the Library of Harvard College.

The next publication of Champlain was in 1619. There
was a re-iffue of the fame in 1620 and likewife in 1627.
The title of the laft-mentioned iffue is as follows: —

3. *Voyages et Defcovvertvres faites en la Novvelle France,
depuis l'année 1615. iufques à la fin de l'année 1618. Par le
Sieur de Champlain, Cappitaine ordinaire pour le Roy en la
Mer du Ponant. Seconde Edition. A Paris, chez Clavde Collet, au Palais, en la gallerie des Prifonniers. M.D.C.XXVII.
Avec privilege dv Roy.* 12mo. 8 preliminary leaves. Text
158 leaves, 6 plates. The title-page contains, in addition,

a

LES
VOYAGES
du Sʳ de Cha-
mplain Capita-
ine ordinaire
pour le ROY
et la nouuelle
France es an-
nées 1615
et 1618.

dediés au
ROY e.

chez C. Collet. au
Pallais a Paris.

a fub-title, giving an outline of the contents. The edition of 1627, belonging to the Library of Harvard College, contains likewife an illuminated title-page, which we here give in heliotype. As this illuminated title-page bears the date of 1619, it was probably that of the original edition of that date.

The next and laft publication of Champlain was iffued in 1632, with the following title : —

4. *Les Voyages de la Nouvelle France occidentale, dicte Canada, faits par le S<sup>r</sup> de Champlain Xainctongeois, Capitaine pour le Roy en la Marine du Ponant, & toutes les Defcouuertes qu'il a faites en ce païs depuis l'an* 1603. *iufques en l'an* 1629. *Où fe voit comme ce pays a efté premierement defcouuert par les François, fous l'authorité de nos Roys tref-Chreftiens, iufques au regne de fa Majefté à prefent regnante Lovis XIII. Roy de France & de Navarre. A Paris. Chez Clavde Collet au Palais, en la Gallerie des Prifonniers, à l'Eftoille d'Or. M. DC. XXXII. Auec Priuilege du Roy.* There is alfo a long fub-title, with a ftatement that the volume contains what occurred in New France in 1631. The volume is dedicated to Cardinal Richelieu. 4to. 16 preliminary pages. Text 308 pages. 6 plates, which are the fame as thofe in the edition of 1619. "Seconde Partie," 310 pages. One large general map; table explanatory of map, 8 pages. "Traitté de la Marine," 54 pages. 2 plates. "Doctrine Chreftienne" and "L'Oraifon Dominicale," 20 pages. Another copy gives the name of Seveftre as publifher, and another that of Pierre Le-Mvr.

The publication of 1632 is ftated by Laverdière to have been reiffued in 1640, with a new title and date, but without

further

further changes. This, however, is not found in the National
Library at Paris, which contains all the other editions and
iffues. The copies of the edition of 1632 which we have
confulted are in the Harvard College Library and in the
Bofton Athenæum.

It is of importance to refer, as we have done, to the particular copy ufed, for it appears to have been the cuftom in
the cafe of books printed as early as the above, to keep the
type ftanding, and print iffues at intervals, fometimes without any change in the title-page or date, and yet with alter-
ations to fome extent in the text. For inftance, the copy of
the publication of 1613 in the Harvard College Library
differs from that in Mrs. Brown's Library, at Providence, in
minor points, and particularly in reference to fome changes
in the fmall map. The fame is true of the publication of
1603. The variations are probably in part owing to the
lack of uniformity in fpelling at that period.

None of Champlain's works had been reprinted until 1830,
when there appeared, in two volumes, a reprint of the publication of 1632, "at the expenfe of the government, in order
to give work to printers." Since then there has been publifhed the elaborate work, with extenfive annotations, of the
Abbé Laverdière, as follows : —

ŒUVRES DE CHAMPLAIN, PUBLIÉES SOUS LE PATRONAGE DE
L'UNIVERSITÉ LAVAL. PAR L'ABBÉ C. H. LAVERDIÈRE, M. A.
SECONDE ÉDITION. 6 TOMES. 4TO. QUÉBEC: IMPRIMÉ AU
SÉMINAIRE PAR GEO. E. DESBARATS. 1870.

This contains all the works of Champlain above mentioned,
and the text is a faithful reprint from the early Paris editions. It includes, in addition to this, Champlain's narrative
of

of his voyage to the Weſt Indies, in 1598, of which the following is the title : —

*Brief Diſcovrs des choſes plvs remarqvables qve Sammvel Champlain de Brovage a reconneues aux Indes Occidentalles au voiage qu'il en a faiᴄt en icelles en l'année mil vᶜ iiij.ˣˣ. xix. & en l'année mil vjᶜ. j. comme enſuit.*

This had never before been publiſhed in French, although a tranſlation of it had been iſſued by the Hakluyt Society in 1859. The *MS.* is the only one of Champlain's known to exiſt, excepting a letter to Richelieu, publiſhed by Laverdière among the " Pièces Juſtificatives." When uſed by Laverdière it was in the poſſeſſion of M. Féret, of Dieppe, but has ſince been advertiſed for ſale by the Paris bookſellers, Maiſonneuve & Co., at the price of 15,000 francs, and is now in the poſſeſſion of M. Pinart.

The volume printed in 1632 has been frequently compared with that of 1613, as if the former were merely a ſecond edition of the latter. But this conveys an erroneous idea of the relation between the two. In the firſt place, the volume of 1632 contains what is not given in any of the previous publications of Champlain. That is, it extends his narrative over the period from 1620 to 1632. It likewiſe goes over the ſame ground that is covered not only by the volume of 1613, but alſo by the other ſtill later publications of Champlain, up to 1620. It includes, moreover, a treatiſe on navigation. In the ſecond place, it is an abridgment, and not a ſecond edition in any proper ſenſe. It omits for the most part perſonal details and deſcriptions of the manners and cuſtoms of the Indians, ſo that very much that is eſſential to the full comprehenſion of Champlain's work

as

as an obferver and explorer is gone. Moreover, there feems to be fome internal evidence indicating that this abridgment was not made by Champlain himfelf, and Laverdière fuggefts that the work has been tampered with by another hand. Thus, all favorable allufions to the Récollets, to whom Champlain was friendly, are modified or expunged, while the Jefuits are made to appear in a prominent and favorable light. This queftion has been fpecially confidered by Laverdière in his introduction to the iffue of 1632, to which the reader is referred.

The language ufed by Champlain is effentially the claffic French of the time of Henry IV. The dialect or patois of Saintonge, his native province, was probably underftood and fpoken by him ; but we have not difcovered any influence of it in his writings, either in refpect to idiom or vocabulary. An occafional appearance at court, and his conftant official intercourfe with public men of prominence at Paris and elfewhere, rendered neceffary ftrict attention to the language he ufed.

But though ufing in general the language of court and literature, he offends not unfrequently againft the rules of grammar and logical arrangement. Probably his bufy career did not allow him to read, much lefs ftudy, at leaft in reference to their ftyle, fuch mafterpieces of literature as the " Effais " of Montaigne, the tranflations of Amyot, or the " Hiftoire Univerfelle" of D'Aubigné. The voyages of Cartier he undoubtedly read ; but, although fuperior in point of literary merit to Champlain's writings, they were by no means without their blemifhes, nor were they worthy of being compared with the claffical authors to which we have alluded. But

Champlain's

Champlain's difcourfe is fo ftraightforward, and the thought
fo fimple and clear, that the meaning is feldom obfcure, and
his occafional violations of grammar and loofenefs of ftyle
are quite pardonable in one whofe occupations left him little
time for correction and revifion. Indeed, one rather wonders that the unpretending explorer writes fo well. It is the
thought, not the words, which occupies his attention. Sometimes, after beginning a period which runs on longer than
ufual, his intereft in what he has to narrate feems fo completely to occupy him that he forgets the way in which he
commenced, and concludes in a manner not in logical accordance with the beginning. We fubjoin a paffage or two
illuftrative of his inadvertencies in refpect to language. They
are from his narrative of the voyage of 1603, and the text of
the Paris edition is followed:

1. " Au dit bout du lac, il y a des peuples qui font caban-
nez, puis on entre dans trois autres riuieres, quelques trois
ou quatre iournees dãs chacune, où au bout defdites riuieres,
il y a deux ou trois manieres de lacs, d'où prend la fource
du Saguenay." Chap. iv.

2. " Cedit iour rengeant toufiours ladite cofte du Nort,
iufques à vn lieu où nous relachafmes pour les vents qui
nous eftoiẽt contraires, où il y auoit force rochers & lieux
fort dangereux, nous feufmes trois iours en attendant le beau
temps." Chap. v.

3. " Ce feroit vn grand bien qui pourroit trouuer à la cofte
de la Floride quelque paffage qui allaft donner proche du
fufdit grand lac." Chap. x.

4. " lefquelles [riuieres] vont dans les terres, où le pays y
eft tref-bon & fertille, & de fort bons ports." Chap. x.

5.

222 Preface to the Translation.

5. " Il y a auffi vne autre petite riuiere qui va tomber comme à moitié chemin de celle par où reuint ledict fieur Preuert, où font comme deux manieres de lacs en cefte-dicte riuiere." Chap. xii.

The following paffages are taken at random from the voyages of 1604-10, as illuftrative of Champlain's ftyle in general:

1. Explorations in the Bay of Fundy, Voyage of 1604-8.

" De la riuiere fainct Iean nous fufmes à quatre ifles, en l'vne defquelles nous mifmes pied à terre, & y trouuafmes grande quantité d'oifeaux appellez Margos, dont nous prifmes force petits, qui font auffi bons que pigeonneaux. Le fieur de Poitrincourt f'y penfa efgarer : Mais en fin il reuint à noftre barque comme nous l'allions cerchant autour de ifle, qui eft efloignee de la terre ferme trois lieues." Chap. iii.

2. Explorations in the Vineyard Sound. Voyage of 1604-8.

" Comme nous eufmes fait quelques fix ou fept lieues nous eufmes cognoiffance d'vne ifle que nous nommafmes la foupçonneufe, pour auoir eu plufieurs fois croyance de loing que ce fut autre chofe qu'vne ifle, puis le vent nous vint contraire, qui nous fit relafcher au lieu d'où nous eftions partis, auquel nous fufmes deux on trois jours fans que durant ce temps il vint aucū fauuage fe prefenter à nous." Chap. xv.

3. Fight with the Indians on the Richelieu. Voyage of 1610.

" Les Yroquois f'eftonnoient du bruit de nos arquebufes, & principalemēt de ce que les balles perfoient mieux que leurs flefches ; & eurent tellement l'efpouuāte de l'effet qu'elles faifoient, voyāt plufieurs de leurs cōpaignons tombez morts, & bleffez, que de crainte qu'ils auoient, croyans
ans

ans ces coups eftre fans remede ils fe icttoient par terre, quand ils entendoient le bruit: auffi ne tirions gueres à faute, & deux ou trois balles à chacun coup, & auios la plufpart du temps nos arquebufes appuyees fur le bord de leur barricade." Chap. ii.

The following words, found in the writings of Champlain, are to be noted as ufed by him in a fenfe different from the ordinary one, or as not found in the dictionaries. They occur in the voyages of 1603 and 1604–11. The numbers refer to the continuous pagination in the Quebec edition :

*appoil*, 159. A fpecies of duck. (?)

*catalougue*, 266. A cloth ufed for wrapping up a dead body. Cf. Spanifh *catalogo*.

*déferter*, 211, *et paffim.* In the fenfe of to clear up a new country by removing the trees, &c.

*efplan*, 166. A fmall fifh, like the *équille* of Normandy.

*eftaire*, 250. A kind of mat. Cf. Spanifh *eftera*.

*fleurir*, 247. To break or foam, fpoken of the waves of the fea.

*legueux*, 190. Watery. (?) Or for *ligneux*, fibrous. (?)

*marmette*, 159. A kind of fea-bird.

*Matachias*, 75, *et paffim.* Indian word for ftrings of beads, ufed to ornament the perfon.

*papefi*, 381. Name of one of the fails of a veffel.

*petunoir*, 79. Pipe for fmoking.

*Pilotua*, 82, *et paffim.* Word ufed by the Indians for foothfayer or medicine-man.

*fouler*, 252. In fenfe of, to be wont, accuftomed.

*truitière*, 264. Trout-brook.

The firft and main aim of the tranflator has been to give the

the exact fenfe of the original, and he has endeavored alfo to reproduce as far as poffible the fpirit and tone of Champlain's narrative. The important requifite in a tranflation, that it fhould be pure and idiomatic Englifh, without any transfer of the mode of expreffion peculiar to the foreign language, has not, it is hoped, been violated, at leaft to any great extent. If, perchance, a French term or ufage has been tranf-ferred to the tranflation, it is becaufe it has feemed that the fenfe or fpirit would be better conveyed in this way. At beft, a tranflation comes fhort of the original, and it is perhaps pardonable at times to admit a foreign term, if by this means the fenfe or ftyle feems to be better preferved. It is hoped that the prefent work has been done fo as to fatisfy the demands of the hiftorian, who may find it convenient to ufe it in his inveftigations.

C. P. O.

BOSTON, June 17, 1880.

# THE SAVAGES

OR VOYAGE OF

## SAMUEL DE CHAMPLAIN

OF BROUAGE,

Made in New France in the year 1603.

DESCRIBING,

The customs, mode of life, marriages, wars, and dwellings of the
Savages of Canada. Discoveries for more than four hundred and
fifty leagues in the country. The tribes, animals, rivers, lakes,
islands, lands, trees, and fruits found there. Discoveries on the
coast of La Cadie, and numerous mines existing there according
to the report of the Savages.

PARIS.

Claude de Monstr'œil, having his store in the Court of the Palace,
under the name of Jesus.

*WITH AUTHORITY OF THE KING.*

# DEDICATION.

To the very noble, high and powerful Lord Charles De Montmorency, Chevalier of the Orders of the King, Lord of Ampuille and of Meru, Count of Secondigny, Viscount of Melun, Baron of Chateauneuf and of Gonnort, Admiral of France and of Brittany.

*My Lord,*

*Although many have written about the country of Canada, I have nevertheless been unwilling to rest satisfied with their report, and have visited these regions expressly in order to be able to render a faithful testimony to the truth, which you will see, if it be your pleasure, in the brief narrative which I address to you, and which I beg you may find agreeable, and I pray God for your ever increasing greatness and prosperity, my Lord, and shall remain all my life,*

*Your most humble*
*and obedient servant,*
*S. CHAMPLAIN.*

## EXTRACT FROM THE LICENSE.

BY licenfe of the King, given at Paris on the 15th of November, 1603, figned Brigard.

Permiffion is given to Sieur de Champlain to have printed by fuch printer as may feem good to him, a book which he has compofed, entitled, " The Savages, or Voyage of Sieur de Champlain, made in the Year 1603;" and all book-fellers and printers of this kingdom are forbidden to print, fell, or diftribute faid book, except with the confent of him whom he fhall name and choofe, on penalty of a fine of fifty crowns, of confifcation, and all expenfes, as is more fully ftated in the licenfe.

Said Sieur de Champlain, in accordance with his licenfe, has chofen and given permiffion to Claude de Monftr'œil, book-feller to the Univerfity of Paris, to print faid book, and he has ceded and transferred to him his licenfe, fo that no other perfon can print or have printed, fell, or diftribute it, during the time of five years, except with the confent of faid Monftr'œil, on the penalties contained in the faid licenfe.

# THE SAVAGES.

OR

## VOYAGE OF SIEUR DE CHAMPLAIN

### MADE IN THE YEAR 1603.

---

### CHAPTER I.

E fet out from Honfleur on the 15th of March, 1603. On the fame day we put back to the roadftead of Havre de Grâce, the wind not being favorable. On Sunday following, the 16th, we fet fail on our route. On the 17th. we fighted d'Orgny and Grenefey,[181] iflands between the coaft of Normandy and England. On the 18th of the fame month, we faw the coaft of Brittany. On the 19th, at 7 o'clock in the evening we reckoned that we were off Oueffant.[182] On the 21ft, at 7 o'clock in the morning, we met feven Flemifh veffels, coming,

---

[181] Alderney and Guernfey. French maps at the prefent day for Alderney have d'Aurigny.

[182] The iflands lying off Finiftère, on the weftern extremity of Brittany in France.

ing, as we thought, from the Indies. On Eaſter day, the 30th of the ſame month, we encountered a great tempeſt, which ſeemed to be more lightning than wind, and which laſted for ſeventeen days, though not continuing ſo ſevere as it was on the firſt two days. During this time, we loſt more than we gained. On the 16th of April, to the delight of all, the weather began to be more favorable, and the ſea calmer than it had been, ſo that we continued our courſe until the 28th, when we fell in with a very lofty iceberg. The next day we ſighted a bank of ice more than eight leagues long, accompanied by an infinite number of ſmaller banks, which prevented us from going on. In the opinion of the pilot, theſe maſſes of ice were about a hundred or a hundred and twenty leagues from Canada. We were in latitude 45° 40′, and continued our courſe in 44°.

On the 2nd of May we reached the Bank at 11 o'clock in the forenoon, in 44° 40′. On the 6th of the ſame month we had approached ſo near to land that we heard the ſea beating on the ſhore, which, however, we could not ſee on account of the denſe fog, to which theſe coaſts are ſubject.[133] For this reaſon we put out to ſea again a few leagues, until the next morning, when the weather being clear, we ſighted land, which was Cape St. Mary.[134]

On the 12th we were overtaken by a ſevere gale, laſting two days. On the 15th we ſighted the iſlands of St. Peter.[135] On the 17th we fell in with an ice-bank near Cape Ray, ſix leagues in length, which led us to lower ſail for the entire night

that

[133] The ſhore which they approached was probably Cape Pine, eaſt of Placentia Bay, Newfoundland.

[134] In Placentia Bay, on the ſouthern coaſt of Newfoundland.

[135] Weſt of Placentia Bay.

that we might avoid the danger to which we were expofed. On the next day we fet fail and fighted Cape Ray,[126] the iflands of St. Paul, and Cape St. Lawrence.[127] The latter is on the mainland lying to the fouth, and the diftance from it to Cape Ray is eighteen leagues, that being the breadth of the entrance to the great bay of Canada.[128] On the fame day, about ten o'clock in the morning, we fell in with another bank of ice, more than eight leagues in length. On the 20th, we fighted an ifland fome twenty-five or thirty leagues long, called *Anticofty*,[129] which marks the entrance to the river of Canada. The next day, we fighted Gafpé,[130] a very high land, and began

[126] Cape Ray is northweft of the iflands of St. Peter.

[127] Cape St. Lawrence, now called Cape North, is the northern extremity of the ifland of Cape Breton, and the ifland of St. Paul is a few miles north of it.

[128] The Gulf or Bay of St. Lawrence. It was fo named by Jacques Cartier on his fecond voyage, in 1535. Nous nommafmes la dicte baye la Sainct Laurens. *Brief Récit,* 1545, D'Avezac ed. p. 8. The northeaftern part of it is called on De Laet's map, "Grand Baye."

[129] "This ifland is about one hundred and forty miles long, thirty-five miles broad in its wideft part, with an average breadth of twenty-feven and one-half miles."—*Le Moine's Chronicles of the St. Lawrence,* p. 100. It was named by Cartier in 1535, the Ifland of the Affumption, having been difcovered on the 15th of Auguft, the feftival of the Affumption. Nous auons nommes l'yfle de l'Affumption. — *Brief Récit,* 1545, D'Avezac's ed. p. 9. Alfonfe, in his report of his voyage of 1542, calls it the *Ifle de l'Afcenfion,* probably by miftake. "The Ifle of Afcenfion is a goodly ifle and a goodly champion land, without

any hills, ftanding all vpon white rocks and Alabafter, all couered with wild beafts, as bears, Luferns, Porkefpicks." *Hakluyt,* Vol. III. p. 292. Of this ifland De Laet fays, "Elle eft nommee en langage des Sauuages *Natifcotec.*"—*Hift. du Nouveau Monde,* a Leyde, 1640, p. 42. *Vide alfo Wyet's Voyage* in Hakluyt, Vol. III. p. 241. Laverdière fays the Montagnais now call it *Natafconeh,* which fignifies, *where the bear is caught.* He cites Thevet, who fays it is called by the favages *Naticoufti,* by others *de Laiffle.* The ufe of the name Anticofti by Champlain, now fpelled Anticofti, would imply that its corruption from the original, *Natifcotec,* took place at a very early date. Or it is poffible that Champlain wrote it as he heard it pronounced by the natives, and his orthography may beft reprefent the original.

[130] *Gachepé,* fo written in the text, fubfequently written by the author *Gafpey,* but now generally Gafpé. It is fuppofed to have been derived from the Abnaquis word *Katfepi ooi,* which means what is feparated from the reft, and to have reference to a remarkable rock, three miles above Cape Gafpé, feparated from the fhore by the violence of the waves,

gan to enter the river of Canada, coafting along the fouth side as far as Montanne,[131] diftant fixty-five leagues from Gafpé. Proceeding on our courfe, we came in fight of the Bic,[132] twenty leagues from Mantanne and on the fouthern fhore; continuing farther, we croffed the river to Tadouffac, fifteen leagues from the Bic. All this region is very high, barren, and unproductive.

On the 24th of the month, we came to anchor before Ta-douffac,[133] and on the 26th entered this port, which has the form of a cove. It is at the mouth of the river Saguenay, where there is a current and tide of remarkable fwiftnefs and a great depth of water, and where there are fometimes troublefome winds,[134] in confequence of the cold they bring. It is ftated that it is fome forty-five or fifty leagues up to the firft fall in this river, and that it flows from the northweft. The harbor of Tadouffac is fmall, in which only ten or twelve

veffels

waves, the incident from which it takes its name. — *Vide Voyages de Champlain,* ed. 1632, p. 91; *Chronicles of the St. Lawrence,* by J. M. Le Moine, p. 9.

[131] A river flowing into the St. Lawrence from the fouth in latitude 48° 52' and in longitude weft from Greenwich 67° 32', now known as the Matane.

[132] For Bic, Champlain has *Pic,* which is probably a typographical error. It feems probable that Bic is derived from the French word *bicoque,* which means a place of fmall confideration, a little paltry town. Near the fite of the an-cient Bic, we now have, on modern maps, *Bicoque* Rocks, *Bicquette* Light, *Bic* Ifland, *Bic* Channel, and *Bic* Anchor-age. As fuggefted by Laverdière, this appears to be the identical harbor en-tered by Jacques Cartier, in 1535, who named it the Ifles of Saint John, be-caufe he entered it on the day of the

beheading of St. John, which was the 29th of Auguft. Nous les nommafmes les Yfleaux fainct Jehan, parce que nous y entrafmes le iour de la decollation du-dict fainct. *Brief Récit,* 1545, D'Ave-zac's ed. p. 11. Le Jeune fpeaks of the *Ifle du Bic* in 1635. *Vide Relation des Jéfuites,* p. 19.

[133] *Tadouffac,* or *Tadouchac,* is derived from the word *totouchac,* which in Mon-tagnais means *breafts,* and Saguenay fignifies *water which fprings forth,* from the Montagnais word *faki-nip.* — *Vide Laverdière in loco.* Tadouffac, or the breafts from which water fprings forth, is naturally fuggefted by the rocky elevations at the bafe of which the Saguenay flows.

[134] *Impetueux,* plainly intended to mean *troublefome,* as may be feen from the context.

veffels could lie; but there is water enough on the eaft, fheltered from the river Saguenay, and along a little mountain, which is almoft cut off by the river. On the fhore there are very high mountains, on which there is little earth, but only rocks and fand, which are covered with pine, cyprefs and fir,[135] and a fmallifh fpecies of trees. There is a fmall pond near the harbor, enclofed by wood-covered mountains. At the entrance to the harbor, there are two points: the one on the weft fide extending a league out into the river, and called St. Matthew's Point;[136] the other on the foutheaft fide extending out a quarter of a league, and called All-Devils' Point. This harbor is expofed to the winds from the fouth, foutheaft, and fouth-fouthweft. The diftance from St. Matthew's Point to All-Devils' Point is nearly a league; both points are dry at low tide.

CHAPTER II.

[135] Pine, *pins.* The white pine, *Pinus ftrobus,* or *Strobus Americanus,* grows as far north as Newfoundland, and as far fouth as Georgia. It was obferved by Captain George Weymouth on the Kennebec, and hence deals afterward imported into England were called *Weymouth pine.* — *Vide Chronological Hiftory of Plants,* by Charles Pickering, M.D., Bofton, 1879, p. 809. This is probably the fpecies here referred to by Champlain. Cyprefs, *Cyprez.* This was probably the American arbor vitæ, *Thuja occidentalis,* a fpecies which, according to the Abbé Laverdière, is found in the neighborhood of the Saguenay. Champlain employed the fame word to defignate the American favin, or red cedar, *Juniperus Virginiana,* which he found on Cape Cod. — *Vide* Vol. II. p. 82. Note 168.

Fir, *fapins.* The fir may have been the white fpruce, *Abies alba,* or the black fpruce, *Abies nigra,* or the balfam fir or Canada balfam, *Abies balfamea,*

or yet the hemlock fpruce, *Abies Canadenfis.*

[136] *St. Matthew's Point,* now known as Point aux Allouettes, or Lark Point. — *Vide* Vol. II. p 165, note 292. *All-Devils' Point,* now called *Pointe aux Vaches.* Both of thefe points had changed their names before the publication of Champlain's ed., 1632. — *Vide* p. 119 of that edition. The laft mentioned was called by Champlain, in 1632, *pointe aux roches.* Laverdière thinks *roches* was a typographical error, as Sagard, about the fame time, writes *vaches.* — *Vide Sagard, Hiftoire du Canada,* 1636, Strofs. ed., Vol.1. p. 150. We naturally afk why it was called *pointe aux vaches,* or point of cows. An old French apothegm reads *Le diable eft aux vaches,* the devil is in the cows, for which in Englifh we fay, "the devil is to pay." May not this proverb have fuggefted *vaches* as a fynonyme of *diables?*

## CHAPTER II.

FAVORABLE RECEPTION GIVEN TO THE FRENCH BY THE GRAND SAGAMORE OF
THE SAVAGES OF CANADA. — THE BANQUETS AND DANCES OF THE LATTER.
— THEIR WAR WITH THE IROQUOIS. — THE MATERIAL OF WHICH THEIR
CANOES AND CABINS ARE MADE, AND THEIR MODE OF CONSTRUCTION. —
INCLUDING ALSO A DESCRIPTION OF ST. MATTHEW'S POINT.

N the 27th, we went to vifit the favages at St.
Matthew's point, diftant a league from Tadouffac, accompanied by the two favages whom
Sieur du Pont Gravé took to make a report
of what they had feen in France, and of the
friendly reception the king had given them.  Having landed,
we proceeded to the cabin of their grand Sagamore[37] named
*Anadabijou*, whom we found with fome eighty or a hundred
of his companions celebrating a *tabagie*, that is a banquet.
He received us very cordially, and according to the cuftom
of his country, feating us near himfelf, with all the favages
arranged in rows on both fides of the cabin.  One of
the favages whom we had taken with us began to make
an addrefs, fpeaking of the cordial reception the king had
given them, and the good treatment they had received in
France, and faying they were affured that his Majefty was
favorably difpofed towards them, and was defirous of peo-
pling their country, and of making peace with their enemies,
the Iroquois, or of fending forces to conquer them.  He alfo
told them of the handfome manors, palaces, and houfes they
had

[37] *Sagamo*, thus written in the
French.  According to Laflèche, as
cited by Laverdière, this word, in the
Montagnais language, is derived from
*tchi*. great. and *okimau*. chief, and
confequently fignifies the Great Chief.

had feen, and of the inhabitants and our mode of living. He was liftened to with the greateft poffible filence. Now, after he had finifhed his addrefs, the grand Sagamore, Anadabijou, who had liftened to it attentively, proceeded to take fome tobacco, and give it to Sieur du Pont Gravé of St. Malo, myfelf, and fome other Sagamores, who were near him. After a long fmoke, he began to make his addrefs to all, fpeaking with gravity, ftopping at times a little, and then refuming and faying, that they truly ought to be very glad in having his Majefty for a great friend. They all anfwered with one voice, *Ho, ho, ho,* that is to fay *yes, yes.* He continuing his addrefs faid that he fhould be very glad to have his Majefty people their land, and make war upon their enemies; that there was no nation upon earth to which they were more kindly difpofed than to the French: finally he gave them all to underftand the advantage and profit they could receive from his Majefty. After he had finifhed his addrefs, we went out of his cabin, and they began to celebrate their *tabagie* or banquet, at which they have elk's meat, which is fimilar to beef, alfo that of the bear, feal and beaver, thefe being their ordinary meats, including alfo quantities of fowl. They had eight or ten boilers full of meats, in the middle of this cabin, feparated fome fix feet from each other, each one having its own fire. They were feated on both fides, as I ftated before, each one having his porringer made of bark. When the meat is cooked, fome one diftributes to each his portion in his porringer, when they eat in a very filthy manner. For when their hands are covered with fat, they rub them on their heads or on the hair of their dogs, of which they have large numbers for hunting. Before their
meat

meat was cooked, one of them arofe, took a dog and hopped around thefe boilers from one end of the cabin to the other. Arriving in front of the great Sagamore, he threw his dog violently to the ground, when all with one voice exclaimed, *Ho, ho, ho,* after which he went back to his place. Inftantly another arofe and did the fame, which performance was continued until the meat was cooked. Now after they had finifhed their *tabagie,* they began to dance, taking the heads of their enemies, which were flung on their backs, as a fign of joy. One or two of them fing, keeping time with their hands, which they ftrike on their knees: fometimes they ftop, exclaiming, *Ho, ho, ho,* when they begin dancing again, puffing like a man out of breath. They were having this celebration in honor of the victory they had obtained over the Iroquois, feveral hundred of whom they had killed, whofe heads they had cut off and had with them to contribute to the pomp of their feftivity. Three nations had engaged in the war, the Etechemins, Algonquins, and Montagnais.[18] Thefe, to the number of a thoufand, proceeded to make war upon the Iroquois, whom they encountered at the mouth of the river of the Iroquois, and of whom they killed a hundred. They carry on war only by furprifing their enemies; for they would not dare to do fo otherwife, and fear too much the Iroquois, who are more numerous than the Montagnais, Etechemins, and Algonquins.

On

---

[18] The Etechemins may be faid in general terms to have occupied the territory from St. John. N. B., to Mount Defert Ifland. in Maine, and perhaps ftill further weft, but not fouth of Saco. The Algonquins here referred to were thofe who dwelt on the Ottawa River. The Montagnais occupied the region on both fides of the Saguenay. having their trading centre at Tadouffac War had been carried on for a period we know not how long, perhaps for feveral centuries, between thefe allied tribes and the Iroquois.

On the 28th of this month they came and erected cabins at the harbor of Tadouffac, where our veffel was. At daybreak their grand Sagamore came out from his cabin and went about all the others, crying out to them in a loud voice to break camp to go to Tadouffac, where their good friends were. Each one immediately took down his cabin in an incredibly fhort time, and the great captain was the firft to take his canoe and carry it to the water, where he embarked his wife and children, and a quantity of furs. Thus were launched nearly two hundred canoes, which go wonderfully faft; for, although our fhallop was well manned, yet they went fafter than ourfelves. Two only do the work of propelling the boat, a man and a woman. Their canoes are fome eight or nine feet long, and a foot or a foot and a half broad in the middle, growing narrower towards the two ends. They are very liable to turn over, if one does not underftand how to manage them, for they are made of the bark of trees called *bouille*,[19] ftrengthened on the infide by little ribs of wood ftrongly and neatly made. They are fo light that a man can eafily carry one, and each canoe can carry the weight of a pipe. When they wifh to go overland to fome river where they have bufinefs, they carry their canoes with them.

Their cabins are low and made like tents, being covered with the fame kind of bark as that before mentioned. The whole

[19] *Bouille* for *bouleau*, the birch-tree. *Betula papyracea*, popularly known as the paper or canoe birch. It is a large tree, the bark white, and fplitting into thin layers. It is common in New England, and far to the north. The white birch, *Betula alba*, of Europe and Northern Afia, is ufed for boat-building at the prefent day.—*Vide Chronological Hiftory of Plants*, by Charles Pickering, M.D., Bofton, 1879, p. 134.

whole top for the fpace of about a foot they leave uncovered,
whence the light enters; and they make a number of fires
directly in the middle of the cabin, in which there are fometimes ten families at once.  They fleep on fkins, all together,
and their dogs with them.'⁴⁰

They were in number a thoufand perfons, men, women
and children.  The place at St. Matthew's Point, where they
were firft encamped, is very pleafant.  They were at the foot
of a fmall flope covered with trees, firs and cypreffes.  At
St. Matthew's Point there is a fmall level place, which is feen
at a great diftance.  On the top of this hill there is a level
tract of land, a league long, half a league broad, covered with
trees.  The foil is very fandy, and contains good pafturage.
Elfewhere there are only rocky mountains, which are very
barren.  The tide rifes about this flope, but at low water
leaves it dry for a full half league out.

CHAPTER III.

⁴⁰ The dog was the only domeftic
animal found among the aborigines of
this country.  "The Auftralians," fays
Dr. Pickering, "appear to be the only
confiderable portion of mankind deftitute of the companionfhip of the dog.
The American tribes, from the Arctic
Sea to Cape Horn, had the companionfhip of the dog, and certain remarkable
breeds had been developed before the
vifit of Columbus (F. Columbus 25);
further, according to Coues, the crofs
between the coyote and female dog is
regularly procured by our northweftern
tribes, and, according to Gabb, "dogs
one-fourth coyote are pointed out; the
fact therefore feems eftablifhed that the
coyote or American barking wolfe,
*Canis latrans*, is the dog in its original
wild ftate."—*Vide Chronological Hiftory
of Plants*, etc., by Charles Pickering,
M.D., Bofton, 1879, p. 20.

"It was believed by fome for a length
of time that the wild dog was of recent
introduction to Auftralia; this is not
fo."—*Vide Aborigines of Victoria*, by
R. Brough Smyth, London, 1878, Vol. I.
p. 149.  The bones of the wild dog
have recently been difcovered in Auftralia, at a depth of excavation, and in
circumftances, which prove that his exiftence there antedates the introduction
of any fpecies of the dog by Europeans.
The Auftralians appear, therefore, to be
no exception to the univerfal companionfhip of the dog with man.

## CHAPTER III.

THE REJOICINGS OF THE INDIANS AFTER OBTAINING A VICTORY OVER THEIR
ENEMIES. — THEIR DISPOSITION, ENDURANCE OF HUNGER, AND MALICIOUS-
NESS. — THEIR BELIEFS AND FALSE OPINIONS, COMMUNICATION WITH EVIL
SPIRITS. — THEIR GARMENTS, AND HOW THEY WALK ON THE SNOW. —
THEIR MANNER OF MARRIAGE, AND THE INTERMENT OF THEIR DEAD.

N the 9th of June the favages proceeded to have
a rejoicing all together, and to celebrate their
*tabagie*, which I have before defcribed, and to
dance, in honor of their victory over their enemies. Now, after they had feafted well, the
Algonquins, one of the three nations, left their cabins and
went by themfelves to a public place. Here they arranged
all their wives and daughters by the fide of each other, and
took pofition themfelves behind them, all finging in the
manner I have defcribed before. Suddenly all the wives
and daughters proceeded to throw off their robes of fkins,
prefenting themfelves ftark naked, and expofing their fexual
parts. But they were adorned with *matachiats*, that is beads
and braided ftrings, made of porcupine quills, which they dye
in various colors. After finifhing their fongs, they all faid
together, *Ho, ho, ho :* at the fame inftant all the wives and
daughters covered themfelves with their robes, which were
at their feet. Then, after ftopping a fhort time, all fuddenly
beginning to fing throw off their robes as before. They do
not ftir from their pofition while dancing, and make various
geftures and movements of the body, lifting one foot and
then the other, at the fame time ftriking upon the ground.
Now, during the performance of this dance, the Sagamore

31                                    of

of the Algonquins, named *Beſouat*, was ſeated before theſe
wives and daughters, between two ſticks, on which were hung
the heads of their enemies. Sometimes he aroſe and went
haranguing, and ſaying to the Montagnais and Etechemins :
" Look ! how we rejoice in the victory that we have obtained
over our enemies ; you muſt do the ſame, ſo that we may be
ſatisfied." Then all ſaid together, *Ho, ho, ho*. After returning to his poſition, the grand Sagamore together with all his
companions removed their robes, making themſelves ſtark
naked except their ſexual parts, which are covered with a
ſmall piece of ſkin. Each one took what ſeemed good to
him, as *matachiats*, hatchets, ſwords, kettles, fat, elk fleſh,
ſeal, in a word each one had a preſent, which they proceeded
to give to the Algonquins. After all theſe ceremonies, the
dance ceaſed, and the Algonquins, men and women, carried
their preſents into their cabins. Then two of the moſt agile
men of each nation were taken, whom they cauſed to run,
and he who was the faſteſt in the race, received a preſent.

All theſe people have a very cheerful diſpoſition, laughing
often ; yet at the ſame time they are ſomewhat phlegmatic.
They talk very deliberately, as if deſiring to make themſelves
well underſtood, and ſtopping ſuddenly, they reflect for a
long time, when they reſume their diſcourſe. This is their
uſual manner at their harangues in council, where only the
leading men, the elders, are preſent, the women and children
not attending at all.

All theſe people ſuffer ſo much ſometimes from hunger,
on account of the ſevere cold and ſnow, when the animals
and fowl on which they live go away to warmer countries,
that they are almoſt conſtrained to eat one another. I am of
opinion

opinion that if one were to teach them how to live, and inftruct them in the cultivation of the foil and in other refpects, they would learn very eafily, for I can teftify that many of them have good judgment and refpond very appropriately to whatever queftion may be put to them."[141]   They have the vices of taking revenge and of lying badly, and are people in whom it is not well to put much confidence, except with caution and with force at hand.   They promife well, but keep their word badly.

Moft of them have no law, fo far as I have been able to obferve or learn from the great Sagamore, who told me that they really believed there was a God, who created all things. Whereupon I faid to him : that, " Since they believed in one fole God, how had he placed them in the world, and whence was their origin."   He replied : that, " After God had made all things, he took a large number of arrows, and put them in the ground ; whence fprang men and women, who had been multiplying in the world up to the prefent time, and that this was their origin."   I anfwered that what he faid was falfe, but that there really was one only God, who had created all things upon earth and in the heavens.   Seeing all thefe things fo perfect, but that there was no one to govern here on earth, he took clay from the ground, out of which he created Adam our firft father.   While Adam was fleeping, God took a rib from his fide, from which he formed Eve, whom he gave to him as a companion, and, I told him, that it was true that they and ourfelves had our origin in this manner, and not from arrows, as they fuppofe.   He faid nothing, except that he acknowledged what I faid, rather than

what

[141] *Vide* Vol. II. of this work, p. 190.

what he had aſſerted. I aſked him alſo if he did not believe
that there was more than one only God. He told me their
belief was that there was a God, a Son, a Mother, and the
Sun, making four; that God, however, was above all, that
the Son and the Sun were good, ſince they received good
things from them; but the Mother, he ſaid, was worthleſs,
and ate them up; and the Father not very good. I remon-
ſtrated with him on his error, and contraſted it with our
faith, in which he put ſome little confidence. I aſked him
if they had never ſeen God, nor heard from their anceſtors
that God had come into the world. He ſaid that they had
never ſeen him; but that formerly there were five men who
went towards the ſetting ſun, who met God, who aſked
them : " Where are you going ? " they anſwered : " We are
going in ſearch of our living." God replied to them : " You
will find it here." They went on, without paying attention
to what God had ſaid to them, when he took a ſtone and
touched two of them with it, whereupon they were changed
to ſtones; and he ſaid again to the three others : " Where are
you going ? " They anſwered as before, and God ſaid to
them again : " Go no farther, you will find it here." And
ſeeing that nothing came to them, they went on ; when God
took two ſticks, with which he touched the two firſt, whereupon they were transformed into ſticks, when the fifth one
ſtopped, not wiſhing to go farther. And God aſked him
again : "Where are you going ? " " I am going in ſearch of
my living." " Stay and thou ſhalt find it." He ſtaid without advancing farther, and God gave him ſome meat, which
he ate. After making good cheer, he returned to the other
ſavages, and related to them all the above.

He

He told me alfo that another time there was a man who
had a large quantity of tobacco (a plant from which they
obtain what they fmoke), and that God came to this man,
and afked him where his pipe was. The man took his pipe,
and gave it to God, who fmoked much. After fmoking to
his fatisfaction, God broke the pipe into many pieces, and
the man afked: " Why haft thou broken my pipe? thou
feeft in truth that I have not another." Then God took one
that he had, and gave it to him, faying: " Here is one that
I will give you, take it to your great Sagamore; let him
keep it, and if he keep it well, he will not want for any thing
whatever, neither he nor all his companions." The man
took the pipe, and gave it to his great Sagamore; and while
he kept it, the favages were in want of nothing whatever: but
he faid that afterwards the grand Sagamore loft this pipe,
which was the caufe of the fevere famines they fometimes
have. I afked him if he believed all that; he faid yes, and
that it was the truth. Now I think that this is the reafon
why they fay that God is not very good. But I replied,
" that God was in all refpects good, and that it was doubtlefs the Devil who had manifefted himfelf to thofe men, and
that if they would believe as we did in God they would not
want for what they had need of; that the fun which they
faw, the moon and the ftars, had been created by this great
God, who made heaven and earth, but that they have no
power except that which God has given them; that we believe in this great God, who by His goodnefs had fent us
His dear Son who, being conceived of the Holy Spirit, was
clothed with human flefh in the womb of the Virgin Mary,
lived thirty years on earth, doing an infinitude of miracles,
raifing

raising the dead, healing the sick, driving out devils, giving
sight to the blind, teaching men the will of God his Father,
that they might serve, honor and worship Him, shed his
blood, suffered and died for us, and our sins, and ransomed
the human race; that, being buried, he rose again, descended
into hell, and ascended into heaven, where he is seated on
the right hand of God his Father." [149]   I told him that this
was the faith of all Christians who believe in the Father,
Son, and Holy Spirit; that these, nevertheless, are not three
Gods, but one the same and only God, and a trinity in which
there is no before nor after, no greater nor smaller; that the
Virgin Mary, mother of the Son of God, and all the men and
women who have lived in this world doing the commandments
of God, and enduring martyrdom for his name, and who by
the permission of God have done miracles, and are saints in
heaven in his paradise, are all of them praying this Great
Divine Majesty to pardon us our errors and sins which we
commit against His law and commandments.   And thus, by
the prayers of the saints in heaven and by our own prayers
to his Divine Majesty, He gives what we have need of, and
the devil has no power over us and can do us no harm.   I
told them that if they had this belief, they would be like us,
and that the devil could no longer do them any harm, and
that they would not lack what they had need of.

Then this Sagamore replied to me that he acknowledged
what I said.   I asked him what ceremonies they were accustomed to in praying to their God.   He told me that they were
not accustomed to any ceremonies, but that each prayed in his
heart

[149] This summary of the Christian faith is nearly in the words of the Apostles
Creed.

heart as he defired.  This is why I believe that they have
no law, not knowing what it is to worfhip and pray to God,
and living, the moft of them, like brute beafts.  But I think
that they would fpeedily become good Chriftians, if people
were to colonize their country, of which moft of them were
defirous.

There are fome favages among them whom they call *Pilotoua*,[43] who have perfonal communications with the devil.
Such an one tells them what they are to do, not only in regard to war, but other things; and if he fhould command
them to execute any undertaking, as to kill a Frenchman or
one of their own nation, they would obey his command at
once.

They believe, alfo, that all dreams which they have are
real; and many of them, indeed, fay that they have feen in
dreams things which come to pafs or will come to pafs.
But, to tell the truth in the matter, thefe are vifions of the
devil, who deceives and mifleads them.  This is all that
I have been able to learn from them in regard to their matters of belief, which is of a low, animal nature.

All thefe people are well proportioned in body, without
any deformity, and are alfo agile.  The women are well-
fhaped, full and plump, and of a fwarthy complexion, on
account of the large amount of a certain pigment with
which they rub themfelves, and which gives them an olive
color.  They are clothed in fkins, one part of their body
being covered and the other left uncovered.  In winter they
provide for their whole body, for they are dreffed in good
furs, as thofe of the elk, otter, beaver, feal, ftag, and hind,
which

[43] On *Pilotoua* or *Pilotois, vide* Vol. II. note 341.

which they have in large quantities. In winter, when the fnows
are heavy, they make a fort of *raquette*,[144] two or three times
as large as thofe in France. Thefe they attach to their feet,
and thus walk upon the fnow without finking in ; for without
them, they could not hunt or make their way in many places.

Their manner of marriage is as follows: When a girl
attains the age of fourteen or fifteen years, fhe may have
feveral fuitors and friends, and keep company with fuch as
fhe pleafes. At the end of fome five or fix years fhe may
choofe that one to whom her fancy inclines as her hufband,
and they will live together until the end of their life, unlefs,
after living together a certain period, they fail to have children, when the hufband is at liberty to divorce himfelf and
take another wife, on the ground that his own is of no worth.
Accordingly, the girls are more free than the wives ; yet as
foon as they are married they are chafte, and their hufbands
are for the moft part jealous, and give prefents to the father
or relatives of the girl whom they marry. This is the manner of marriage, and conduct in the fame.

In regard to their interments, when a man or woman dies,
they make a trench, in which they put all their property, as
kettles, furs, axes, bows and arrows, robes, and other things.
Then they put the body in the trench, and cover it with
earth, laying on top many large pieces of wood, and erecting
over all a piece of wood painted red on the upper part.
They believe in the immortality of the foul, and fay that
when they die themfelves, they fhall go to rejoice with their
relatives and friends in other lands.

CHAPTER IV.

[144] *Vue maniere de raquette.* The
fnow-fhoe, which much refembles the
racket or battledore, an inftrument ufed
for ftriking the ball in the game of ten-
nis. This name was given for the want
of one more fpecific.

## CHAPTER IV.

### THE RIVER SAGUENAY AND ITS SOURCE.

N the 11th of June, I went fome twelve or fifteen leagues up the Saguenay, which is a fine river, of remarkable depth. For I think, judging from what I have heard in regard to its fource, that it comes from a very high place, whence a torrent of water defcends with great impetuofity. But the water which proceeds thence is not capable of producing fuch a river as this, which, however, only extends from this torrent, where the firft fall is, to the harbor of Tadouffac, at the mouth of the Saguenay, a diftance of fome forty-five or fifty leagues, it being a good league and a half broad at the wideft place, and a quarter of a league at the narroweft; for which reafon there is a ftrong current. All the country, fo far as I faw it, confifted only of rocky mountains, moftly covered with fir, cyprefs, and birch; a very unattractive region in which I did not find a level tract of land either on the one fide or the other. There are fome iflands in the river, which are high and fandy. In a word, thefe are real deferts, uninhabitable for animals or birds. For I can teftify that when I went hunting in places which feemed to me the moft attractive, I found nothing whatever but little birds, like nightingales and fwallows, which come only in fummer, as I think, on account of the exceffive cold there, this river coming from the northweft.

They told me that, after paffing the firft fall, whence this torrent comes, they pafs eight other falls, when they go a day's

journey without finding any ; then they pafs ten other falls
and enter a lake ¹⁴⁵ which it requires two days to crofs, they
being able to make eafily from twelve to fifteen leagues a day.
At the other extremity of the lake is found a people who
live in cabins.   Then you enter three other rivers, up each
of which the diftance is a journey of fome three or four
days.   At the extremity of thefe rivers are two or three bodies of water, like lakes, in which the Saguenay has its fource,
from which to Tadouffac is a journey of ten days in their
canoes.   There is a large number of cabins on the border of
thefe rivers, occupied by other tribes which come from the
north to exchange with the Montagnais their beaver and
marten fkins for articles of merchandife, which the French
veffels furnifh to the Montagnais.   Thefe favages from the
north fay that they live within fight of a fea which is falt.   If
this is the cafe, I think that it is a gulf of that fea which flows
from the north into the interior, and in faƈt it cannot be
otherwife.¹⁴⁶   This is what I have learned in regard to the
River Saguenay.

CHAPTER V.

¹⁴⁵ This was Lake St. John.   This
defcription is given nearly *verbatim* in
Vol. II. p. 169. — *Vide* notes in the
fame volume, 294, 295.
¹⁴⁶ Champlain appears to have obtained from the Indians a very correƈt
idea not only of the exiftence but of the
charaƈter of Hudfon's Bay, although
that bay was not difcovered by Hudfon
till about feven years later than this.

## CHAPTER V.

DEPARTURE FROM TADOUSSAC FOR THE FALL. — DESCRIPTION OF HARE
ISLAND, ISLE DU COUDRE, ISLE D'ORLÉANS, AND SEVERAL OTHERS. —
OUR ARRIVAL AT QUEBEC

N Wednefday, the eighteenth day of June, we fet out from Tadouffac for the Fall.[147] We paffed near an ifland called Hare Ifland,[148] about two leagues from the northern fhore and fome feven leagues from Tadouffac and five leagues from the fouthern fhore. From Hare Ifland we proceeded along the northern coaft about half a league, to a point extending out into the water, where one muft keep out farther. This point is one league [149] from an ifland called *Ifle au Coudre*, about two leagues wide, the diftance from which to the northern fhore is a league. This ifland has a pretty even furface, growing narrower towards the two ends. At the weftern end there are meadows and rocky points, which extend out fome diftance into the river. This ifland is very pleafant on account of the woods furrounding it. It has a great deal of flate-rock, and the foil is very gravelly; at its extremity there is a rock extending half a league out into the

---

[147] *Saut de St. Louis*, about three leagues above Montreal.

[148] *Ifle au Lieure*. Hare Ifland, fo named by Cartier from the great number of hares which he found there. Le foir feufmes à ladiête yfle, ou trouuafmes grand nôbre de lieures, defquelz eufmes quâtité : & par ce la nômafmes l'yfle es lieures. — *Brief Récit*, par Jacques Cartier, 1545, D'Avezac ed. p. 45.

The diftances are here overeftimated. From Hare Ifland to the northern fhore the diftance is four nautical miles, and to the fouthern fix.

[149] The point neareft to Hare Ifland is Cape Salmon, which is about fix geographical miles from the Ifle au Coudres, and we fhould here correêt the error by reading not one but two leagues. The author did not probably intend to be exaêt.

the water. We went to the north of this ifland,[150] which is twelve leagues diftant from Hare Ifland.

On the Thurfday following, we fet out from here and came to anchor in a dangerous cove on the northern fhore, where there are fome meadows and a little river,[151] and where the favages fometimes erect their cabins. The fame day, continuing to coaft along on the northern fhore, we were obliged by contrary winds to put in at a place where there were many very dangerous rocks and localities. Here we ftayed three days, waiting for fair weather. Both the north-ern and fouthern fhores here are very mountainous, refembling in general thofe of the Saguenay.

On Sunday, the twenty-fecond, we fet out for the Ifland of Orleans,[152] in the neighborhood of which are many iflands on the fouthern fhore. Thefe are low and covered with trees, feem to be very pleafant, and, fo far as I could judge, fome of them are one or two leagues and others half a league in length. About thefe iflands there are only rocks and fhallows, fo that the paffage is very dangerous.

They are diftant fome two leagues from the mainland on the fouth. Thence we coafted along the Ifland of Orleans on the fouth. This is diftant a league from the mainland on the north, is very pleafant and level, and eight leagues long. The coaft on the fouth is low for fome two leagues inland ; the country

---

[150] *Ifle au Coudre.* — *Vide Brief Récit, par Jacques Cartier,* 1545, D'Avezac ed. p. 44 ; alfo Vol. II. of this work, p. 172. Charlevoix fays, whether from tra-dition or on good authority we know not, that "in 1663 an earthquake rooted up a mountain, and threw it upon the Ifle au Coudres, which made it one-half larger than before." — *Letters to the Duchefs of Lefdiguieres,* London, 1763, p. 15.

[151] This was probably about two leagues from the Ifle aux Coudres, where is a fmall ftream which ftill bears the name La Petite Rivière.

[152] *Ifle d'Orléans.* — *Vide* Vol. II. p. 173.

country begins to be low at this ifland, which is perhaps two leagues diftant from the fouthern fhore. It is very danger-ous paffing on the northern fhore, on account of the fand-banks and rocks between the ifland and mainland, and it is almoft entirely dry here at low tide.

At the end of this ifland I faw a torrent of water [153] which defcended from a high elevation on the River of Canada. Upon this elevation the land is uniform and pleafant, al-though in the interior high mountains are feen fome twenty or twenty-five leagues diftant, and near the firft fall of the Saguenay.

We came to anchor at Quebec, a narrow paffage in the River of Canada, which is here fome three hundred paces broad.[154] There is, on the northern fide of this paffage, a very high elevation, which falls off on two fides. Elfe-where the country is uniform and fine, and there are good tracts full of trees, as oaks, cypreffes, birches, firs, and af-pens, alfo wild fruit-trees and vines which, if they were culti-vated, would, in my opinion, be as good as our own. Along the fhore of Quebec, there are diamonds in fome flate-rocks, which are better than thofe of Alençon. From Quebec to Hare Ifland is a diftance of twenty-nine leagues.

CHAPTER VI.

[153] On Champlain's map of the harbor of Quebec he calls this "torrent" *le grand faut de Montmorency,* the grand fall of Montmorency. It was named by Champlain himfelf, and in honor of the "noble, high, and powerful Charles de Montmorency," to whom the jour-nal of this voyage is dedicated. The ftream is fhallow; "in fome places," Charlevoix fays, "not more than ankle deep." The grandeur or impreffive-nefs of the fall, if either of thefe quali-ties can be attributed to it, arifes from its height and not from the volume of water. — *Vide* ed. 1632, p. 123. On Bellin's Atlas Maritime, 1764, its height is put down at *fixty-five feet.* Bay-field's Chart more correctly fays 251 feet above high water fpring tides. — *Vide* Vol. II. of this work, note 308.

[154] *Nous vinfmes mouiller l'ancre à Quebec, qui eft vn deftroict de laditt riuiere de Canadas.* Thefe words very clearly

## CHAPTER VI.

OF THE POINT ST. CROIX AND THE RIVER BATISCAN. — OF THE RIVERS,
ROCKS, ISLANDS, LANDS, TREES, FRUITS, VINES, AND FINE COUNTRY
BETWEEN QUEBEC AND THE TROIS RIVIÈRES.

N Monday, the 23d of this month, we fet out
from Quebec, where the river begins to widen,
fometimes to the extent of a league, then a
league and a half or two leagues at moft. The
country grows finer and finer; it is everywhere
low, without rocks for the moft part. The northern fhore is
covered with rocks and fand-banks ; it is neceffary to go along
the fouthern one about half a league from the fhore. There
are fome fmall rivers, not navigable, except for the canoes of
the favages, and in which there are a great many falls. We
came to anchor at St. Croix, fifteen leagues diftant from
Quebec ; a low point rifing up on both fides.[15]  The country is fine and level, the foil being the beft that I had feen,
with extenfive woods, containing, however, but little fir
and cyprefs. There are found there in large numbers vines,
pears, hazel-nuts, cherries, red and green currants, and certain little radifhes of the fize of a fmall nut, refembling truf-
fles in tafte, which are very good when roafted or boiled.
All this foil is black, without any rocks, excepting that there
is

clearly define the meaning of Quebec,
which is an Indian word, fignifying a
narrowing or a contraction. — *Vide* Vol.
II. p. 175, note 309. The breadth of
the river at this point is undereftimated.
It is not far from 1320 feet, or three-
quarters of a mile.

[16]  The Point of St. Croix, where they
anchored, muft have been what is now
known as Point Platon. Champlain's
diftances are rough eftimates, made
under very unfavorable circumftances,
and far from accurate. Point Platon is
about thirty-five miles from Quebec.

a large quantity of flate. The foil is very foft, and, if well cultivated, would be very productive.

On the north fhore there is a river called Batifcan,[156] extending a great diftance into the interior, along which the Algonquins fometimes come. On the fame fhore there is another river,[157] three leagues below St. Croix, which was as far as Jacques Cartier went up the river at the time of his explorations.[158] The above-mentioned river is pleafant, extending a confiderable diftance inland. All this northern fhore is very even and pleafing.

On Wednefday,[159] the 24th, we fet out from St. Croix, where we had ftayed over a tide and a half in order to proceed the next day by daylight, for this is a peculiar place on account of the great number of rocks in the river, which is almoft entirely dry at low tide; but at half-flood one can begin to advance without difficulty, although it is neceffary to keep a good watch, lead in hand. The tide rifes here nearly three fathoms and a half.

The farther we advanced, the finer the country became. After going fome five leagues and a half, we came to anchor on the northern fhore. On the Wednefday following, we fet out from this place, where the country is flatter than the preceding

---

[156] Champlain does not mention the rivers precifely in their order. On his map of 1612, he has *Contree de Baftifquan* on the weft of Trois Rivières. The river Batifcan empties into the St. Lawrence about four miles weft of the St. Anne. — *Vide Atlas Maritime*, by Bellin, 1764; *Atlas of the Dominion of Canada*, 1875.

[157] River Jacques Cartier, which is in fact about five miles eaft of Point Platon.

[158] Jacques Cartier did, in fact, afcend the St. Lawrence as far as Hochelaga, or Montreal. The Abbé Laverdière fuggefts that Champlain had not at this time feen the reports of Cartier. Had he feen them he would hardly have made this ftatement. Pont Gravé had been here feveral times, and may have been Champlain's incorrect informant. *Vide Laverdière in loco.*

[159] Read Tuefday.

preceding and heavily wooded, as at St. Croix. We paffed
near a fmall ifland covered with vines, and came to anchor on
the fouthern fhore, near a little elevation, upon afcending
which we found a level country. There is another fmall ifland
three leagues from St. Croix, near the fouthern fhore.¹⁶⁰ We
fet out on the following Thurfday from this elevation, and
paffed by a little ifland near the northern fhore. Here I
landed at fix or more fmall rivers, up two of which boats
can go for a confiderable diftance. Another is fome three
hundred feet broad, with fome iflands at its mouth. It extends far into the interior, and is the deepeft of all.¹⁶¹ Thefe
rivers are very pleafant, their fhores being covered with
trees which refemble nut-trees, and have the fame odor; but,
as I faw no fruit, I am inclined to doubt. The favages told
me that they bear fruit like our own.

 Advancing ftill farther, we came to an ifland called St.
Éloi;¹⁶² alfo another little ifland very near the northern fhore.
We paffed between this ifland and the northern fhore, the
diftance from one to the other being fome hundred and fifty
feet; that from the fame ifland to the fouthern fhore, a league
and a half. We paffed alfo near a river large enough for
canoes. All the northern fhore is very good, and one can
fail along there without obftruction; but he fhould keep the
lead in hand in order to avoid certain points. All this fhore
                                                    along

---

¹⁶⁰ Richelieu Ifland, fo called by the
French, as early as 1635, nearly oppofite
Dechambeau Point. — *Vide Laurie's
Chart.* It was called St. Croix up to
1633. *Laverdière in loco.* The Indians
called it *Ka ouapaffinfkakhi.* — *Jefuit
Relations,* 1635, p. 13.

¹⁶¹ This river is now known as the
Sainte Anne. Champlain fays they
named it *Rivière Saincte Marie.* —
*Vide* Quebec ed. Tome III. p. 175;
Vol. II. p. 201 of this work.
¹⁶² An inconfiderable ifland near Batifcan, not laid down on the charts.

along which we coafted confifts of fhifting fands, but a fhort diftance in the interior the land is good.

The Friday following, we fet out from this ifland, and continued to coaft along the northern fhore very near the land, which is low and abundant in trees of good quality as far as the Trois Rivières. Here the temperature begins to be fomewhat different from that of St. Croix, fince the trees are more forward here than in any other place that I had yet feen. From the Trois Rivières to St. Croix the diftance is fifteen leagues. In this river [161] there are fix iflands, three of which are very fmall, the others being from five to fix hundred feet long, very pleafant, and fertile fo far as their fmall extent goes. There is one of thefe in the centre of the above-mentioned river, confronting the River of Canada, and commanding a view of the others, which are diftant from the land from four to five hundred feet on both fides. It is high on the fouthern fide, but lower fomewhat on the northern. This would be, in my judgment, a favorable place in which to make a fettlement, and it could be eafily fortified, for its fituation is ftrong of itfelf, and it is near a large lake which is only fome four leagues diftant. This river extends clofe to the River Saguenay, according to the report of the favages, who go nearly a hundred leagues northward, pafs numerous falls, go overland fome five or fix leagues, enter a lake from which principally
the

[161] The St. Maurice, anciently known as *Trois Rivièrs*, becaufe two iflands in its mouth divide it into three channels. Its Indian name, according to Père Le Jeune, was *Metaberoutin*. It appears to be the fame river mentioned by Cartier in his fecond voyage, which he explored and reported as fhallow and of no importance. He found in it four fmall iflands, which may afterward have been fubdivided into fix. He named it *La Riuiere du Foues.* — *Brief Récit*, par Jacques Cartier, D'Avezac ed. p. 28. *Vide Relations des Jésuites*, 1635, p. 13.

33

the Saguenay has its fource, and thence go to Tadouffac.[184]
I think, likewife, that the fettlement of the Trois Rivières
would be a boon for the freedom of fome tribes, who dare
not come this way in confequence of their enemies, the Iroquois, who occupy the entire borders of the River of Canada; but, if it were fettled, thefe Iroquois and other favages
could be made friendly, or, at leaft, under the protection of
this fettlement, thefe favages would come freely without fear
or danger, the Trois Rivières being a place of paffage. All
the land that I faw on the northern fhore is fandy. We afcended this river for about a league, not being able to proceed farther on account of the ftrong current. We continued
on in a fkiff, for the fake of obfervation, but had not gone
more than a league when we encountered a very narrow fall,
about twelve feet wide, on account of which we could not go
farther. All the country that I faw on the borders of this
river becomes conftantly more mountainous, and contains a
great many firs and cypreffes, but few trees of other kinds.

CHAPTER VII.

[184] An eaftern branch of the St. Maurice River rifes in a fmall lake, from
which Lake St. John, which is an affluent of the Saguenay, may be reached
by a land portage of not more than five
or fix leagues.

## CHAPTER VII.

LENGTH, BREADTH, AND DEPTH OF A LAKE. — OF THE RIVERS THAT FLOW
INTO IT, AND THE ISLANDS IT CONTAINS. — CHARACTER OF THE SUR-
ROUNDING COUNTRY. — OF THE RIVER OF THE IROQUOIS AND THE FOR-
TRESS OF THE SAVAGES WHO MAKE WAR UPON THEM.

N the Saturday following, we fet out from the Trois Rivières, and came to anchor at a lake four leagues diftant. All this region from the Trois Rivières to the entrance to the lake is low and on a level with the water, though fome-what higher on the fouth fide. The land is very good and the pleafanteft yet feen by us. The woods are very open, fo that one could eafily make his way through them.

The next day, the 29th of June,[165] we entered the lake, which is fome fifteen leagues long and feven or eight wide.[166] About a league from its entrance, and on the fouth fide, is a river[167] of confiderable fize and extending into the interior fome fixty or eighty leagues. Farther on, on the fame fide, there is another fmall river, extending about two leagues inland, and, far in, another little lake, which has a length of perhaps

[165] They entered the lake on St. Peter's day, the 29th of June, and, for this reafon doubtlefs, it was fubfe-quently named Lake St. Peter, which name it ftill retains. It was at firft called Lake Angoulême. — *Vide* marginal note in Hakluyt, Vol. III. p. 271. Laverdière cites Thévet to the fame effect.

[166] From the point at which the river flows into the lake to its exit, the dif-tance is about twenty-feven miles and its width about feven miles. Cham-plain's diftances, founded upon rough eftimates made on a firft voyage of diffi-cult navigation, are exceedingly inaccu-rate, and, independent of other data, cannot be relied upon for the identifica-tion of localities.

[167] The author appears to have con-fufed the relative fituations of the two rivers here mentioned. The fmaller one fhould, we think, have been mentioned firft. The larger one was plainly the St. Francis, and the fmaller one the Nicolette.

perhaps three or four leagues.[18] On the northern fhore,
where the land appears very high, you can fee for fome
twenty leagues; but the mountains grow gradually fmaller
towards the weft, which has the appearance of being a flat
region. The favages fay that on thefe mountains the land
is for the moft part poor. The lake above mentioned is
fome three fathoms deep where we paffed, which was nearly
in the middle. Its longitudinal direction is from eaft to
weft, and its lateral one from north to fouth. I think that it
muft contain good fifh, and fuch varieties as we have at
home. We paffed through it this day, and came to anchor
about two leagues up the river, which extends its courfe
farther on, at the entrance to which there are thirty little
iflands.[19] From what I could obferve, fome are two leagues
in extent, others a league and a half, and fome lefs. They
contain numerous nut-trees, which are but little different
from our own, and, as I am inclined to think, the nuts are
good in their feafon. I faw a great many of them under the
trees, which were of two kinds, fome fmall, and others an
inch long; but they were decayed. There are alfo a great
many vines on the fhores of thefe iflands, moft of which,
however, when the waters are high, are fubmerged. The
country here is fuperior to any I have yet feen.

The laft day of June, we fet out from here and went to
the

[18] This would feem to be the *Baie la Vallière*, at the fouthweftern extremity of Lake St. Peter.
[19] The author here refers to the iflands at the weftern extremity of Lake St. Peter, which are very numerous. On Charlevoix's Carte de la Rivière de Richelieu they are called *Ifles de Richelieu*. The more prominent are Monk Ifland, Ifle de Grace, Bear Ifland, Ifle St. Ignace, and Ifle du Pas. Champlain refers to thefe iflands again in 1609, with perhaps a fuller defcription —*Vide* Vol. II. p. 206.

the entrance of the River of the Iroquois,[170] where the favages were encamped and fortified who were on their way to
make war with the former.[171] Their fortrefs is made of a
large number of ftakes clofely preffed againft each other. It
borders on one fide on the fhore of the great river, on the
other on that of the River of the Iroquois. Their canoes
are drawn up by the fide of each other on the fhore, fo that
they may be able to flee quickly in cafe of a furprife from
the Iroquois ; for their fortrefs is covered with oak bark, and
ferves only to give them time to take to their boats.

We went up the River of the Iroquois fome five or fix
leagues, but, becaufe of the ftrong current, could not proceed farther in our barque, which we were alfo unable to
drag overland, on account of the large number of trees on
the fhore. Finding that we could not proceed farther, we
took our fkiff to fee if the current were lefs ftrong above ;
but, on advancing fome two leagues, we found it ftill ftronger,
and were unable to go any farther.[172] As we could do nothing elfe, we returned in our barque. This entire river is
fome three to four hundred paces broad, and very unob-
ftructed. We faw there five iflands, diftant from each other
a quarter or half a league, or at moft a league, one of which,
the neareft, is a league long, the others being very fmall.
All

[170] The Richelieu, flowing from Lake Champlain to the St. Lawrence. For defcription of this river, fee Vol. II. p. 210, note 337. In 1535 the Indians at Montreal pointed out this river as leading to Florida. — *Vide Brief Récit*, par Jacques Cartier, 1545, D'Avezac ed.

[171] The Hurons, Algonquins, and Montagnais were at war with the Iroquois, and the favages affembled here were compofed of fome or all of thefe tribes.

[172] The rapids in the river here were too ftrong for the French barque, or even the fkiff, but were not difficult to pafs with the Indian canoe, as was fully proved in 1609. — *Vide* Vol. II. p. 207 of this work.

All this country is heavily wooded and low, like that which
I had before feen ; but there are more firs and cypreffes than
in other places.   The foil is good, although a little fandy.
The direction of this river is about fouthweft.[173]

The favages fay that fome fifteen leagues from where we
had been there is a fall [174] of great length, around which they
carry their canoes about a quarter of a league, when they
enter a lake, at the entrance to which there are three iflands,
with others farther in.   It may be fome forty or fifty leagues
long and fome twenty-five wide, into which as many as ten
rivers flow, up which canoes can go for a confiderable diftance.[175]   Then, at the other end of this lake, there is another
fall, when another lake is entered, of the fame fize as the
former,[176] at the extremity of which the Iroquois are encamped.   They fay alfo that there is a river [177] extending to
the coaft of Florida, a diftance of perhaps fome hundred or
hundred and forty leagues from the latter lake.   All the
country of the Iroquois is fomewhat mountainous, but has a
very good foil, the climate being moderate, without much
winter.

CHAPTER VIII.

[173] The courfe of the Richelieu is
nearly from the fouth to the north.
[174] The rapids of Chambly.
[175] Lake Champlain, difcovered by
him in 1609. — *Vide* Vol. II. ch. ix.
[176] Lake George.  Champlain either
did not comprehend his Indian inform-
ants, or they greatly exaggerated the
comparative fize of this lake.
[177] The Hudfon River. — *Vide* Vol.
II. p. 218, note 347.

## CHAPTER VIII.

ARRIVAL AT THE FALL. — DESCRIPTION OF THE SAME AND ITS REMARK-
ABLE CHARACTER. — REPORTS OF THE SAVAGES IN REGARD TO THE
END OF THE GREAT RIVER.

ETTING out from the River of the Iroquois, we came to anchor three leagues from there, on the northern fhore. All this country is low, and filled with the various kinds of trees which I have before mentioned.

On the firft day of July we coafted along the northern fhore, where the woods are very open; more fo than in any place we had before feen. The foil is alfo everywhere favorable for cultivation.

I went in a canoe to the fouthern fhore, where I faw a large number of iflands,[178] which abound in fruits, fuch as grapes, walnuts, hazel-nuts, a kind of fruit refembling cheft-nuts, and cherries; alfo in oaks, afpens, poplar, hops, afh, maple, beech, cyprefs, with but few pines and firs. There were, moreover, other fine-looking trees, with which I am not acquainted. There are alfo a great many ftrawberries, rafpberries, and currants, red, green, and blue, together with numerous fmall fruits which grow in thick grafs. There are alfo many wild beafts, fuch as orignacs, ftags, hinds, does, bucks, bears, porcupines, hares, foxes, beavers, otters, mufk-rats, and fome other kinds of animals with which I am not acquainted, which are good to eat, and on which the favages fubfift.[179]

We

[178] Ifle Plat, and at leaft ten other iflets along the fhore before reaching the Verchères. — *Vide* Laurie's Chart.

[179] The reader will obferve that the catalogue of fruits, trees, and animals mentioned above, includes only fuch as are

We paffed an ifland having a very pleafant appearance, fome

are important in commerce. They are, we think, without an exception, of American fpecies, and, confequently, the names given by Champlain are not accurately defcriptive. We notice them in order, and in italics give the name affigned by Champlain in the text.

Grapes. *Vignes*, probably the froft grape, *Vitis cordifolia.* — Pickering's *Chronological Hiftory of Plants*, p. 875.

Walnuts. *Noix*, this name is given in France to what is known in commerce as the Englifh or European walnut, *Juglans regia*, a Perfian fruit now cultivated in moft countries in Europe. For want of a better, Champlain ufed this name to fignify probably the butternut, *Juglans cinerea*, and five varieties of the hickory; the fhag-bark, *Carya alba*, the mocker-nut, *Carya tomentofa*, the fmall-fruited *Carya microcarpa*, the pig-nut, *Carya glabra*, bitter-nut, *Carya amara*, all of which are exclufively American fruits, and are ftill found in the valley of the St. Lawrence. — *MS. Letter of J. M. Le Moine*, of Quebec; Jeffrie's *Natural Hiftory of French Dominions in America*, London, 1760, p. 41.

Hazel-nuts, *noyfettes*. The American filbert or hazel-nut, *Corylus Americana*. The flavor is fine, but the fruit is fmaller and the fhell thicker than that of the European filbert.

"Kind of fruit refembling cheftnuts." This was probably the cheftnut, *Caftanea Americana*. The fruit much refembles the European, but is fmaller and fweeter.

Cherries, *cerifes*. Three kinds may here be included, the wild red cherry, *Prunus Pennfylvanica*, the choke cherry, *Prunus Virginiana*, and the wild black cherry, *Prunus ferotina*.

Oaks, *chefnes*. Probably the more noticeable varieties, as the white oak, *Quercus alba*, and red oak, *Quercus rubra*.

Afpens, *trembles*. The American afpen, *Populus tremuloides*.

Poplar, *pible*. For *piboule*, as fuggefted by Laverdière, a variety of poplar.

Hops, *houblon*. *Humulus lupulus*, found in northern climates, differing from the hop of commerce, which was imported from Europe.

Afh, *frefne*. The white afh, *Fraxinus Americana*, and black afh, *Fraxinus fambucifolia*.

Maple, *érable*. The tree here obferved was probably the rock or fugar maple, *Acer faccharinum*. Several other fpecies belong to this region.

Beech, *heftre*. The American beech, *Fagus ferruginea*, of which there is but one fpecies. — *Vide*, Vol. II. p. 113, note 205.

Cyprefs, *cypres.* — *Vide antea*, note 135.

Strawberry, *fraifes*. The wild ftrawberry, *Fragaria vefca*, and *Fragaria Virginiana*, both fpecies, are found in this region. — *Vide* Pickering's *Chronological Hiftory of Plants*, p. 873.

Rafpberries, *framboifes*. The American rafpberry, *Rubus ftrigofus*.

Currants, red, green, and blue, *groifelles rouges, vertes*, and *bleues*. The firft mentioned is undoubtedly the red currant of our gardens. *Ribes rubrum*. The fecond may have been the unripe fruit of the former. The third doubtlefs the black currant, *Ribes nigrum*, which grows throughout Canada. — *Vide Chronological Hiftory of Plants*, Pickering, p. 871; alfo Vol. II. note 138.

*Orignas*, fo written in the original text. This is, I think, the earlieft mention of this animal under this Algonquin name. It was written, by the French, fometimes *orignac, orignat*, and *orignal. — Vide Jéfuit Relations*, 1635, p. 16; 1636, p. 11, *et paffim*; Sagard, *Hift. du Canada*, 1636, p. 749; *Defcription*

*da*

fome four leagues long and about half a league wide.[180]  I

faw

*de l'Amerique*, par Denys, 1672, p. 27. *Orignac* was ufed interchangeably with *élan*, the name of the elk of northern Europe, regarded by fome as the fame fpecies. — *Vide Mammals*, by Spenfer F. Baird. But the *orignac* of Champlain was the moofe, *Alce Americanus*, peculiar to the northern latitudes of America. Moofe is derived from the Indian word *moofóô*. This animal is the largeft of the *Cervus* family. The males are faid to attain the weight of eleven or twelve hundred pounds. Its horns fometimes weigh fifty or fixty pounds. It is exceedingly fhy and difficult to capture.

Stags, *cerfs*. This is undoubtedly a reference to the caribou, *Cervus tarandus*. Sagard (1636) calls it *Caribou ou afne Sauuages*, caribou or wilde afs. — *Hift. du Canada*, p. 750. La Hontan, 1686, fays harts and caribous are killed both in fummer and winter after the fame manner with the elks (moofes), excepting that the caribous, which are a kind of wild affes, make an eafy efcape when the fnow is hard by virtue of their broad feet (Voyages, p. 59). There are two varieties, the *Cervus tarandus arcticus* and the *Cervus tarandus fylveftris*. The latter is that here referred to and the larger and finer animal, and is ftill found in the forefts of Canada.

Hinds, *biches*, the female of *cerfs*, and does, *dains*, the female of *daim*, the fallow deer. Thefe may refer to the females of the two preceding fpecies, or to additional fpecies as the common red deer, *Cervus Virginianus*, and fome other fpecies or variety. La Hontan in the paffage cited above fpeaks of three, the *elk* which we have fhown to be the moofe, the well-known *caribou*, and the *hart*, which was undoubtedly the common red deer of this region, *Cervus*

*Virginianus*. I learn from Mr. J. M. LeMoine of Quebec, that the Wapiti, *Elaphus Canadenfis* was found in the valley of the St. Lawrence a hundred and forty years ago, feveral horns and bones having been dug up in the foreft, efpecially in the Ottawa diftrict. It is now extinct here, but is ftill found in the neighborhood of Lake Winipeg and further weft. Cartier, in 1535, fpeaks of *dains* and *cerfs*, doubtlefs referring to different fpecies.— *Vide Brief Récit*, D'Avezac ed. p. 31 *verfo*.

Bears, *ours*. The American black bear, *Urfus Americanus*. The grifly bear, *Urfus ferox*, was found on the Ifland of Anticofti. — *Vide Hift. du Canada*, par Sagard, 1636, pp. 148, 750. *La Hontan's Voyages*, 1687, p. 66.

Porcupines, *porc-efpics*. The Canada porcupine, *Hyftrix pilofus*. A nocturnal rodent quadruped, armed with barbed quills, his chief defence when attacked by other animals.

Hares, *lapins*. The American hare, *Lepus Americanus*.

Foxes, *reynards*. Of the fox, *Canis vulpes*, there are feveral fpecies in Canada. The moft common is of a carroty red color, *Vulpes fulvus*. The American crofs fox, *Canis decuffatus*, and the black or filver fox, *Canis argentatus*, are varieties that may have been found there at that period, but are now rarely if ever seen.

Beavers, *caftors*. The American beaver, *Caftor Americanus*. The fur of the beaver was of all others the moft important in the commerce of New France.

Otters, *loutres*. This has reference only to the river otter, *Lutra Canadenfis*. The fea otter, *Lutra marina*, is only

found

faw on the fouthern fhore two high mountains, which appeared to be fome twenty leagues in the interior.[181] The
favages told me that this was the firft fall of the River of the
Iroquois.

On Wednefday following, we fet out from this place, and
made fome five or fix leagues. We faw numerous iflands;
the land on them was low, and they were covered with trees
like thofe of the River of the Iroquois. On the following
day we advanced fome few leagues, and paffed by a great
number of iflands,[182] beautiful on account of the many meadows, which are likewife to be feen on the mainland as well as
on the iflands. The trees here are all very fmall in compar-
ifon with thofe we had already paffed.

We arrived finally, on the fame day, having a fair wind,
at the entrance to the fall. We came to an ifland almoft in
the middle of this entrance, which is a quarter of a league
long.[183] We paffed to the fouth of it, where there were from
three to five feet of water only, with a fathom or two in fome
places, after which we found fuddenly only three or four
feet. There are many rocks and little iflands without any
wood at all, and on a level with the water. From the lower
extremity of the above-mentioned ifland in the middle of the
entrance, the water begins to come with great force. Although

we

found in America on the north-weft
Pacific coaft.

Mufkrat, *rats mufquets.* The mufkrat, *Fiber sibethecus,* fometimes called
mufquafh from the Algonquin word,
*mooʃkooʃʃʃoo,* is found in three varieties, the black, and rarely the pied and
white. For a defcription of this animal
*vide Le Jeune, Jéſuit Relations,* 1635,
pp. 18, 19.

[181] Summits of the Green Mountains.

[182] From the Verchères to Montreal,
the St. Lawrence is full of iflands,
among them St. Therefe and namelefs
others.

[183] This was the Ifland of St. Hélène,
a favorite name given to feveral other
places. He fubfequently called it St.
Hélène, probably from Hélène Boullé,
his wife. Between it and the mainland
on the north flows the *Rapide de Ste.
Marie.* — *Vide Laurie's Chart.*

we had a very favorable wind, yet we could not, in fpite
of all our efforts, advance much. Still, we paffed this ifland
at the entrance of the fall. Finding that we could not proceed, we came to anchor on the northern fhore, oppofite a
little ifland, which abounds in moft of the fruits before mentioned.[184] We at once got our fkiff ready, which had been
expreffly made for paffing this fall, and Sieur Du Pont Gravé
and myfelf embarked in it, together with fome favages whom
we had brought to fhow us the way. After leaving our
barque, we had not gone three hundred feet before we had
to get out, when fome failors got into the water and dragged
our fkiff over. The canoe of the favages went over eafily.
We encountered a great number of little rocks on a level
with the water, which we frequently ftruck.

There are here two large iflands; one on the northern
fide, fome fifteen leagues long and almoft as broad,[185] begins
in the River of Canada, fome twelve leagues towards the
River of the Iroquois, and terminates beyond the fall. The
ifland on the fouth fhore is fome four leagues long and half
a league wide.[186] There is, befides, another ifland [187] near
that on the north, which is perhaps half a league long and a
quarter wide. There is ftill another fmall ifland between that
on the north and the other farther fouth, where we paffed
the entrance to the fall.[188] This being paffed, there is a kind
of

[184] This landing was on the prefent fite of the city of Montreal, and the little ifland, according to Laverdière, is now joined to the mainland by quays.
[185] The ifland of Montreal, here re-ferred to, not including the Ifle Jéfus, is about thirty miles long and nine miles in its greateft width.

[186] The Ifle Perrot is about feven or eight miles long and about three miles wide.
[187] Ifland of St. Paul, fometimes called Nuns' Ifland.
[188] Round Ifland, fituated juft below St. Hélène's, on the eaft, fay about fifty yards diftant.

of lake, in which are all thefe iflands, and which is fome five leagues long and almoft as wide, and which contains a large number of little iflands or rocks. Near the fall there is a mountain,[189] vifible at a confiderable diftance, alfo a fmall river coming from this mountain and falling into the lake.[190] On the fouth, fome three or four mountains are feen, which feem to be fifteen or fixteen leagues off in the interior. There are alfo two rivers; the one [191] reaching to the firft lake of the River of the Iroquois, along which the Algonquins fometimes go to make war upon them, the other near the fall and extending fome feet inland.[192]

On approaching this fall [193] with our little fkiff and the canoe, I faw, to my aftonifhment, a torrent of water defcending with an impetuofity fuch as I have never before witneffed, although it is not very high, there being in fome places only a fathom or two, and at moft but three. It defcends

[189] The mountain in the rear of the city of Montreal, 700 feet in height, difcovered in October, 1535, by Jacques Cartier, to which he gave the name after which the city is called. "Nous nommafmes la dicte montaigne le mont Royal." — *Brief Récit,* 1545, D'Avezac's ed. p. 23. When Cartier made his vifit to this place in 1535, he found on or near the fite of the prefent city of Montreal the famous Indian town called *Hochelaga.* Champlain does not fpeak of it in the text, and it had of courfe entirely difappeared. — *Vide* Cartier's defcription in *Brief Récit,* above cited.

[190] Rivière St. Pierre. This little river is formed by two fmall ftreams flowing one from the north and the other from the fouth fide of the mountain. Bellin and Charlevoix denominate it *La Petite Rivière.* Thefe fmall ftreams do not appear on modern maps, and have probably now entirely difappeared. — *Vide Charlevoix's Carte de l'Ifle de Montreal; Atlas Maritime,* par Sieur Bellin; likewife *Atlas of the Dominion of Canada,* 1875.

[191] The River St. Lambert, according to Laverdière, a fmall ftream from which by a fhort portage the Indian with his canoe could eafily reach Little River, which flows into the bafin of Chambly, the lake referred to by Champlain. This was the route of the Algonquins, at leaft on their return from their raids upon the Iroquois. — *Vide* Vol. II. p. 225.

[192] Laverdière fuppofes this infignificant ftream to be La rivière de la Tortue.

[193] The Falls of St. Louis, or the Lachine rapids.

fcends as if by fteps, and at each defcent there is a remarkable boiling, owing to the force and fwiftnefs with which the
water traverfes the fall, which is about a league in length.
There are many rocks on all fides, while near the middle
there are fome very narrow and long iflands. There are
rapids not only by the fide of thofe iflands on the fouth
fhore, but alfo by thofe on the north, and they are fo dangerous that it is beyond the power of man to pafs through with
a boat, however fmall. We went by land through the woods
a diftance of a league, for the purpofe of feeing the end of
the falls, where there are no more rocks or rapids; but the
water here is fo fwift that it could not be more fo, and this
current continues three or four leagues; fo that it is impoffible to imagine one's being able to go by boats through
thefe falls. But any one defiring to pafs them, fhould provide himfelf with the canoe of the favages, which a man can
eafily carry. For to make a portage by boat could not be
done in a fufficiently brief time to enable one to return to
France, if he defired to winter there. Befides this firft fall,
there are ten others, for the moft part hard to pafs; fo that
it would be a matter of great difficulty and labor to fee and
do by boat what one might propofe to himfelf, except at
great coft, and the rifk of working in vain. But in the canoes
of the favages one can go without reftraint, and quickly,
everywhere, in the fmall as well as large rivers. So that, by
ufing canoes as the favages do, it would be poffible to fee all
there is, good and bad, in a year or two.

The territory on the fide of the fall where we went overland confifts, fo far as we faw it, of very open woods, where
one can go with his armor without much difficulty. The air
is

is milder and the foil better than in any place I have before feen. There are extenfive woods and numerous fruits, as in all the places before mentioned. It is in latitude 45° and fome minutes.

Finding that we could not advance farther, we returned to our barque, where we afked our favages in regard to the continuation of the river, which I directed them to indicate with their hands; fo, alfo, in what direction its fource was. They told us that, after paffing the firft fall,[194] which we had feen, they go up the river fome ten or fifteen leagues with their canoes,[195] extending to the region of the Algonquins, fome fixty leagues diftant from the great river, and that they then pafs five falls, extending, perhaps, eight leagues from the firft to the laft, there being two where they are obliged to carry their canoes.[196] The extent of each fall may be an eighth of a league, or a quarter at moft. After this, they enter a lake,[197] perhaps fome fifteen or fixteen leagues long. Beyond this they enter a river a league broad, and in which they go feveral leagues.[198] Then they enter another lake fome four or five leagues long.[199] After reaching the end of this, they pafs five other falls,[200] the diftance from the firft to the laft being about twenty-five or thirty leagues.
Three

[194] Lachine Rapids.

[195] Paffing through Lake St. Louis, they come to the River Ottawa, fometimes called the River of the Algonquins.

[196] The Cafcades, Cedres and Rapids du Côteau du Lac with fubdivifions. *Laverdière.* La Hontan mentions four rapids between Lake St. Louis and St. Francis, as *Cafcades, Le Cataracte du Trou, Sauts des Cedres,* and *du Buiffon.*

[197] Lake St. Francis, about twenty-five miles long.

[198] Long Saut.

[199] Hardly a lake but rather the river uninterrupted by falls or rapids.

[200] The fmaller rapids, the Galops, Point Cardinal, and others.—*Vide* La Hontan's defcription of his paffage up this river, *New Voyages to N. America,* London, 1735. Vol. I. p. 30.

Three of thefe they pafs by carrying their canoes, and the other two by dragging them in the water, the current not being fo ftrong nor bad as in the cafe of the others. Of all thefe falls, none is fo difficult to pafs as the one we faw. Then they come to a lake fome eighty leagues long,[201] with a great many iflands; the water at its extremity being frefh and the winter mild. At the end of this lake they pafs a fall,[202] fomewhat high and with but little water flowing over. Here they carry their canoes overland about a quarter of a league, in order to pafs the fall, afterwards entering another lake [203] fome fixty leagues long, and containing very good water. Having reached the end, they come to a ftrait [204] two leagues broad and extending a confiderable diftance into the interior. They faid they had never gone any farther, nor feen the end of a lake [205] fome fifteen or fixteen leagues diftant from where they had been, and that thofe relating this to them had not feen any one who had feen it; that fince it was fo large, they would not venture out upon it, for

fear

[201] Lake Ontario. It is one hundred and eighty miles long. —*Garneau.*

[202] Niagara Falls. Champlain does not appear to have obtained from the Indians any adequate idea of the grandeur and magnificence of this fall. The expreffion, *qui eft quelque peu éleué, où il y a peu d'eau, laquelle defcend,* would imply that it was of moderate if not of an inferior character. This may have arifen from the want of a fuitable medium of communication, but it is more likely that the intenfely practical nature of the Indian did not enable him to appreciate or even obferve the beauties by which he was furrounded. The immenfe volume of water and the perpendicular fall of 160 feet render it unfurpaffed in grandeur by any other cataract in the world. Although Champlain appears never to have feen this fall, he had evidently obtained a more accurate defcription of it before 1629.—*Vide* note No. 90 to map in ed. 1632.

[203] Lake Erie, 250 miles long. —*Garneau.*

[204] Detroit river, or the ftrait which connects Lake Erie and Lake St. Clair. —*Atlas of the Dominion of Canada.*

[205] Lake Huron, denominated on early maps *Mer Douce,* the fweet fea of which the knowledge of the Indian guides was very imperfect.

fear of being furprifed by a tempeſt or gale.  They fay that
in fummer the fun fets north of this lake, and in winter
about the middle ; that the water there is very bad, like that
of this fea.²⁰⁶

I aſked them whether from this laſt lake, which they had
feen, the water defcended continuouſly in the river extending
to Gafpé.  They faid no ; that it was from the third lake
only that the water came to Gafpé, but that beyond the laſt
fall, which is of confiderable extent, as I have faid, the water
was almoſt ſtill, and that this lake might take its courfe by
other rivers extending inland either to the north or fouth, of
which there are a large number there, and of which they do
not fee the end.  Now, in my judgment, if fo many rivers flow
into this lake, it muſt of neceſſity be that, having fo fmall a
difcharge at this fall, it ſhould flow off into fome very large
river.  But what leads me to believe that there is no river
through which this lake flows, as would be expeſted, in view
of the large number of rivers that flow into it, is the faſt
that the favages have not feen any river taking its courfe
into the interior, except at the place where they have been.
This leads me to believe that it is the fouth fea which is falt,
as they fay.  But one is not to attach credit to this opinion
without more complete evidence than the little adduced.

This is all that I have aſtually feen refpeſting this matter,
or heard from the favages in refponfe to our interrogatories.

CHAPTER IX.

²⁰⁶ The Indians with whom Cham- | plain came in contaſt on this haſty | vifit in 1603 appear to have had fome | notion of a falt fea, or as they fay | water that is very bad like the fea, | lying in an indefinite region, which | neither they nor their friends had ever | vifited.  The falt fea to which they oc- cafionally referred was probably Hud- | fon's Bay, of which fome knowledge | may have been tranfmitted from the | tribes dwelling near it to others more | remote, and thus paffing from tribe to | tribe till it reached, in rather an inde- | finite ſhape, thofe dwelling on the St. | Lawrence.

## CHAPTER IX.

RETURN FROM THE FALL TO TADOUSSAC. — TESTIMONY OF SEVERAL SAV-
AGES IN REGARD TO THE LENGTH AND COMMENCEMENT OF THE GREAT
RIVER OF CANADA, NUMBER OF THE FALLS, AND THE LAKES WHICH IT
TRAVERSES.

E fet out from the fall on Friday, the fourth of June,[207] and returned the fame day to the river of the Iroquois. On Sunday, the fixth of June, we fet out from here, and came to anchor at the lake. On Monday following, we came to anchor at the Trois Rivières. The fame day, we made fome four leagues beyond the Trois Rivières. The following Tuefday we reached Quebec, and the next day the end of the ifland of Orleans, where the Indians, who were encamped on the mainland to the north, came to us. We queftioned two or three Algonquins, in order to afcertain whether they would agree with thofe whom we had interrogated in regard to the extent and commencement of the River of Canada.

They faid, indicating it by figns, that two or three leagues after paffing the fall which we had feen, there is, on the northern fhore, a river in their territory; that, continuing in the faid great river, they pafs a fall, where they carry their canoes; that they then pafs five other falls comprifing, from the firft to the laft, fome nine or ten leagues, and that thefe falls are not hard to pafs, as they drag their canoes in the
moft

[207] As they were at Lake St. Peter on the 29th of June, it is plain that this fhould read *July.*

35

moſt of them, except at two, where they carry them. After
that, they enter a river which is a ſort of lake, compriſing
ſome ſix or ſeven leagues; and then they paſs five other
falls, where they drag their canoes as before, except at two,
where they carry them as at the firſt; and that, from the
firſt to the laſt, there are ſome twenty or twenty-five leagues.
Then they enter a lake ſome hundred and fifty leagues in
length, and ſome four or five leagues from the entrance of
this lake there is a river ²⁰⁴ extending northward to the Algonquins, and another towards the Iroquois,²⁰⁰ where the ſaid
Algonquins and the Iroquois make war upon each other.
And a little farther along, on the ſouth ſhore of this lake,
there is another river,²¹⁰ extending towards the Iroquois;
then, arriving at the end of this lake, they come to another
fall, where they carry their canoes; beyond this, they enter
another very large lake, as long, perhaps, as the firſt. The
latter they have viſited but very little, they ſaid, and have
heard that, at the end of it, there is a ſea of which they have
not ſeen the end, nor heard that any one has, but that the
water at the point to which they have gone is not ſalt, but
that they are not able to judge of the water beyond, ſince they
have not advanced any farther; that the courſe of the water
is from the weſt towards the eaſt, and that they do not know
whether, beyond the lakes they have ſeen, there is another
watercourſe towards the weſt; that the ſun ſets on the right
of this lake; that is, in my judgment, northweſt more or
leſs; and that, at the firſt lake, the water never freezes, which
                                                        leads

---

²⁰⁴ This river extending north from        ²⁰⁰ The Oſwego River.
Lake Ontario is the river-like Bay of      ²¹⁰ The Geneſee River, after which
Quinté.                                     they come to Niagara Falls.

leads me to conclude that the weather there is moderate."' They faid, moreover, that all the territory of the Algonquins is low land, containing but little wood; but that on the fide of the Iroquois the land is mountainous, although very good and productive, and better than in any place they had feen. The Iroquois dwell fome fifty or fixty leagues from this great lake. This is what they told me they had feen, which differs but very little from the ftatement of the former favages.

On the fame day we went about three leagues, nearly to the Ifle aux Coudres. On Thurfday, the tenth of the month, we came within about a league and a half of Hare Ifland, on the north fhore, where other Indians came to our barque, among whom was a young Algonquin who had travelled a great deal in the aforefaid great lake. We queftioned him very particularly, as we had the other favages. He told us that, fome two or three leagues beyond the fall we had feen, there is a river extending to the place where the Algonquins dwell, and that, proceeding up the great river, there are five falls, fome eight or nine leagues from the firft to the laft, paft three of which they carry their canoes, and in the other two drag them; that each one of thefe falls is, perhaps, a quarter of a league long. Then they enter a lake fome fifteen leagues in extent, after which they pafs five other falls, extending from the firft to the laft fome twenty to twenty-five leagues, only two of which they pafs in their canoes, while at the three others they drag them. After this, they enter a very large lake, fome three hundred leagues in length.
Proceeding

211 We can eafily recognize Lake although this account is exceedingly Ontario, Lake Erie and Niagara Falls, coufufed and inaccurate.

Proceeding fome hundred leagues in this lake, they come to a very large ifland, beyond which the water is good; but that, upon going fome hundred leagues farther, the water has become fomewhat bad, and, upon reaching the end of the lake, it is perfectly falt.   That there is a fall about a league wide, where a very large mafs of water falls into faid lake ; that, when this fall is paffed, one fees no more land on either fide, but only a fea fo large that they have never feen the end of it, nor heard that any one has ; that the fun fets on the right of this lake, at the entrance to which there is a river extending towards the Algonquins, and another towards the Iroquois, by way of which they go to war; that the country of the Iroquois is fomewhat mountainous, though very fertile, there being there a great amount of Indian corn and other products which they do not have in their own country.   That the territory of the Algonquins is low and fertile.

I afked them whether they had knowledge of any mines. They told us that there was a nation called the good Iroquois,[21] who come to barter for the articles of merchandife which the French veffels furnifh the Algonquins, who fay that, towards the north, there is a mine of pure copper, fome bracelets made from which they fhowed us, which they had obtained from the good Iroquois ;[22] that, if we wifhed

to

---

[21] Reference is here made to the Hurons who were nearly related to the Iroquois.   They were called by the French the good Iroquois in diftinction from the Iroquois in the State of New York, with whom they were at war.
[22] A fpecimen of pure copper was

fubfequently prefented to Champlain. — Vol. II. p. 236:  *Vide* a brochure on *Pre-hiftoric Copper Implements.* by the editor, reprinted from the New England Hiftorical and Genealogical Regifter for Jan. 1879 ; alfo reprinted in the Collections of Wis. Hift. Soc., Vol. VIII. 1880.

to go there, they would guide thofe who might be deputed for this object.

This is all that I have been able to afcertain from all parties, their ftatements differing but little from each other, except that the fecond ones who were interrogated faid that they had never drunk falt water; whence it appears that they had not proceeded fo far in faid lake as the others. They differ, alfo, but little in refpect to the diftance, fome making it fhorter and others longer; fo that, according to their ftatement, the diftance from the fall where we had been to the falt fea, which is poffibly the South Sea, is fome four hundred leagues. It is not to be doubted, then, according to their ftatement, that this is none other than the South Sea, the fun fetting where they fay.

On Friday, the tenth of this month,[214] we returned to Tadouffac, where our veffel lay.

## CHAPTER X.

VOYAGE FROM TADOUSSAC TO ISLE PERCÉE. — DESCRIPTION OF MOLUËS BAY, THE ISLAND OF BONAVENTURE, BAY OF CHALEUR: ALSO SEVERAL RIVERS, LAKES, AND COUNTRIES WHERE THERE ARE VARIOUS KINDS OF MINES.

AT once, after arriving at Tadouffac, we embarked for Gafpé, about a hundred leagues diftant. On the thirteenth day of the month, we met a troop of favages encamped on the fouth fhore, nearly half way between Tadouffac and Gafpé. The name of the Sagamore who led them is Armouchides, who is

---

[214] Friday, July 11th.

is regarded as one of the moſt intelligent and daring of the
ſavages. He was going to Tadouſſac to barter their arrows
and orignac meat[214] for beavers and martens[215] with the
Montagnais, Etchemins, and Algonquins.

On the 15th day of the month we arrived at Gaſpé, ſituated on the northern ſhore of a bay, and about a league and
a half from the entrance. This bay is ſome ſeven or eight
leagues long, and four leagues broad at its entrance. There
is a river there extending ſome thirty leagues inland.[217]
Then we ſaw another bay, called *Moluës Bay*,[218] ſome three
leagues long and as many wide at its entrance. Thence we
come to Iſle Percée,[219] a ſort of rock, which is very high and
ſteep on two ſides, with a hole through which ſhallops and
boats can paſs at high tide. At low tide, you can go from
the mainland to this iſland, which is only ſome four or five
hundred feet diſtant. There is alſo another iſland, about a
league ſoutheaſt of Iſle Percée, called the Iſland of Bonaventure, which is, perhaps, half a league long. Gaſpé,
Moluës Bay, and Iſle Percée are all places where dry and
green fiſhing is carried on.

Beyond Iſle Percée there is a bay, called *Baye de Chaleurs*,[220]
extending

[214] *Orignac.* Mooſe. — *Vide antea,*
note 179.

[215] Martens, *martres.* This may in-
clude the pine-marten, *Muſtela martes,*
and the pecan or fiſher, *Muſtela Cana-
denſis,* both of which were found in large
numbers in New France.

[216] York River.

[217] Molues Bay, *Baye des Moluès.*
Now known as Mal-Bay, from *morue,*
codfiſh, a corruption from the old orthography *molue* and *baie,* codfiſh bay,
the name having been originally ap-

plied on account of the excellent fiſh
of the neighborhood. The harbor of
Mal-Bay is encloſed between two points,
Point Peter on the north, and a high
rocky promontory on the ſouth, whoſe
cliffs riſe to the height of 666 feet. —
*Vide Charts of the St. Lawrence by
Captain H. W. Bayfield.*

[219] *Iſle Percée.* — *Vide* Vol. II. note
290.

[220] *Baye de Chaleurs.* This bay was
ſo named by Jacques Cartier on account
of the exceſſive heat, *chaleur,* experienced

extending fome eighty leagues weft-fouthweft inland, and fome fifteen leagues broad at its entrance. The Canadian favages fay that fome fixty leagues along the fouthern fhore of the great River of Canada, there is a little river called Mantanne, extending fome eighteen leagues inland, at the end of which they carry their canoes about a league by land, and come to the Baye de Chaleurs,[221] whence they go fometimes to Ifle Percée. They alfo go from this bay to Tregate[222] and Mifamichy.[223]

Proceeding along this coaft, you pafs a large number of rivers, and reach a place where there is one called *Souricoua*, by way of which Sieur Prevert went to explore a copper mine. They go with their canoes up this river for two or three days, when they go overland fome two or three leagues to the faid mine, which is fituated on the feafhore fouthward. At the entrance to the above-mentioned river there is an ifland[224] about a league out, from which ifland to Ifle Percée is a diftance of fome fixty or feventy leagues. Then, continuing along this coaft, which runs towards the eaft, you come to a ftrait about two leagues broad and twenty-five long.

rienced there on his firft voyage in 1634. — *Vide Voyage de Jacques Cartier*, Mechelant, ed. Paris, 1865, p. 50. The depth of the bay is about ninety miles and its width at the entrance is about eighteen. It receives the Riftigouche and other rivers.

[221] By a portage of about three leagues from the river Matane to the Matapedia, the Bay of Chaleur may be reached by water.

[222] *Tregaté*, Tracadie. By a very fhort portage between Bafs River and the Big Tracadie River, this place may be reached.

[223] *Mifamichy*, Miramichi. This is reached by a fhort portage from the Nepifiguit to the head waters of the Miramichi.

[224] It is obvious from this defcription that the ifland above mentioned is Shediac Ifland, and the river was one of the feveral emptying into Shediac Bay, and named *Souricoua*, as by it the Indians went to the Souriquois or Micmacs in Nova Scotia.

long.[1]   On the eaſt ſide of it is an iſland named *St. Law-*
*rence*,[2] on which is Cape Breton, and where a tribe of ſavages called the *Souriquois* winter.  Paſſing the ſtrait of the
Iſland of St. Lawrence, and coaſting along the ſhore of La
Cadie, you come to a bay [3] on which this copper mine is ſituated.  Advancing ſtill farther, you find a river [4] extending
ſome ſixty or eighty leagues inland, and nearly to the Lake
of the Iroquois, along which the ſavages of the coaſt of La
Cadie go to make war upon the latter.

One would accompliſh a great good by diſcovering, on the
coaſt of Florida, ſome paſſage running near to the great lake
before referred to, where the water is ſalt ; not only on account of the navigation of veſſels, which would not then be
expoſed to ſo great riſks as in going by way of Canada, but
alſo on account of the ſhortening of the diſtance by more
than three hundred leagues.  And it is certain that there
are rivers on the coaſt of Florida, not yet diſcovered, extending into the interior, where the land is very good and fertile,
and containing very good harbors.  The country and coaſt
of Florida may have a different temperature and be more
productive in fruits and other things than that which I have
ſeen ; but there cannot be there any lands more level nor of
a better quality than thoſe we have ſeen.

The ſavages ſay that, in this great Baye de Chaleurs, there
is a river extending ſome twenty leagues into the interior,
at

---

[3] The Strait of Canſeau.
[2] *St. Lawrence.*  This iſland had
then borne the name of the *Iſland of
Cape Breton* for a hundred years.
[1] The Bay of Fundy.

[4] The River St. John by which they
reached the St. Lawrence, and through
the River Richelieu the lake of the Iroquois.  It was named Lake Champlain
in 1609.  *Vide* Vol. II. p. 223.

at the extremity of which is a lake [229] fome twenty leagues in extent, but with very little water; that it dries up in fummer, when they find in it, a foot or foot and a half under ground, a kind of metal refembling the filver which I fhowed them, and that in another place, near this lake, there is a copper mine.

This is what I learned from thefe favages.

## CHAPTER XI.

RETURN FROM ISLE PERCÉE TO TADOUSSAC. — DESCRIPTION OF THE COVES, HARBORS, RIVERS, ISLANDS, ROCKS, FALLS, BAYS, AND SHALLOWS ALONG THE NORTHERN SHORE.

E fet out from Ifle Percée on the nineteenth of the month, on our return to Tadouffac. When we were fome three leagues from Cape Évêque [230] we encountered a tempeft, which lafted two days, and obliged us to put into a large cove and wait for fair weather. The next day we fet out from there and again encountered another tempeft. Not wifhing to put back, and thinking that we could make our way, we proceeded to the north fhore on the 28th of July, and came to anchor in a cove which is very dangerous on account of its rocky banks. This cove is in latitude 51° and fome minutes. [231]

The

[229] By traverfing the Riftigouche River, the Matapediac may be reached, the lake here defignated.

[230] *Évefque.* This cape cannot be identified.

[231] On paffing to the northern fhore of the St. Lawrence, they entered, according to the conjecture of Laverdière, Moifie Bay. It feems to us, however, more likely that they entered a cove fome-where

The next day we anchored near a river called St. Margaret,
where the depth is fome three fathoms at full tide, and a fathom and a half at low tide. It extends a confiderable diftance
inland. So far as I obferved the eaftern fhore inland, there is
a waterfall fome fifty or fixty fathoms in extent, flowing into
this river; from this comes the greater part of the water
compofing it. At its mouth there is a fand-bank, where there
is, perhaps, at low tide, half a fathom of water. All along
the eaftern fhore there is moving fand ; and here there is a
point fome half a league from the above mentioned river,²²
extending out half a league, and on the weftern fhore there
is a little ifland. This place is in latitude 50°. All thefe
lands are very poor, and covered with firs. The country is
fomewhat high, but not fo much fo as that on the fouth fide.

After going fome three leagues, we paffed another river,²³
apparently very large, but the entrance is, for the moft part,
filled with rocks. Some eight leagues diftant from there,
is a point ²⁴ extending out a league and a half, where there
is only a fathom and a half of water. Some four leagues
beyond

beyond this point, there is another, where there is water enough.²³⁵  All this coaſt is low and ſandy.

Some four leagues beyond there is a cove into which a river enters.²³⁶  This place is capable of containing a large number of veſſels on its weſtern ſide.  There is a low point extending out about a league.  One muſt ſail along the eaſtern ſide for ſome three hundred paces in order to enter.  This is the beſt harbor along all the northern coaſt; yet it is very dangerous ſailing there on account of the ſhallows and ſand-banks along the greater part of the coaſt for nearly two leagues from the ſhore.

Some ſix leagues farther on is a bay,²³⁷ where there is a ſandy iſland.  This entire bay is very ſhoal, except on the eaſtern ſide, where there are ſome four fathoms of water.  In the channel which enters this bay, ſome four leagues from there, is a fine cove, into which a river flows.  There is a large fall on it.  All this coaſt is low and ſandy.  Some five leagues beyond, is a point extending out about half a league,²³⁸ in which there is a cove; and from one point to the other is a diſtance of three leagues; which, however, is only ſhoals with little water.

Some two leagues farther on, is a ſtrand with a good harbor

²³⁵ Point St. Nicholas. — *Laverdière.* This is probably the point referred to, although the diſtance is again three times too great.

²³⁶ The Manicouagan River.—*Laverdière.* The diſtance is ſtill exceſſive, but in other reſpects the deſcription in the text identifies this river.  On Bellin's map this river is called Rivière Noire.

²³⁷ Outard Bay.  The iſland does not now appear.  It was probably an iſland of ſand, which has ſince been ſwept away, unleſs it was the ſandy peninſula lying between Outard and Manicoua-gan Rivers.  The fall is laid down on Bayfield's chart.

²³⁸ Berſimis Point.  Walker and Miles have *Betſiamites,* Bellin, *Berſiamites,* Laverdière, *Betſiamis,* and Bayfield, *Ber-ſimis.*  The text deſcribes the locality with ſufficient accuracy.

bor and a little river, in which there are three iflands,[339] and in which veffels could take fhelter.

Some three leagues from there, is a fandy point,[340] extending out about a league, at the end of which is a little ifland. Then, going on to the Efquemin,[341] you come to two fmall, low iflands and a little rock near the fhore. Thefe iflands are about half a league from the Efquemin, which is a very bad harbor, furrounded by rocks and dry at low tide, and, in order to enter, one muft tack and go in behind a little rocky point, where there is room enough for only one veffel. A little farther on, is a river extending fome little diftance into the interior; this is the place where the Bafques carry on the whale-fifhery.[342] To tell the truth, the harbor is of no account at all.

We went thence to the harbor of Tadouffac, on the third of Auguft. All thefe lands above-mentioned along the fhore are low, while the interior is high. They are not so attractive or fertile as thofe on the fouth fhore, although lower.

This is precifely what I have feen of this northern fhore.

CHAPTER XII.

[339] Jeremy Ifland. Bellin, 1764, lays down three iflands, but Bayfield, 1834, has but one. Two of them appear to have been fwept away or united in one.
[340] Three leagues would indicate Point Colombier. But Laverdière fuggefts Mille Vaches as better conforming to the defcription in the text, although the diftance is three times too great.

[341] *Efquemin*. Walker and Miles have *Efcoumain*, Bellin, *Lefquemin*, Bayfield, *Efquamine*, and Laverdière, *Efcoumins*. The river half a league diftant is now called River Romaine.
[342] The River Leffumen, a fhort diftance from which is *Anfe aux Bafques*, or Bafque Cove. This is probably the locality referred to in the text.

## CHAPTER XII.

CEREMONIES OF THE SAVAGES BEFORE ENGAGING IN WAR. — OF THE AL-
MOUCHICOIS SAVAGES AND THEIR STRANGE FORM. — NARRATIVE OF
STEUR DE PREVERT OF ST. MALO ON THE EXPLORATION OF THE LA
CADIAN COAST; WHAT MINES THERE ARE THERE; THE EXCELLENCE
AND FERTILITY OF THE COUNTRY.

PON arriving at Tadouffac, we found the favages,
whom we had met at the River of the Iroquois,
and who had had an encounter at the firft lake
with three Iroquois canoes, there being ten
of the Montagnais. The latter brought back
the heads of the Iroquois to Tadouffac, there being only
one Montagnais wounded, which was in the arm by an arrow; and in cafe he fhould have a dream, it would be neceffary for all the ten others to execute it in order to fatisfy
him, they thinking, moreover, that his wound would thereby
do better. If this favage fhould die, his relatives would
avenge his death either on his own tribe or others, or it
would be neceffary for the captains to make prefents to the
relatives of the deceafed, in order to content them, otherwife, as I have faid, they would practife vengeance, which is
a great evil among them.

Before thefe Montagnais fet out for the war, they all gathered together in their richeft fur garments of beaver and
other fkins, adorned with beads and belts of various colors.
They affembled in a large public place, in the prefence of a
fagamore named Begourat, who led them to the war. They
were arranged one behind the other, with their bows and
arrows, clubs, and round fhields with which they provide
themfelves

themfelves for fighting. They went leaping one after the
other, making various geftures with their bodies, and many
fnail-like turns. Afterwards they proceeded to dance in the
cuftomary manner, as I have before defcribed ; then they
had their *tabagie*, after which the women ftripped themfelves
ftark naked, adorned with their handfomeft *matachiats*. Thus
naked and dancing, they entered their canoes, when they
put out upon the water, ftriking each other with their oars,
and throwing quantities of water at one another. But they
did themfelves no harm, fince they parried the blows hurled
at each other. After all thefe ceremonies, the women withdrew to their cabins, and the men went to the war againft
the Iroquois.

On the fixteenth of Auguft we fet out from Tadouffac,
and arrived on the eighteenth at Ifle Percée, where we found
Sieur Prevert of St. Malo, who came from the mine where he
had gone with much difficulty, from the fear which the favages
had of meeting their enemies, the Almouchicois,[343] who are
favages of an exceedingly ftrange form, for their head is
fmall and body fhort, their arms flender as thofe of a fkele-
ton, fo alfo the thighs, their legs big and long and of uniform fize, and when they are feated on the ground, their
knees extend more than half a foot above the head, fomething ftrange and feemingly abnormal. They are, however,
very agile and refolute, and are fettled upon the beft lands
of

[343] *Almouchiquois.* Champlain here
writes *Armouchicois.* The account here
given to Prevert, by the Souriquois or
Micmacs, as they have been more re-
cently called, of the Almouchicois or    Indians found fouth of Saco, on the coaft
of Maffachufetts, if accurately reported,
is far from correct. *Vide* Champlain's
defcription of them, Vol. II. p. 63, *et
paffim.*

of all the coaft of La Cadie; [244] fo that the Souriquois fear them greatly. But with the affurance which Sieur de Pre-vert gave them, he took them to the mine, to which the fav-ages guided him.[245] It is a very high mountain, extending fomewhat feaward, glittering brightly in the funlight, and containing a large amount of verdigris, which proceeds from the before mentioned copper mine. At the foot of this mountain, he faid, there was at low water a large quantity of bits of copper, fuch as he fhowed us, which fall from the top of the mountain. Going on three or four leagues in the direction of the coaft of La Cadie, one finds another mine; alfo a fmall river extending fome diftance in a foutherly di-rection, where there is a mountain containing a black pig-ment with which the favages paint themfelves. Then, fome fix leagues from the fecond mine, going feaward about a league, and near the coaft of La Cadie, you find an ifland containing a kind of metal of a dark brown color, but white when it is cut. This they formerly ufed for their arrows and knives, which they beat into fhape with ftones, which leads me to believe that it is neither tin nor lead, it being fo hard; and, upon our fhowing them fome filver, they faid that the metal of this ifland was like it, which they find fome one or two feet under ground. Sieur Prevert gave to the

[244] *Coaft of La Cadie.* This extent given to La Cadie correfponds with the charter of De Monts, which covered the territory from 40° north latitude to 46°. The charter was obtained in the autumn of this fame year, 1603, and be-fore the account of this voyage by Champlain was printed. — *Vide* Vol. II. note 155.

[245] Prevert did not make this explora-tion, perfonally, although he pretended that he did. He fent fome of his men with Secondon, the chief of St. John, and others. His report is therefore fecond-hand, confufed, and inaccurate. Champlain expofes Prevert's attempt to deceive in a fubfequent reference to him. Compare Vol. II. pp. 26, 97, 98.

the favages wedges and chifels and other things neceffary to extract the ore of this mine, which they promifed to do, and on the following year to bring and give the fame to Sieur Prevert.

They fay, alfo, that, fome hundred or hundred and twenty leagues diftant, there are other mines, but that they do not dare to go to them, unlefs accompanied by Frenchmen to make war upon their enemies, in whofe poffeffion the mines are.

This place where the mine is, which is in latitude 44° and fome minutes,[246] and fome five or fix leagues from the coaft of La Cadie, is a kind of bay fome leagues broad at its entrance, and fomewhat more in length, where there are three rivers which flow into the great bay near the ifland of St. John,[247] which is fome thirty or thirty-five leagues long and fome fix leagues from the mainland on the fouth. There is alfo another fmall river emptying about half way from that by which Sieur Prevert returned, in which there are two lake-like bodies of water. There is alfo ftill another fmall river, extending in the direction of the pigment mountain. All thefe rivers fall into faid bay nearly foutheaft of the ifland where thefe favages fay this white mine is. On the north fide of this bay are the copper mines, where there is a good harbor for veffels, at the entrance to which is a fmall ifland. The bottom is mud and fand, on which veffels can be run.

From

---

[246] *44° and fome minutes.* The Bafin of Mines, the place where the copper was faid to be, is about 45° 30′.

[247] *Ifland of St. John.* Prince Edward Ifland. It was named the Ifland of St. John by Cartier, having been difcovered by him on St. John's Day, the 24th of June, 1534. — *Vide Voyage de Jacques Cartier,* 1534, Michelant, ed. Paris, 1865, p. 33. It continued to be fo called for the period of *two hundred and fixty-five* years, when it was changed to *Prince Edward Ifland* by an act of its legiflature, in November, 1798, which was confirmed by the king in council, Feb. 1, 1799.

From this mine to the mouth of the above rivers is a diftance of fome fixty or eighty leagues overland. But the diftance to this mine, along the feacoaft, from the outlet between
the Ifland of St. Lawrence and the mainland is, I fhould
think, more than fifty or fixty leagues.²⁴⁸

All this country is very fair and flat, containing all the
kinds of trees we faw on our way to the firft fall of the great
river of Canada, with but very little fir and cyprefs.

This is an exaçt ftatement of what I afcertained from
Sieur Prevert.

## CHAPTER XIII.

A TERRIBLE MONSTER, WHICH THE SAVAGES CALL GOUGOU. — OUR SHORT
AND FAVORABLE VOYAGE BACK TO FRANCE.

HERE is, moreover, a ftrange matter, worthy of
being related, which feveral favages have affured
me was true ; namely, near the Bay of Chaleurs,
towards the fouth, there is an ifland where a
terrible monfter refides, which the favages call
*Gougou,* and which they told me had the form of a woman,
though very frightful, and of fuch a fize that they told me
the tops of the mafts of our veffel would not reach to his
middle, fo great do they picture him ; and they fay that he
has often devoured and ftill continues to devour many favages;
thefe he puts, when he can catch them, into a great pocket,
and afterwards eats them ; and thofe who had efcaped the
jaws

²⁴⁸ That is, from the Strait of Canfeau round the coaft of Nova Scotia to
the Bay of Mines.

37

jaws of this wretched creature faid that its pocket was fo great that it could have put our veffel into it. This monfter makes horrible noifes in this ifland, which the favages call the *Gougou;* and when they fpeak of him, it is with the greateft poffible fear, and feveral have affured me that they have feen him. Even the above-mentioned Prevert from St. Malo told me that, while going in fearch of mines, as mentioned in the previous chapter, he paffed fo near the dwelling-place of this frightful creature, that he and all thofe on board his veffel heard ftrange hiffings from the noife it made, and that the favages with him told him it was the fame creature, and that they were fo afraid that they hid themfelves wherever they could, for fear that it would come and carry them off. What makes me believe what they fay is the fact that all the favages in general fear it, and tell fuch ftrange things about it that, if I were to record all they fay, it would be regarded as a myth; but I hold that this is the dwelling-place of fome devil that torments them in the above-mentioned manner.⁴⁰ This is what I have learned about this Gougou.

Before

⁴⁰ The defcription of this enchanted ifland is too indefinite to invite a conjecture of its identity or location. The refounding noife of the breaking waves, mingled with the whiftling of the wind, might well lay a foundation for the fears of the Indians, and their excited imaginations would eafily fill out and complete the picture. In Champlain's time, the belief in the active agency of good and evil fpirits, particularly the latter, in the affairs of men, was univerfal. It culminated in this country in the tragedies of the Salem witchcraft in 1692. It has fince been gradually fubfiding, but neverthelefs ftill exifts under the mitigated form of fpiritual communications. Champlain, fharing the credulity of his times, very naturally refers thefe ftrange phenomena reported by the favages, whofe ftatements were fully accredited and corroborated by the teftimony of his countryman, M. Prevert, to the agency of fome evil demon, who had taken up his abode in that region in order to vex and terrify thefe unhappy Indians. As a faithful hiftorian, he could not omit this ftory, but it probably made no more impreffion

Before leaving Tadouffac on our return to France, one of the fagamores of the Montagnais, named *Bechourat*, gave his fon to Sieur Du Pont Gravé to take to France, to whom he was highly commended by the grand fagamore, Anadabijou, who begged him to treat him well and have him fee what the other two favages, whom we had taken home with us, had feen. We afked them for an Iroquois woman they were going to eat, whom they gave us, and whom, alfo, we took with this favage. Sieur de Prevert alfo took four favages: a man from the coaft of La Cadie, a woman and two boys from the Canadians.

On the 24th of Auguft, we fet out from Gafpé, the veffel of Sieur Prevert and our own. On the 2d of September we calculated that we were as far as Cape Race; on the 5th, we came upon the bank where the fifhery is carried on; on the 16th, we were on foundings, fome fifty leagues from Oueffant; on the 20th we arrived, by God's grace, to the joy of all, and with a continued favorable wind, at the port of Havre de Grâce.

impreffion upon his mind than did the thoufand others of a fimilar character with which he muft have been familiar. He makes no allufion to it in the edition of 1613, when fpeaking of the copper mines in that neighborhood, nor yet in that of 1632, and it had probably paffed from his memory.

# CHAMPLAIN'S EXPLANATION

OF THE

# CARTE DE LA NOVVELLE FRANCE.

## 1632.

TABLE FOR FINDING THE PROMINENT PLACES ON
THE MAP.

A. *Baye des Ifles.*[1]
B. *Calefme.*[2]
C. *Baye des Trefpaffez.*
D. *Cap de Leuy.*[3]
E. *Port du Cap de Raye*, where the cod-fifhery is carried on.
F. The north-weft coaft of Newfoundland, but little known.
G. Paffage to the north at the 52d degree.[4]
H. *Ifle St. Paul*, near Cape St. Lawrence.

I.

[1] It is to be obferved that fome of the letters and figures are not found on the map. Among the reft, the letter A is wanting. It is impoffible of courfe to tell with certainty to what it refers, particularly as the places referred to do not occur in confecutive order. The Abbé Laverdière thinks this letter points to the bay of Bofton or what we commonly call Maffachufetts Bay, or to the Bay of all Ifles as laid down by Champlain on the eaftern coaft of Nova Scotia.

[2] On the fouthern coaft of Newfoundland, now known as *Placentia Bay.*

[3] Point Levi, oppofite Quebec.

[4] The letter G is wanting, but the reference is plainly to the Straits of Belle Ifle, as may be feen by reference to the map.

# 294 Champlain's Explanation of the

I. *Ifle de Safinou*, between Monts Déferts and Ifles aux Corneilles.[8]

K. *Ifle de Mont-réal*, at the Falls of St. Louis, fome eight or nine leagues in circuit.[6]

L. *Riuière Jeannin.*[7]

M. *Riuière St. Antoine.*[8]

N. Kind of falt water difcharging into the fea, with ebb and flood, abundance of fifh and fhell-fifh, and in fome places oyfters of not very good flavor.[9]

P. *Port aux Coquilles*, an ifland at the mouth of the River St. Croix, with good fifhing.[10]

Q. Iflands where there is fifhing.[11]

R. *Lac de Soiffons.*[12]

S. *Baye du Gouffre.*[13]

T. *Ifle de Monts Déferts*, very high.

V. *Ifle S. Barnabé*, in the great river near the Bic.

X. *Lefquemain*, where there is a fmall river, abounding in falmon and trout, near which is a little rocky iflet, where there was formerly a ftation for the whale fifhery.[14]

Y. *La Pointe aux Alloüettes*, where, in the month of September, there are numberlefs larks, alfo other kinds of game and fhell-fifh.

Z.

[8] This ifland was fomewhere between Mount Defert and Jonefport; not unlikely it was that now known as Petit Manan. It was named after Safanou, chief of the River Kennebec. *Vide* Vol. II. p. 58.

[6] The undereftimate is fo great, that it is probable that the author intended to fay that the length of the ifland is eight or nine leagues.

[7] The Boyer, eaft of Quebec. It appears to have been named after the Prefident Jeannin. *Vide antea*, p. 112.

[8] A river eaft of the Ifland of Orleans now called Rivière du Sud.

[9] N is wanting.

[10] A harbor at the north-eaftern extremity of the ifland of Campobello. *Vide* Vol. II. p. 100.

[11] Q is wanting. The reference is perhaps to the iflands in Penobfcot Bay.

[12] Lac de Soiffons. So named after Charles de Bourbon, Count de Soiffons, a Viceroy of New France in 1612. *Vide antea*, p. 112. Now known as the Lake of Two Mountains.

[13] A bay at the mouth of a river of this name now called St. Paul's Bay, near the Ifle aux Coudres. *Vide* Vol. II. note 305.

[14] *Vide antea*, note 241.

Z. *Isle aux Liéures*, fo named becaufe fome hares were captured there when it was firft difcovered.[15]

2. *Port à Lefquille*, dry at low tide, where are two brooks coming from the mountains.[16]

3. *Port au Saulmon*, dry at low tide. There are two fmall iflands here, abounding, in the feafon, with ftrawberries, rafpberries, and *bluets*.[17] Near this place is a good roadftead for veffels, and two fmall brooks flowing into the harbor.

4. *Riuière Platte*, coming from the mountains, only navigable for canoes. It is dry here at low tide a long diftance out. Good anchorage in the offing.

5. *Isles aux Couldres*, fome league and a half long, containing in their feafon great numbers of rabbits, partridges, and other kinds of game. At the fouthweft point are meadows, and reefs feaward. There is anchorage here for veffels between this ifland and the mainland on the north.

6. *Cap de Tourmente*, a league from which Sieur de Champlain had a building erected, which was burned by the Englifh in 1628. Near this place is Cap Bruflé, between which and Ifle aux Coudres is a channel, with eight, ten, and twelve fathoms of water. On the fouth the fhore is muddy and rocky. To the north are high lands, &c.

7. *Isle d'Orléans*, fix leagues in length, very beautiful on account of its variety of woods, meadows, vines, and nuts. The weftern point of this ifland is called Cap de Condé.

8. *Le Sault de Montmorency*, twenty fathoms high,[18] formed by a river coming from the mountains, and difcharging into the St. Lawrence, a league and a half from Quebec.

9.

[15] An ifland in the River St. Lawrence weft of Tadouffac, ftill called Hare Ifland. *Vide antea*, note 148.

[16] Figure 2 is not found on the map, and it is difficult to identify the place referred to.

[17] Bluets, *Vaccinium Canadenfe*, the Canada blueberry. Champlain fays it is a fmall fruit very good for eating. *Vide* Quebec ed. Voyage of 1615, p. 509.

[18] *Vide* Vol. II. p. 176.

9. *Riuière S. Charles*, coming from Lac S. Jofeph,[19] very beautiful with meadows at low tide. At full tide barques can go up as far as the firft fall. On this river are built the churches and quarters of the reverend Jéfuit and Récolleét Fathers. Game is abundant here in fpring and autumn.

10. *Riuière des Etechemins*,[20] by which the favages go to Quinebequi, croffing the country with difficulty, on account of the falls and little water. Sieur de Champlain had this exploration made in 1628, and found a favage tribe, feven days from Quebec, who till the foil, and are called the Abenaquiuoit.

11. *Riuière de Champlain*, near that of Batifquan, north-weft of the Grondines.

12. *Riuière de Sauuages*.[21]

13. *Ifle Verte*, five or fix leagues from Tadouffac.[22]

14. *Ifle de Chaffe*.

15. *Riuière Batifquan*, very pleafant, and abounding in fifh.

16. *Les Grondines*, and fome neighboring iflands. A good place for hunting and fifhing.

17. *Riuière des Efturgeons & Saulmons*, with a fall of water from fifteen to twenty feet high, two leagues from Sainéte Croix, which defcends into a fmall pond difcharging into the great river St. Lawrence.[23]

18. *Ifle de St. Eloy*, with a paffage between the ifland and the mainland on the north.[24]

19. *Lac S. Pierre*, very beautiful, three to four fathoms in depth, and abounding in fifh, furrounded by hills and level traéts, with

[19] For *Lac S. Jofeph*, read Lac S. Charles.

[20] Champlain here calls the *Chaudière* the River of the Etechemins, notwithftanding he had before given the name to that now known as the St. Croix. *Vide* Vol. II. pp. 30, 47, 60. There is ftill a little eaft of the Chaudière a river now known as the Etechemin ; but the channel of the Chau-

dière would be the courfe which the Indians would naturally take to reach the head-waters of the Kennebec, where dwelt the Abenaquis.

[21] River Verte, entering the St. Lawrence on the fouth of Green Ifland, oppofite to Tadouffac.

[22] Green Ifland.

[23] Jacques Cartier River.

[24] Near the Batifcan.

with meadows in places. Several fmall ftreams and brooks flow into it.

20. *Riuière du Gaft*, very pleafant, yet containing but little water.[25]
21. *Riuière Sainct Antoine.*[26]
22. *Riuière Sainéte Suzanne.*[27]
23. *Riuière des Yrocois*, very beautiful, with many iflands and meadows. It comes from Lac de Champlain, five or fix days' journey in length, abounding in fifh and game of different kinds. Vines, nut, plum, and cheftnut trees abound in many places. There are meadows and very pretty iflands in it. To reach it, it is neceffary to pafs one large and one fmall fall.[28]
24. *Sault de Riuière du Saguenay*, fifty leagues from Tadouffac, ten or twelve fathoms high.[29]
25. *Grand Sault*, which falls fome fifteen feet, amid a large number of iflands. It is half a league in length and three leagues broad.[30]
26. *Port au Mouton.*
27. *Baye de Campfeau.*
28. *Cap Baturier*, on the Ifle de Sainét Jean.
29. A river by way of which they go to the Baye Françoife.[31]
30. *Chaffe des Eflans.*[32]
31. *Cap de Richelieu*, on the eaftern part of the Ifle d'Orleans.[33]
32. A fmall bank near Ifle du Cap Breton.
33. *Riuière des Puans*, coming from a lake where there is a mine of pure red copper.[34]

34.

[25] Nicolet. *Vide* Laverdière's note, Quebec ed. Vol. III. p. 328.
[26] River St. Francis.
[27] Rivière du Loup.
[28] River Richelieu.
[29] This number is wanting.
[30] The Falls of St. Louis, above Montreal. The figures are wanting.
[31] One of the fmall rivers between Cobequid Bay and Cumberland Strait.
[32] Moofe Hunting, on the weft of Gafpé.
[33] Argentenay. — *Laverdière.*
[34] Champlain had not been in this region, and confequently obtained his information from the favages. There is no fuch lake as he reprefents on his map, and this ifland producing pure copper may have been Ifle Royale, in Lake Superior.

34. *Sault de Gaſton*, nearly two leagues broad, and diſcharging into the *Mer Douce*. It comes from another very large lake, which, with the *Mer Douce*, have an extent of thirty days' journey by canoe, according to the report of the ſavages.[35]

*Returning to the Gulf of St. Lawrence and Coaſt of La Cadie.*

35. *Riuière de Gaſpey.*[36]
36. *Riuière de Chaleu.*[37]
37. Several Iſlands near Miſcou and the harbor of Miſcou, between two iſlands.
38. *Cap de l'Iſle Sainct Jean.*[38]
39. *Port au Roſſignol.*
40. *Riuière Platte.*[39]
41. *Port du Cap Naigrt.* On the bay by this cape there is a French ſettlement, where Sieur de la Tour commands, from whom it was named Port la Tour. The Reverend Récollect Fathers dwelt here in 1630.[40]
42. *Baye du Cap de Sable.*
43. *Baye Saine.*[41]
44. *Baye Courante*, with many iſlands abounding in game, good fiſhing, and places favorable for veſſels.[42]
45. *Port du Cap Fourchu*, very pleaſant, but very nearly dry at low tide. Near this place are many iſlands, with good hunting.
47. *Petit Paſſage de Iſle Longue.* Here there is good cod-fiſhing.
48. *Cap des Deux Bayes.*[43]
49. *Port des Mines*, where, at low tide, ſmall pieces of very pure copper are to be found in the rocks along the ſhore.[44]

50.

[35] The Falls of St. Mary.
[36] York River.
[37] The Riſtigouche.
[38] Now called North Point.
[39] Probably Gold River, flowing into Mahone Bay.
[40] Still called Port La Tour.
[41] Halifax Harbor. *Vide* Vol. II. note 266.
[42] *Vide* Vol. II. note 192.
[44] Now Cape Chignecto, in the Bay of Fundy.
[44] Advocates' Harbor.

50. *Iſles de Bacchus,* very pleaſant, containing many vines, nut, plum, and other trees.[45]
51. Iſlands near the mouth of the river Chouacoet.
52. *Iſles Aſſez Hautes,* three or four in number, two or three leagues diſtant from the land, at the mouth of Baye Longue.[46]
53. *Baye aux Iſles,* with ſuitable harbors for veſſels. The country is very good, and ſettled by numerous ſavages, who till the land. In theſe localities are numerous cypreſſes, vines, and nut-trees.[47]
54. *La Soupçonneuſe,* an iſland nearly a league diſtant from the land.[48]
55. *Baye Longue.*[49]
56. *Les Sept Iſles.*[50]
57. *Riuière des Etechemins.*[51]

*The Virginias, where the Engliſh are ſettled, between the 36th and 37th degrees of latitude. Captains Ribaut and Laudonnière made explorations 36 or 37 years ago along the coaſts adjoining Florida, and eſtabliſhed a ſettlement.*[52]

58. Several rivers of the Virginias, flowing into the Gulf.
59. Coaſt inhabited by ſavages who till the ſoil, which is very good.
60. *Poinɕle Confort.*[53]
61. *Immeſtan.*[54]
62. *Cheſapeacq Bay.*
63. *Bedabedec,* the coaſt weſt of the river Pemetegoet.[55]
64. *Belles Prairies.* 65.

[45] Richmond Iſland. *Vide* note 42 Vol. I. and note 123 Vol. II. of this work.
[46] The Iſles of Shoals. *Vide* Vol. II. note 142.
[47] Boſton Bay.
[48] Martha's Vineyard. *Vide* Vol. II. note 227.
[49] Merrimac Bay, as it may be appropriately called, ſtretching from Little Boar's Head to Cape Anne.

[50] Theſe iſlands appear to be in Caſco Bay.
[51] The figures are not on the map. The reference is to the Scoudic, commonly known as the River St. Croix.
[52] There is probably a typographical error in the figures. The paſſage ſhould read "66 or 67 years ago."
[53] Now Old Point Comfort.
[54] Jameſtown, Virginia.
[55] *Vide* Vol. II. note 95.

300 *Champlain's Explanation of the*

65. Place on Lac Champlain where the Yroquois were defeated by Sieur Champlain in 1606.[66]

66. *Petit Lac*, by way of which they go to the Yroquois, after paffing over that of Champlain.[67]

67. *Baye des Trefpaffez*, on the ifland of Newfoundland.

68. *Chappeau Rouge.*

69. *Baye du Sainct Efprit.*

70. *Les Vierges.*

71. *Port Breton*, near Cap Sainct Laurent, on Ifle du Cap Breton.

72. *Les Bergeronnettes*, three leagues from Tadouffac.

73. *Le Cap d'Efpoir*, near Ifle Percée.[88]

74. *Forillon*, at Poincte de Gafpey.

75. *Ifle de Mont-réal*, at the Falls of St. Louis, in the River St. Lawrence.[89]

76. *Riuière des Prairies*, coming from a lake at the Falls of St. Louis, where there are two iflands, one of which is Mont-réal. For feveral years this has been a ftation for trading with the favages.[90]

77. *Sault de la Chaudière*, on the river of the Algonquins, fome eighteen feet high, and defcending among rocks with a great roar.[91]

78. *Lac de Nibachis*, the name of a favage captain who dwells here and tills a little land, where he plants Indian corn.[92]

79. Eleven lakes, near each other, one, two, and three leagues in extent, and abounding in fifh and game. Sometimes the favages go this way in order to avoid the Fall of the Calu-mets,

---

[66] This fhould read 1609. *Vide* Vol. II. note 348.

[67] Lake George. *Vide antea*, note 63, p. 93.

[88] This cape ftill bears the fame name.

[89] This number is wanting.

[90] This river comes from the Lake of Two Mountains, is a branch of the Ottawa feparating the Ifland of Mont-real from the Ifle Jéſus. and flows into the main channel of the Ottawa two or three miles before it reaches the eaftern end of the Ifland of Montreal.

[91] The Chaudière Falls are near the fite of the city of Ottawa. *Vide antea*, p. 120.

[92] Mufkrat Lake.

mets, which is very dangerous. Some of thefe localities abound in pines, yielding a great amount of refin.[62]

80. *Sault des Pierres à Calunmet*, which refemble alabafter.

81. *Ifle de Tefouac*, an Algonquin captain (*Tefouac*) to whom the favages pay a toll for allowing them paffage to Quebec.[64]

82. *La Riuière de Tefouac*, in which there are five falls.[65]

83. A river by which many favages go to the North Sea, above the Saguenay, and to the Three Rivers, going fome diftance overland.[66]

84. The lakes by which they go to the North Sea.

85. A river extending towards the North Sea.

86. Country of the Hurons, fo called by the French, where there are numerous communities, and feventeen villages fortified by three palifades of wood, with a gallery all around in the form of a parapet, for defence againft their enemies. This region is in latitude 44° 30′, with a fertile foil cultivated by the favages.

87. Paffage of a league overland, where the canoes are carried.

88. A river difcharging into the *Mer Douce*.[67]

89. Village fortified by four palifades, where Sieur de Champlain went in the war againft the Antouhonorons, and where feveral favages were taken prifoners.[68]

90. Falls at the extremity of the Falls of St. Louis, very high, where many fifh come down and are ftunned.[69]

91. A fmall river near the Sault de la Chaudière, where there is a waterfall nearly twenty fathoms high, over which the water flows

---

[62] This number is wanting on the map. Mufkrat Lake is one of this fucceffion of lakes, which extends eafterly towards the Ottawa.

[64] Allumette Ifland, in the River Ottawa, about eighty-five miles above the capital of the Dominion of Canada.

[65] That part of the River Ottawa which, after its bifurcation, fweeps around and forms the northern boundary of Allumette Ifland.

[66] The Ottawa beyond its junction with the Matawan.

[67] French River.

[68] *Vide antea*, note 83, p. 130.

[69] Plainly Lake St. Louis, now the Ontario, and not the *Falls* of St. Louis. The reference is here to Niagara Falls.

*Champlain's Explanation of the*

flows in such volume and with such velocity that a long arcade is made, beneath which the savages go for amusement, without getting wet. It is a fine sight.[70]

92. This river is very beautiful, with numerous islands of various sizes. It passes through many fine lakes, and is bordered by beautiful meadows. It abounds in deer and other animals, with fish of excellent quality. There are many cleared tracts of land upon it, with good soil, which have been abandoned by the savages on account of their wars. It discharges into Lake St. Louis, and many tribes come to these regions to hunt and obtain their provision for the winter.[71]

93. Chestnut forest, where there are great quantities of chestnuts, on the borders of Lac St. Louis. Also many meadows, vines, and nut-trees.[72]

94. Lake-like bodies of salt water at the head of Baye François, where the tide ebbs and flows. Islands containing many birds, many meadows in different localities, small rivers flowing into these species of lakes, by which they go to the Gulf of St. Lawrence, near Isle S. Jean.[73]

95. *Isle Haute*, a league in circuit, and flat on top. It contains fresh water and much wood. It is a league distant from Port aux Mines and Cap des Deux Bayes. It is more than forty fathoms high on all sides, except in one place, where it slopes, and where there is a pebbly point of a triangular shape. In the centre is a pond with salt water. Many birds make their nests in this island.

δ *La Riuière des Algommequins*, extending from the Falls of St. Louis nearly to the Lake of the Bissereni, containing more than eighty falls, large and small, which must be passed by

going

[70] The River Rideau.
[71] The River Trent discharges into the Bay of Quinté, an arm of Lake Ontario or Lac St. Louis.
[72] On the borders of Lake Ontario in the State of New York.
[73] The head-waters of the Bay of Fundy.

going around, by rowing, or by hauling with ropes. Some of thefe falls are very dangerous, particularly in going down.[74]

*Gens de Petun.* This is a tribe cultivating this herb (*tobacco*), in which they carry on an extenfive traffic with the other tribes. They have large towns, fortified with wood, and they plant Indian corn.

*Cheveux Releues.* Thefe are favages who wear nothing about the loins, and go ftark naked, except in winter, when they clothe themfelves in robes of fkins, which they leave off when they quit their houfes for the fields. They are great hunters, fifh-ermen, and travellers, till the foil, and plant Indian corn. They dry *bluets*[75] and rafpberries, in which they carry on an extenfive traffic with the other tribes, taking in exchange fkins, beads, nets, and other articles. Some of thefe people pierce the nofe, and attach beads to it. They tattoo their bodies, applying black and other colors. They wear their hair very ftraight, and greafe it, painting it red, as they do alfo the face.

*La Nation Neutre.* This is a people that maintains itfelf againft all the others. They engage in war only with the Affiftaque-ronons. They are very powerful, having forty towns well peopled.

*Les Antouhonorons.* They confift of fifteen towns built in ftrong fituations. They are enemies of all the other tribes, except Neutral nation. Their country is fine, with a good climate, and near the river St. Lawrence, the paffage of which they forbid to all the other tribes, for which reafon it is lefs vifited by them. They till the foil, and plant their land.[76]

*Les Yroquois.*

[74] The River Ottawa, here referred to, extends nearly to Lake Nipiffing, here fpoken of as the lake of the *Biffe-reni*.

[75] The Canada blueberry, *Vaccinium Canadenfe*. The aborigines of New England were accuftomed to dry the blueberry for winter's ufe. *Vide 'Joffe-lyn's Rarities*, Tuckerman's ed., Bofton, 1865, p. 113.

[76] This reference is to the *Antouo-ronons*, as given on the map.

*Les Yroquois.* They unite with the Antouhonorons in making war againſt all the other tribes, except the Neutral nation.

*Carantouanis.* This is a tribe that has moved to the ſouth of the Antouhonorons, and dwells in a very fine country, where it is ſecurely quartered. They are friends of all the other tribes, except the above named Antouhonorons, from whom they are only three days' journey diſtant. Once they took as priſoners ſome Flemiſh, but ſent them back again without doing them any harm, ſuppoſing that they were French. Between Lac St. Louis and Sault St. Louis, which is the great river St. Lawrence, there are five falls, numerous fine lakes, and pretty iſlands, with a pleaſing country abounding in game and fiſh, favorable for ſettlement, were it not for the wars which the ſavages carry on with each other.

*La Mer Douce* is a very large lake, containing a countleſs number of iſlands. It is very deep, and abounds in fiſh of all varieties and of extraordinary ſize, which are taken at different times and ſeaſons, as in the great ſea. The ſouthern ſhore is much pleaſanter than the northern, where there are many rocks and great quantities of caribous.

*Le Lac des Biſſerenis* is very beautiful, ſome twenty-five leagues in circuit, and containing numerous iſlands covered with woods and meadows. The ſavages encamp here, in order to catch in the river ſturgeon, pike, and carp, which are excellent and of very great ſize, and taken in large numbers. Game is alſo abundant, although the country is not particularly attractive, it being for the moſt part rocky.

NOTE. — The following are marked on the map as places where the French have had ſettlements: 1. Grand Cibou; 2. Cap Naigre; 3. Port du Cap Fourchu; 4. Port Royal; 5. St. Croix; 6. Iſle des Monts Déſerts; 7. Port de Miſcou; 8. Tadouſſac; 9. Quebec; 10. St. Croix, near Quebec.

MER DU NORT GLACIALE.

THE PRINCE SOCIETY.

# Commonwealth of Massachusetts.

---

## IN THE YEAR ONE THOUSAND EIGHT HUNDRED AND SEVENTY-FOUR.

---

## AN ACT TO INCORPORATE THE PRINCE SOCIETY.

*Be it enacted by the Senate and House of Representatives, in General Court assembled, and by the authority of the same, as follows :*

SECTION 1. John Ward Dean, J. Wingate Thornton, Edmund F. Slafter, and Charles W. Tuttle, their associates and successors, are made a corporation by the name of the PRINCE SOCIETY, for the purpose of preserving and extending the knowledge of American History, by editing and printing such manuscripts, rare tracts, and volumes as are mostly confined in their use to historical students and public libraries.

SECTION 2. Said corporation may hold real and personal estate to an amount not exceeding thirty thousand dollars.

SECTION 3. This act shall take effect upon its passage.

Approved March 18, 1874.

---

NOTE. — The Prince Society was organized on the 25th of May, 1858. What was undertaken as an experiment has proved successful. This ACT OF INCORPORATION has been obtained to enable the Society better to fulfil its object, in its expanding growth.

# THE PRINCE SOCIETY.

## CONSTITUTION.

ARTICLE I. — This Society fhall be called THE PRINCE SOCIETY; and it fhall have for its objeçt the publication of rare works, in print or manufcript, relating to America.

ARTICLE II. — The officers of the Society fhall be a Prefident, four Vice-Prefidents, a Correfponding Secretary, a Recording Secretary, and a Treafurer; who together fhall form the Council of the Society.

ARTICLE III. — Members may be added to the Society on the recommendation of any member and a confirmatory vote of a majority of the Council.

Libraries and other Inftitutions may hold memberfhip, and be reprefented by an authorized agent.

All members fhall be entitled to and fhall accept the volumes printed by the Society, as they are iffued from time to time, at the prices fixed by the Council; and memberfhip fhall be forfeited by a refufal or neglect fo to accept the faid volumes.

Any perfon may terminate his memberfhip by refignation addreffed in writing to the Prefident; provided, however, that he fhall have previoufly paid for all volumes iffued by the Society after the date of his election as a member.

ARTICLE IV. — The management of the Society's affairs fhall be vefted in the Council, which fhall keep a faithful record of its proceedings,

proceedings, and report the fame to the Society annually, at its
General Meeting in May.

ARTICLE V. — On the anniverſary of the birth of the Rev.
Thomas Prince, — namely, on the twenty-fifth day of May, in every
year (but if this day ſhall fall on Sunday or a legal holiday, on
the following day), — a General Meeting ſhall be held at Boſton, in
Maſſachuſetts, for the purpoſe of electing officers, hearing the
report of the Council, auditing the Treaſurer's account, and tran-
ſacting other buſineſs.

ARTICLE VI. — The officers ſhall be choſen by the Society annually, at the General Meeting ; but vacancies occurring between
the General Meetings may be filled by the Council.

ARTICLE VII. — By-Laws for the more particular government
of the Society may be made or amended at any General Meeting.

ARTICLE VIII. — Amendments to the Conſtitution may be made
at the General Meeting in May, by a three-fourths vote, provided
that a copy of the fame be tranſmitted to every member of the
Society, at leaſt two weeks previous to the time of voting thereon.

## COUNCIL.

### RULES AND REGULATIONS.

1. THE Society ſhall be adminiſtered on the mutual principle,
and ſolely in the intereſt of American hiſtory.

2. A volume ſhall be iſſued as often as practicable, but not more
frequently than once a year.

3. An editor of each work to be iſſued ſhall be appointed, who
ſhall be a member of the Society, whoſe duty it ſhall be to prepare, arrange, and conduct the fame through the preſs ; and, as he
will neceſſarily be placed under obligations to ſcholars and others

for

for affiftance, and particularly for the loan of rare books, he fhall be entitled to receive ten copies, to enable him to acknowledge and return any courtefies which he may have received.

4. All editorial work and official fervice fhall be performed gratuitoufly.

5. All contracts connected with the publication of any work fhall be laid before the Council in diftinct fpecifications in writing, and be adopted by a vote of the Council, and entered in a book kept for that purpofe ; and, when the publication of a volume is completed, its whole expenfe fhall be entered, with the items of its coft in full, in the fame book. No member of the Council fhall be a contractor for doing any part of the mechanical work of the publications.

6. The price of each volume fhall be a hundredth part of the coft of the edition, or as near to that as conveniently may be ; and there fhall be no other affeffments levied upon the members of the Society.

7. A fum, not exceeding one thoufand dollars, may be fet apart by the Council from the net receipts for publications, as a working capital ; and when the faid net receipts fhall exceed that fum, the excefs fhall be divided, from time to time, among the members of the Society, by remitting either a part or the whole coft of a volume, as may be deemed expedient.

8. All moneys belonging to the Society fhall be depofited in the New England Truft Company in Bofton, unlefs fome other banking inftitution fhall be defignated by a vote of the Council ; and faid moneys fhall be entered in the name of the Society, fubject to the order of the Treafurer.

9. It shall be the duty of the Prefident to call the Council together, whenever it may be neceffary for the tranfaction of bufinefs, and to prefide at its meetings.

10. It shall be the duty of the Vice-Prefidents to authorize all bills before their payment, to make an inventory of the property

of

of the Society during the month preceding the annual meeting and to report the fame to the Council, and to audit the accounts of the Treafurer.

11. It fhall be the duty of the Correfponding Secretary to iffue all general notices to the members, and to conduct the general correfpondence of the Society.

12. It fhall be the duty of the Recording Secretary to keep a complete record of the proceedings both of the Society and of the Council, in a book provided for that purpofe.

13. It fhall be the duty of the Treafurer to forward to the members bills for the volumes, as they are iffued ; to fuperintend the fending of the books ; to pay all bills authorized and indorfed by at leaft two Vice-Prefidents of the Society; and to keep an accurate account of all moneys received and difburfed.

14. No books fhall be forwarded by the Treafurer to any member until the amount of the price fixed for the fame fhall have been received ; and any member neglecting to forward the faid amount for one month after his notification, fhall forfeit his memberfhip.

# OFFICERS

OF

# THE PRINCE SOCIETY.

*President.*

THE REV. EDMUND F. SLAFTER, A.M. . . Boston, Mass.

*Vice-Presidents.*

JOHN WARD DEAN, A.M. . . . . . . . Boston, Mass.
WILLIAM B. TRASK, Esq. . . . . . . . Boston, Mass.
THE HON. CHARLES H. BELL, A.M. . . Exeter, N. H.
JOHN MARSHALL BROWN, A.M. . . . . Portland, Me.

*Corresponding Secretary.*

CHARLES W. TUTTLE, Ph.D. . . . . . . Boston, Mass.

*Recording Secretary.*

DAVID GREENE HASKINS, Jr., A.M. . . . Cambridge, Mass.

*Treasurer.*

ELBRIDGE H. GOSS, Esq. . . . . . . . . Boston, Mass.

# THE PRINCE SOCIETY.

1880.

# The Prince Society. 313

| | |
|---|---|
| Jofeph J. Cooke, Efq. | Providence, R.I. |
| Deloraine P. Corey, Efq. | Bofton, Mafs. |
| Eraftus Corning, Efq. | Albany, N.Y. |
| Ellery Bicknell Crane, Efq. | Worcefter, Mafs. |
| Abram E. Cutter, Efq. | Charleftown, Mafs. |
| The Rev. Edwin A. Dalrymple, S.T.D. | Baltimore, Md. |
| William M. Darlington, Efq. | Pittfburg, Pa. |
| John Ward Dean, A.M. | Bofton, Mafs. |
| Charles Deane, LL.D. | Cambridge, Mafs. |
| Edward Denham, Efq. | New Bedford, Mafs. |
| Prof. Franklin B. Dexter, A.M. | New Haven, Ct. |
| The Rev. Henry Martyn Dexter, D.D. | Bofton, Mafs. |
| Samuel Adams Drake, Efq. | Melrofe, Mafs. |
| Henry Thayer Drowne, Efq. | New York, N.Y. |
| Henry H. Edes, Efq. | Charleftown, Mafs. |
| Jonathan Edwards, A.B., M.D. | New Haven, Ct. |
| Janus G. Elder, Efq. | Lewifton, Me. |
| Samuel Eliot, LL.D. | Bofton, Mafs. |
| Alfred Langdon Elwyn, M.D. | Philadelphia, Pa. |
| James Emott, Efq. | New York, N.Y. |
| The Hon. William M. Evarts, LL.D. | New York, N.Y. |
| Jofeph Story Fay, Efq. | Woods Holl, Mafs. |
| John S. H. Fogg, M.D. | Bofton, Mafs. |
| The Rev. Henry W. Foote, A.M. | Bofton, Mafs. |
| Samuel P. Fowler, Efq. | Danvers, Mafs. |
| James E. Gale, Efq. | Haverhill, Mafs. |
| Marcus D. Gilman, Efq. | Montpelier, Vt. |
| The Hon. John E. Godfrey | Bangor, Me. |
| Abner C. Goodell, Jr., A.M. | Salem, Mafs. |
| Elbridge H. Gofs, Efq. | Bofton, Mafs. |
| The Hon. Chief Juftice Horace Gray, LL.D. | Bofton, Mafs. |
| William W. Greenough, A.B. | Bofton, Mafs. |
| Ifaac J. Greenwood, A.M. | New York, N.Y. |
| Charles H. Guild, Efq. | Somerville, Mafs. |
| The Hon. Robert S. Hale, LL.D. | Elizabethtown, N.Y. |
| C. Fifke Harris, A.M. | Providence, R.I. |

David Greene Haſkins, Jr., A.M. . . . . . . Cambridge, Maſs.
The Hon. Francis B. Hayes, A.M. . . . . . Boſton, Maſs.
Thomas Wentworth Higginſon, A.M.. . . . . Cambridge, Maſs.
W. Scott Hill, M.D. . . . . . . . . . Auguſta, Me.
James F. Hunnewell, Eſq. . . . . . . . . Charleſtown, Maſs.
Theodore Irwin, Eſq. . . . . . . . . . Oſwego, N.Y.
The Hon. Clark Jillſon . . . . . . . . Worceſter, Maſs.
Mr. Sawyer Junior . . . . . . . . . . Naſhua, N.H.
George Lamb, Eſq.. . . . . . . . . . Boſton, Maſs.
Edward F. de Lancey, Eſq. . . . . . . . New York, N.Y.
William B. Lapham, M.D. . . . . . . . Auguſta, Me.
Henry Lee, A.M. . . . . . . . . . . Boſton, Maſs.
John A. Lewis, Eſq. . . . . . . . . . Boſton, Maſs.
Orſamus H. Marſhall, Eſq. . . . . . . . Buffalo, N.Y.
William T. R. Marvin, A.M.. . . . . . . Boſton, Maſs.
William F. Matchett, Eſq. . . . . . . . Boſton, Maſs.
Frederic W. G. May, Eſq. . . . . . . . Boſton, Maſs.
The Rev. James H. Means, D.D. . . . . . Boſton, Maſs.
George H. Moore, LL.D.. . . . . . . . New York, N.Y.
The Hon. Henry C. Murphy, LL.D. . . . . Brooklyn, N.Y.
The Rev. James De Normandie, A.M. . . . . Portſmouth, N.H.
The Hon. James W. North . . . . . . . Auguſta, Me.
Prof. Charles E. Norton, A.M. . . . . . . Cambridge, Maſs.
John H. Oſborne, Eſq. . . . . . . . . Auburn, N.Y.
George T. Paine, Eſq.. . . . . . . . . Providence, R.I.
The Hon. John Gorham Palfrey, LL.D. . . . . Cambridge, Maſs.
Daniel Pariſh, Jr., Eſq. . . . . . . . . New York, N. Y.
Francis Parkman, LL.D. . . . . . . . . Boſton, Maſs.
Auguſtus T. Perkins, A.M. . . . . . . . Boſton, Maſs.
The Rt. Rev. William Stevens Perry, D.D., LL.D. Davenport, Iowa.
William Frederic Poole, A.M. . . . . . . Chicago, Ill.
George Prince, Eſq. . . . . . . . . . Bath, Me.
Capt. William Prince, U.S.A. . . . . . . New Orleans, La.
Samuel S. Purple, M.D. . . . . . . . . New York, N.Y.
The Hon. John Phelps Putnam, A.M. . . . . Boſton, Maſs.
Edward Aſhton Rollins, A.M. . . . . . . Philadelphia, Pa.

The Hon. Mark Skinner . . . . . . . . . Chicago, Ill.
The Rev. Carlos Slafter, A.M. . . . . . . . Dedham, Mafs.
The Rev. Edmund F. Slafter, A.M. . . . . . Boston, Mafs.
Charles C. Smith, Efq.. . . . . . . . . . Boston, Mafs.
Samuel T. Snow, Efq. . . . . . . . . . . Boston, Mafs.
Oliver Blifs Stebbins, Efq. . . . . . . . . Boston, Mafs.
George Stevens, Efq. . . . . . . . . . . Lowell, Mafs.
The Hon. Edwin W. Stoughton . . . . . . New York, N.Y.
William B. Trafk, Efq.. . . . . . . . . . Boston, Mafs.
The Hon. William H. Tuthill . . . . . . . Tipton, Iowa.
Charles W. Tuttle, Ph.D. . . . . . . . . Boston, Mafs.
The Rev. Alexander Hamilton Vinton, D.D. . . Pomfret, Ct.
Jofeph B. Walker, A.M. . . . . . . . . . Concord, N.H.
William Henry Wardwell, Efq. . . . . . . . Boston, Mafs.
Mifs Rachel Wetherill . . . . . . . . . . Philadelphia, Pa.
Henry Wheatland, A.M., M.D. . . . . . . . Salem, Mafs.
John Gardner White, A.M. . . . . . . . . Cambridge, Mafs.
William Adee Whitehead, A.M. . . . . . . Newark, N.J.
William H. Whitmore, A.M. . . . . . . . . Boston, Mafs.
Henry Auftin Whitney, A.M. . . . . . . . Boston, Mafs.
The Hon. Marfhall P. Wilder, Ph.D.. . . . . Boston, Mafs.
Henry Winfor, Efq.. . . . . . . . . . . Philadelphia, Pa.
The Hon. Robert C. Winthrop, LL.D. . . . . Boston, Mafs.
Charles Levi Woodbury, Efq. . . . . . . . Boston, Mafs.
Afhbel Woodward, M.D. . . . . . . . . . Franklin, Ct.
J. Otis Woodward, Efq. . . . . . . . . . Albany, N.Y.

#### LIBRARIES.

American Antiquarian Society . . . . . . . Worcefter, Mafs.
Amherft College Library . . . . . . . . . Amherft, Mafs.
Aftor Library . . . . . . . . . . . . . New York, N.Y.
Boston Athenæum . . . . . . . . . . . Boston, Mafs.
Boston Library Society . . . . . . . . . Boston, Mafs.
Britifh Mufeum . . . . . . . . . . . . London, Eng.
Concord Public Library . . . . . . . . . Concord, Mafs.

Eben Dale Sutton Reference Library . . . . . Peabody, Mass.
Free Public Library . . . . . . . . . . . Worcester, Mass.
Grosvenor Library . . . . . . . . . . . . Buffalo, N.Y.
Harvard College Library . . . . . . . . . Cambridge, Mass.
Historical Society of Pennsylvania . . . . . . Philadelphia, Pa.
Library Company of Philadelphia . . . . . . Philadelphia, Pa.
Library of Parliament . . . . . . . . . . Ottawa, Canada.
Library of the State Department . . . . . . Washington, D.C.
Long Island Historical Society . . . . . . . Brooklyn, N.Y.
Maine Historical Society . . . . . . . . . Brunswick, Me.
Maryland Historical Society . . . . . . . . Baltimore, Md.
Massachusetts Historical Society . . . . . Boston, Mass.
Mercantile Library . . . . . . . . . . . New York, N.Y.
Minnesota Historical Society . . . . . . . St. Paul, Minn.
Newburyport Public Library, Peabody Fund . . Newburyport, Mass.
New England Historic Genealogical Society . . Boston, Mass.
Newton Free Library . . . . . . . . . . Newton, Mass.
New York Society Library . . . . . . . New York, N.Y.
Plymouth Public Library . . . . . . . . Plymouth, Mass.
Portsmouth Athenæum . . . . . . . . . Portsmouth, N.H.
Public Library of the City of Boston . . . . Boston, Mass.
Redwood Library . . . . . . . . . . Newport, R.I.
State Library of Massachusetts . . . . . . Boston, Mass.
State Library of New York . . . . . . . Albany, N.Y.
State Library of Rhode Island . . . . . . Providence, R.I.
State Library of Vermont . . . . . . . Montpelier, Vt.
Williams College Library . . . . . . . . Williamstown, Mass.
Yale College Library . . . . . . . . . New Haven, Ct.

# PUBLICATIONS OF THE SOCIETY.

NEW ENGLAND'S PROSPECT.
 A true, lively and experimentall defcription of that part of *America*, commonly called
Nevv England: difcovering the State of that Countrie, both as it ftands to our new-
come *Englifh* Planters; and to the old Natiue Inhabitants. By WILLIAM WOOD.
London, 1634. Preface by Charles Deane, LL.D.

THE HUTCHINSON PAPERS.
 A Collection of Original Papers relative to the Hiftory of the Colony of Maffachu-
fetts-Bay. Reprinted from the edition of 1769. Edited by William H. Whitmore,
A.M., and William S. Appleton, A.M. 2 vols.

JOHN DUNTON'S LETTERS FROM NEW ENGLAND.
 Letters written from New England A.D. 1686. By John Dunton in which are
defcribed his voyages by Sea, his travels on land, and the characters of his friends
and acquaintances. Now firft publifhed from the Original Manufcript in the Bodleian
Library, Oxford. Edited by William H. Whitmore, A.M.

THE ANDROS TRACTS.
 Being a Collection of Pamphlets and Official Papers iffued during the period be-
tween the overthrow of the Andros Government and the eftablifhment of the fecond
Charter of Maffachufetts. Reprinted from the original editions and manufcripts.
With a Memoir of Sir Edmund Andros, by the editor, William H. Whitmore, A.M.
3 vols.

SIR WILLIAM ALEXANDER AND AMERICAN COLONIZATION.
 Including three Royal Charters, iffued in 1621, 1625, 1628; a Tract entitled an
Encouragement to Colonies, by Sir William Alexander, 1624; a Patent, from the
Great Council for New England, of Long Ifland, and a part of the prefent State of
Maine; a Roll of the Knights Baronets of New Scotland; with a Memoir of Sir
William Alexander, by the editor, the Rev. Edmund F. Slafter, A.M.

JOHN WHEELWRIGHT.
 Including his Faft-day Sermon, 1637; his Mercurius Americanus, 1645, and other
writings; with a paper on the genuinenefs of the Indian deed of 1629, and a Memoir
by the editor, Charles H. Bell, A.M.

VOYAGES OF THE NORTHMEN TO AMERICA.

Including extracts from Icelandic Sagas relating to weftern voyages by North-men in the tenth and eleventh centuries, in an Englifh tranflation by North Ludlow Beamifh; with a Synopfis of the hiftorical evidence and the opinion of Profeffor Rafn as to the places vifited by the Scandinavians on the coaft of America. Edited, with an Introduction, by the Rev. Edmund F. Slafter, A.M.

THE VOYAGES OF SAMUEL DE CHAMPLAIN.

Including the Voyage of 1603, and all contained in the edition of 1613, and in that of 1619; tranflated from the French by Charles P. Otis, Ph.D. Edited, with a Memoir and hiftorical illuftrations, by the Rev. Edmund F. Slafter, A.M.

This work confifts of three volumes. Volumes I. and II. have been iffued; Vol. III. will follow as foon as practicable.

---

## VOLUMES IN PREPARATION.

1. CAPTAIN JOHN MASON, the founder of New Hampfhire, including his Tract on Newfoundland, 1620, and the feveral American Charters in which he was a Grantee; with a Memoir and hiftorical illuftrations by CHARLES W. TUTTLE, Ph.D.

2. SIR FERDINANDO GORGES, including his Tract entitled A Brief Narration, 1658, American Charters granted to him, and other papers; with hiftorical illuftrations and a Memoir by the Rev. EDMUND F. SLAFTER, A.M.

3. THE VOYAGES OF SAMUEL DE CHAMPLAIN, including the Voyage of 1603, and all contained in the edition of 1613, and in that of 1619. Tranflated into Englifh by CHARLES P. OTIS, Ph.D. Edited, with a Memoir and hiftorical illuftrations, by the Rev. EDMUND F. SLAFTER, A.M.

Two of the three volumes, of which this work will confift, have already been iffued.

4. SIR HUMPHREY GILBERT, including his Difcourfe to prove a Paffage by the North-Weft to Cathaia and the Eaft Indies; his Letters Patent to difcover and poffefs lands in North America, granted by Queen Elizabeth, June 11, 1578; with hiftorical illuftrations and a Memoir by CHARLES W. TUTTLE, Ph.D.

It is the intention of the Council to iffue at leaft one volume annually, but not neceffarily in the order in which they are placed above.

N. B. Communications to the officers of the Society fhould be directed to 18 Somerfet Street, Bofton, Mafs.

# INDEX.

# INDEX.

41

Champlain, Samuel de, birth, 206;
parentage and home at Brouage
1–11; quarter-mafter in the army,
1–19; his vifit to the Weft Indies,
20–26; his firft voyage to Canada, 26–
35; his fecond voyage and three years
fojourn on the Atlantic coaft of America under De Monts, 35–78; prepares for a voyage to Canada, 78–80;
fettles difficulties at Tadouffac, 80,
81; fails up the St. Lawrence. 81, 82;
he lays the foundations of Quebec,
82; attempt to affaffinate him, 83–
85; his firft winter at Quebec, 86–88;
tour of exploration and difcovery of
Lake Champlain, 89–91; battle at
Ticonderoga, 91–96; his return to
France, 96, 97; returns to Canada,
98; battle at the mouth of the Richelieu, 99–103; he hears of the death
of Henry IV. and returns to France,
103, 104; his marriage, 105; returns
to Canada, 105; he repairs to the
Falls of St. Louis, the rendezvous
for Indian trade, 106–110; returns to
France and reorganizes the company,
110–114; returns to New France,
115; explores the Ottawa, 115–121;
returns to France and takes miffionaries to Canada, 122–124; his exploration of the upper Ottawa, Lake
Nipiffing, Lake Huron, Simcoe, Ontario, penetrates the interior of Weftern New York and gives battle to
the Iroquois, 124–135; goes into winter quarters with the Hurons, 135–
138; explorations during the winter,
138–140; returns to the Falls of St.
Louis, 141, 142; voyages to France,
143; efforts to revive the company,
144–147; takes his wife to Canada,
147; repairs the buildings at Quebec,
148–150; in France two years, 151;
erects a farm-houfe at Cape Tourmente, 151; difficulty with Indians,
152, 153; the peltry and fur trade,
154, 155; the company of New
France, organized, 155, 157; the
Englifh attack New France, 158–
173; receives Capt. Daniel's account
of his colony planted in the Ifland
of Cape Breton, 173–175; he lays
the fubject of the Britifh invafion
before the government at Paris, 175–
177; he attends to the publication of
his works at Paris, 178; returns to
Quebec, and enters upon feveral new
enterprifes, 179–181; his letter to
Richelieu, 181–183; his death, 184,
185; fummary of his character, 186–
204; portrait of, 212; titles of his
publications, 215–219; his dedica-
tion to Charles Montmorency.
Champlain, Lac de, 297, 300.
Champlain, Lake, 93.
Champlain, Madame, 212.
Champlain Rivière de, 70, 296.
Chandler, Peleg W., 156.
Chantrey, 161.
Chantilly, 146.
Chaoufarou, 97.
Chapel of M. de Champlain, 185.
Chappeau Rouge, 300.
Charavay, Étienne, 194, 205.
Charente Inférieure, 206.
Charlefbourg Royal, 30.
Charles I., 161, 169, 172, 176.
Charles II., 193.
Charles VIII., 2.
Charles IX., 3, 14, 16, 186.

Montaigne, 220.

Montmorency, Admiral Charles de, 226, 253.

Montmorency, Charlotte Marguerite de, 113.

Montmorency, Henry, Duke de, 113, 146, 148, 150.

Montmorency, Le Saulte de, 295.

Montreal, 29, 33, 96, 106, 107, 115, 117, 120, 121, 124, 126, 135, 141, 186, 199, 251, 255, 261, 266, 267, 268, 297.

Mont-réal, Ifle de, 294, 300.

Montaut, Sieur de, 4.

Montcalm, Gen'l Louis Jos., 91.

Monts Déferts, Ifle de, 41, 209, 294, 304.

Monte Chrifto, 22.

Moofe, 265.

Morel, Captain, 37.

Morlay, 12.

Morris Ifland, 66.

Mofquitoes, 22.

Motte Bourioli, La, 43.

Mount Defert, 41, 42, 78, 122, 123, 197, 208, 238, 294.

Mourt's Relation, 207.

Mouton, Port au, 297.

Mufcovites, 181.

Mvr, Pierre Le, 217.

Mufhauwomuk, 52.

Mufkrat, 266.

Mufkrat Lake, 118, 300, 301.

Myftic River, 52.

**N.**

Naigré, Port du Cap, 298, 304.

Nantafket, 53.

Nafhaway, 52.

Natel, Antoine, 83.

Natifcotec, 233.

Naufet Harbor, 54, 56, 63, 65, 70, 197.

Navarre, 4, 5, 12, 17, 217.

Navigation, Treatife on, 178.

Nepefiguit River, 279.

Neponfitt, 52.

Neutral Nation, 303, 304.

Neutre, La Nation, 303.

New Brunfwick, 36, 39, 44. 159, 197.

New England, 46, 49, 54, 57, 64, 70, 71, 77, 78, 95, 197, 198, 207, 210, 239, 303.

New England Hiftorical and Genealogical Regifter, vii, 276.

New Foundland, 25, 29, 32, 159, 161, 232, 293, 300.

New France, 36, 37, 62, 99, 104, 105, 111, 113. 114, 116, 123, 146, 148, 149, 151, 156, 157, 159, 171, 172, 177, 178, 180, 181, 183, 185, 187, 188, 195, 213, 216, 225, 265, 278.

New Grenada, 22.

Newport Mountain, 209.

New Scotland, 159, 176, 177.

New York, 93, 136, 143, 152, 170, 199, 200, 276, 302.

New York, Documentary Hift. of, 207.

New York Hift. Society, 93, 132.

Niagara Falls, 271, 274, 275, 301.

Nicaragua, Lake of, 25.

Nicholas, St., 22.

Nichols Pond, 131, 132.

Nicolet River, 297.

Nicolette River, 259.

Nipiffing Lake, 126, 199, 303.

Nipiffings, Indians, 138, 139.

Nipmuck, 52.

Noddle's Ifland, 52.

Nogent-le-Rotrou, 112.

University Press: John Wilson and Son, Cambridge.

www.ingramcontent.com/pod-product-compliance
Lightning Source LLC
Chambersburg PA
CBHW030915270326
41929CB00008B/708